THE SOCIETY OF PUBLICATION DESIGNERS

35th
Publication
Design
Annual

ROCKPORT PUBLISHERS, INC.
ROCKPORT, MASSACHUSETTS

DISTRIBUTED BY
NORTH LIGHT BOOKS
CINCINNATI, OHIO

acknowledgments

The Sponsors
The Society thanks its corporate sponsors
for their continuing support:

Adobe Systems Incorporated
American Express Publishing
Apple Computers, Inc.
Condé Nast Publications, Inc.
Dow Jones & Company, Inc.
Gruner & Jahr
Hachette Filipacchi Magazines, Inc.
Hearst Magazines
McGraw Hill, Inc.
Meredith Corporation
The New York Times
Newsweek
Quad Graphics
Wenner Media
Time Inc.
U.S. News & World Report
Westvaco Corporation

Pub35 Competition
The Co-Chairs, Lynn Staley and D. J. Stout,
would like to extend special thanks to
Angelo Rivello and Dominic Ho of *Newsweek*
and most especially to all the volunteers who
worked so long and hard to make the judging a
successful and exciting event.

Call for Entries Design:
Mimi Park, Design Park Inc.
Paper: Westvaco Corporation
Printing: Quad Graphics

The Gala
PROGRAM DESIGN: Mimi Park
SEPARATIONS: Albert Rufino, Time Imaging
PAPER: Westvaco Corporation
PRINTING: Westbury Press, Englewood, N.J.
SLIDE PRESENTATION & AUDIO VISUAL PROGRAM:
Show & Tell Anagraphics
AWARDS: Nick Fasciano Design, Inc.

Student Competition
CO-CHAIRS: Gail Anderson and Paul Roelofs
POSTER DESIGN: Gail Anderson
SEPARATIONS: Time Inc. People Imaging
PAPER: Westvaco Corporation
PRINTING: Perry-Judd's Inc.

Spots Competition
The Chairperson Christine Curry would like
to extend a special thanks to Suzanne Bennett,
Bob Newman and, of course, Bride Whelan
for keeping us in line and helping us
tally up the ratings for the hundreds and
hundreds of entries.

CALL FOR ENTRIES DESIGN: Christine Curry
SEPARATIONS: Gary Van Dis,
Condé Nast Publications, Inc.
PAPER: Westvaco Corporation
PRINTING: Seiple Lithograph\

The Society of Publication Designers, Inc.

60 East 42nd Street, Suite 721
New York, NY 10165
Telephone: (212) 983-8585
Fax: (212) 983-6043
Email: SPDNYC@aol.com
Web site: HTTP://www.SPD.ORG

Executive Board Officers
President
Robert Newman
Design Director, *Vibe*

Vice Presidents
Diana LaGuardia
Design Director, *Gourmet*

Vice Presidents
Malcolm Frouman
Art Director, *BusinessWeek*

Secretary
Christine Curry
Illustration Editor, *The New Yorker*

Treasurer
Elizabeth Betts
Design Director, *Sports Illustrated for Women*

Executive Director
Bride Whelan
Society of Publication Designers

Board of Directors
Gail Anderson
Senior Art Director, *Rolling Stone*

Janet Froelich
Art Director, *The New York Times Magazine*

David Harris
Art Director, *Vanity Fair*

Steven Hoffman
Creative Director, *Sports Illustrated*

David Matt
Vice President, Circle.com

Mimi Park
Principal, Design Park Inc.

Eric Pike
Design Director, Martha Stewart Living

Paul Roelofs
Art Director, eve.com

Ina Saltz
Design Director, *Golf Magazine*

Veronique Vienne
Principal, Young Vienne, Inc.

Member at Large
David Armario
Art Director, *Los Angeles Magazine*

The SPD 35th Publication Design Annual
Book produced and designed by Mimi Park
Design Park, Inc.,
Jacket Photomosaic™ by Rob Silvers

First published
in the United States of America by:
Rockport Publishers, Inc.
33 Commercial Street
Gloucester, Massachusetts 01930
Telephone: (978) 282-9590
Fax: (978) 283-2742

ISBN 1-56496-716-6

Printed in China

contents

about the society

Established in 1965, the Society of Publication Designers was formed to acknowledge the role of the art director and designer in the visual understanding of the printed word. The art director as a journalist brings a unique skill to the editorial mission of the publication and clarifies the editorial message. The specialized skills of the designer confront the challenges of technology within a constantly expanding industry. ■ The Society provides for its members Speaker Luncheons and Evenings, the monthly newsletter GRIDS, the publication design annual, the Design Exhibition and the annual SPOTS Competition and Exhibition for illustrators, and the SPD Auction and Awards Gala. It has developed a working network of opportunities for job seekers and student interns. It actively participates in related activities that bring together members of the numerous design communities in the New York area.

■ **Bride Whelan,** Executive Director

the pub35 competition

The judging of Pub35 was one of the most spirited and varied in memory. Forty-two design, photography, and illustration professionals spent two days viewing 8,721 submissions from around the world. The 672 merit, 36 silver, 15 gold and the Magazine of the Year awards are the result of their efforts and will be recorded in the SPD 35th Publication Design Annual to be published in October 2000. ■ This judging represented many viewpoints and is a subjective process affected by style and contemporary taste. We hope that certain universal values prevail and that over time this body of work will continue to represent high journalistic standards, innovative problem solving and the pure pleasure of design.

photographs by **Andrew Kist**

competition co-chairs

Lynn Staley, Assistant Managing Editor/Design, Newsweek
D. J. Stout, Partner, Pentagram Design, Austin, TX

blue group CLOCKWISE FROM FRONT ROW CENTER

Steve Hoffman, Design Director, Sports Illustrated (Captain)
Christa Skinner, Art Director, Blue
Christine Curry, Illustration Editor, The New Yorker
Amy Rosenfeld, Art Director, Smart Money
Simon Barnett, Director of Photography, Discover,
Brian Smale, Photographer

orange group CLOCKWISE FROM FRONT ROW CENTER

Melinda Beck, Illustrator
Ted Keller, Art Director, Village Voice
Nicholas Blechman, Art Director Op/Ed, The New York Times
Lesley Vinson, Art Director
Geraldine Hessler, Design Director, Entertainment Weekly
Tom Bentkowski, Design Director,
National Geographic Adventure (Captain)

yellow group CLOCKWISE FROM FRONT ROW CENTER

Toby Fox, Art Director, Garden Design
Michael Lawton, Art Director, Men's Journal
Gail Anderson, Senior Art Director, Rolling Stone (Captain)
Matthew Carter, Principal, Carter & Cone Type, Inc.
Lucie Lacava, President, Lucie Lacava Publication Design, Inc.
Florian Bachleda, Design Director, Maximum Golf

black group CLOCKWISE FROM FRONT ROW LEFT

Joe Dizney, Art Director, The Wall St. Journal
Cathy Gilmore-Barnes, Deputy Art Director,
The New York Times Magazine
Mary Ellen Mark, Photographer
Rodrigo Sanchez, Art Director, El Mundo
Miriam Campiz, Principal, Miriam Campiz Design
Patrick Mitchell, Art Director, Fast Company (Captain)

green group CLOCKWISE FROM FRONT ROW CENTER

Michael Picon, Design Director, New York Magazine
Ina Saltz, Design Director, Golf Magazine (Captain)
Cynthia Hoffman, Deputy Art Director, Time
Peter Yates, Design Director, ESPN
Lloyd Ziff, Creative Director, Time Inc. Custom Publishing
Edward Leida, Group Design Director, W

red group CLOCKWISE FROM FRONT ROW CENTER

Miranda Dempster, Art Director, I.D.
Rena Sokolow, Supervisor/Editorial Design, The Boston Globe
Michael Jones, Principal. Michael Jones Design
Walter Bernard, President, WBMG Inc. (Captain)
Tony Moxham, Art Director, Interview
Ronn Campisi, Principal, Ronn Campisi Design

online group CLOCKWISE FROM FRONT ROW LEFT

Vincent Lacava, Senior Art Director, RGA
Stephen Gullo, Creative Director, Disney Online
Pamela Mead, Director, Meta Design
Robert Raines, V.P. Creative Director, America Online
Lisa Michurski, Creative Director, Time Interactive
Melanie McLaughlin, Art Director,
Feedroom.com (Captain)

design

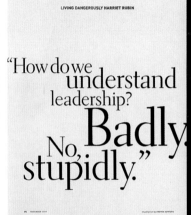

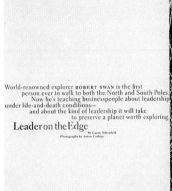

the
magazine
of the
year
winner

1

PUBLICATION Fast Company
ART DIRECTOR Patrick Mitchell
DESIGNERS Patrick Mitchell, Emily Crawford,
Gretchen Smelter, Rebecca Rees
ILLUSTRATORS Brian Cronin, Andrea Ventura
PHOTO EDITOR Alicia Jylkka
PHOTOGRAPHERS Michael McLaughlin, Sean Kennedy, Anton Corbijn
PUBLISHER Fast Company
ISSUES September 1999, October 1999, November 1999
CATEGORY Magazine of the Year

STATE OF THE NEW ECONOMY

FAST COMPANY

What Are You Working On?

21

PLUS

3 MODELS FOR THE NEW MILLENNIUM, 2 RECKONINGS WITH THE PAST, AND 1,004 EXPECTATIONS FOR 2004

A 158-PAGE SPECIAL REPORT TO HELP YOU INVENT YOUR FUTURE

21 Rules for the 21st Century

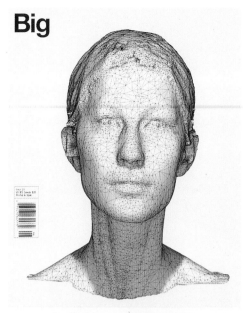

■2
PUBLICATION Big
CREATIVE DIRECTOR Marcelo Jünemann
ART DIRECTORS Markus Kiersztan, Lee Swillingham, Stuart Spalding, Rico Lins
DESIGNERS Garland Lyn, David Lee, Sølve Sündsbø, Alex Rutterford,
Dagmar Rizzolo, Keren Ora Admoni, Thais Lima, Mariana Guimarães
PHOTOGRAPHERS Kishin Shinoyama, Sølve Sündsbø
PUBLISHER Big Magazine, Inc.
ISSUES June 1999, #22, October 1999, #23, December 1999, #26
CATEGORY Magazine of the Year

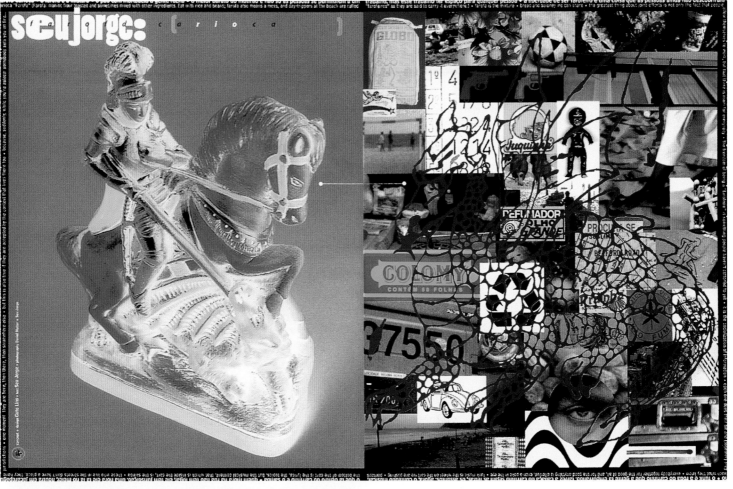

seu jorge: [carioca]

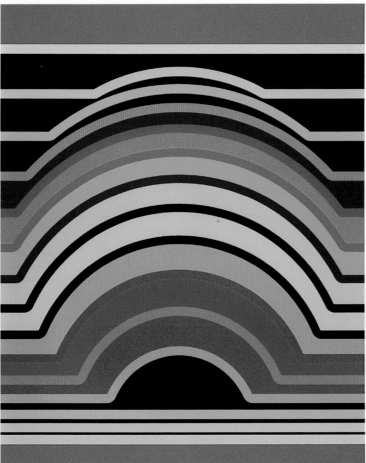

The Seventh Night

It seems that I'm aboard some massive ship.

The ship plows forward, shearing the waves away, day after day, night after night, continuously emitting, without one second's break, a stream of inky smoke. The noise is tremendous; but the destination utterly unknown. All I know is that the sun, burning red like red-hot tongs, bulges up from the bottom of the sea. It rises, seems to hover briefly dead above the tall ship's mast, and then, before we realize what's happening, overtakes the shuddering ship and, plunging dead ahead, sinks back with a sizzling sound, the sound of red-hot tongs, down to the bottom of the sea. Each time it sinks, the blue waves far ahead settle to a blackish red. The ship, making its tremendous noise, pursues the sinking sun. But it never catches up.

One day I buttonholed a sailor, and I asked him: "Is this ship steering west?"

The sailor, a curiously uncertain expression on his face, eyed me briefly and then answered, "Why?"

"Because it seems concerned to chase the setting sun."

The sailor burst into a roar of laughter; and then left me.

I heard the sound of jolly voices chanting:
"Does the sun that travels west
End up in the east?
Is that really true?
Has the sun that leaves the east
Its real home in the west?
Is that also true?
We float on the ocean blue,
Rudders for a pillow,
Sail and sail, on and on."

I went up into the bows where I found a watch of sailors hauling at the halyards.

I began to feel most terribly forlorn. There was no way of knowing when one might get ashore. And, worse, no way of knowing whither we were bound. The only certainties were the streaming of black smoke and the shearing of the sea. The waves stretched wide as wide, blue in their boundlessness. Sometimes they grew purple, though close to the sliding ship, they slavered and went white. I felt most terribly forlorn. I even thought it would be better to throw myself into the sea than to stick with such a ship.

There were many fellow-passengers, most, or so it seemed, foreigners,

though each had a different cast of feature. One day when the sky was clouded and the ship rolling, I saw a woman leaning on the rail, and crying bitterly. The handkerchief with which she wiped her eyes looked white, and her dress, a sort of calico, carried a printed pattern. Seeing her weep, I realized that I was not the only person sad.

One evening when I was alone on deck, watching the stars, a foreigner came up and asked if I knew anything about astronomy. Since I was already contemplating suicide as a means of escape from boredom, it scarcely seemed necessary for one to be acquainted with matters such as astronomy. So I made no answer. The foreigner then told me the story of the seven stars in the neck of the constellation of the Bull, and went on to inform me that the stars and the sea were all of God's creation. He finally asked me if I believed in God. I looked at the sky and said nothing.

Once as I was entering the saloon, I saw a gaudy dressed young woman playing the piano, with her back toward me. At her side a tall man splendid-looking man stood singing. His mouth appeared inordinately large. They seemed completely indifferent to all things other than themselves. They seemed even to have forgotten their being on this ship.

I grew more bored than ever. Finally, I determined to put an end to myself and, one convenient evening when no one was about, I jumped with resolution over the side. However, in that moment when my feet left the deck and my link with the ship was severed, suddenly then life became peculiarly precious. From the bottom of my heart I regretted my rash action. But by then it was too late. Willy-nilly I was committed to the deep. But, possibly because of the ship's high freeboard, my feet for some long time failed to touch water although my body had abandoned ship. Nonetheless, since nothing could check my fall, I dropped closer and closer to the sea. However much I drew in my legs, nearer and still nearer came the sea. The color of the sea was black.

Meanwhile the ship, still as usual streaming its black smoke, steamed straight away. I would have been far better off aboard, even though that ship had no known destination. When I came to that realization, it was too longer possible to make use of my belated wisdom. And so I went down quietly, infinitely regretful, infinitely afraid, down to the black of waves.

Excerpt from Ten Nights of Dream; Hearing Things; The Heredity of Taste, *by Soseki Natsume; translated by Aiko Ito and Graeme Wilson, published by Tuttle Publishing, 153 Milk Street, Boston, MA, 02109, 800 526 2778.*

青

THE BLUE GROUP

11

PUBLICATION ESPN
DESIGN DIRECTOR Peter Yates
ART DIRECTORS Henry Lee, Yvette L. Francis
DESIGNERS Peter Yates, Reyes Meléndez, Jeanine Melnick,
Yvette L. Francis, Gabe Kuo
ILLUSTRATORS Silverkid New York, Todd McFarlane
PHOTO EDITOR Nik Kleinberg
PHOTOGRAPHERS Isabel Snyder, Mary Ellen Mark, Pam Len,
Gregory Heisler, Nitin Vadukul, Eric Tucker
PUBLISHER Disney Publishing Worldwide
ISSUES November 15, 1999, November 29, 1999, December 27, 1999

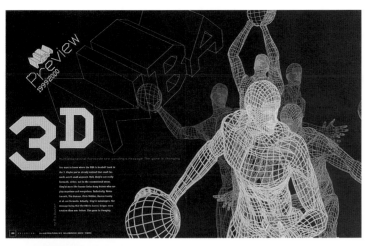

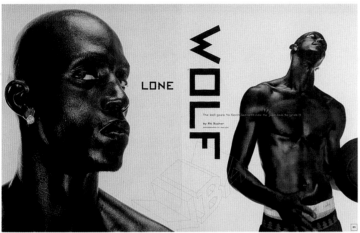

4

PUBLICATION The New York Times Magazine
ART DIRECTORS Janet Froelich, Joele Cuyler
DESIGNERS Joele Cuyler, Ignacio Rodriguez
PHOTO EDITORS Kathy Ryan, Sarah Harbutt
PHOTOGRAPHERS Tom Schierlitz, Dan Winters,
Catherine Chalmers, Joel Peter Witkin, David LaChapelle
PUBLISHER The New York Times
ISSUES April 18, 1999, September 19, 1999, December 5, 1999
CATEGORY Magazine of the Year

CATHERINE CHALMERS
HELLO, COLUMBUS

His arrival ended centuries of isolation — and sparked a monumental exchange between continents.

When Christopher Columbus made landfall in the Bahamas on Oct. 12, 1492, he set in motion a vast ecological transformation. The tide that conveyed Europeans to the New World also brought their cattle, horses, cats and pigs; their wheat, oats, grasses and nettles; their rats, insects and bacilli. Because the Americas had stood in splendid isolation for millenniums, the continent's diverse life forms were no match for the invasion-hardened genes of the Old World. While Europeans lacked the knowledge to carry out biological warfare intentionally, Cortés's conquest of Mexico and Pizarro's conquest of the Inca empire were made easier by smallpox, which preceded their armies and decimated the native populations. Meanwhile clever and thistles, peach trees and dandelions, opportunistic species all, conquered the fields and forests of the untransmuted continent. Christianity, firearms, the Roman alphabet, European styles of clothing, housing and protocol were imposed with minimal difficulty on the dazed and weakened natives. And what did the Old World receive in return? As punishment, only syphilis; very few American weeds were sufficiently aggressive to win retribution on foreign soil. The rewards that traveled east, however, were great: vanilla, maize, tobacco, potatoes, sunflowers, peanuts, tomatoes, indigo, chocolate. European diet and life style were altered profoundly; what started out as novelty quickly became instrumental tradition. These works by Catherine Chalmers depict one of the shock troops of the European invasion, the cockroach, lording it over the bounty of the New World, represented by the tomato. The insect shown in these photographs, painted with an image that festooned Columbus's sails, did so well in its new home that it is now called the American cockroach. ■

Narrate
Or Die
Why Scheherazade keeps on talking.

By A.S. Byatt

The best story ever told? Perhaps the story of the two brothers, both kings, who found that their wives were unfaithful, both bloody vengeance, and set out into the world to travel until they found someone less fortunate than they were...

Photograph by Dan Winters

Start with a rash idea. Add an architect.
Mix in artifacts, argon gas and a dash of irony.
Seal carefully and let sit for 1,000 years.

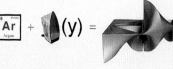

$$ \text{lightbulb} + \text{loom} + \text{tassel} + \boxed{\begin{matrix}18 \\ Ar \\ \text{Argon}\end{matrix}} + \text{iron} + (y) = $$

How to Make a Time Capsule
By Jack Hitt

At the end of the 20th century, the image that comes to most people's minds when they think about time capsules might best be described as terrar-crystal...

JOEL-PETER WITKIN
THE PLAGUE YEARS
Decimation, via the Black Death and AIDS.

Epidemics have been a part of the human story since settled populations first attracted parasites and their trade conveyed them to other vulnerable places. The plague that fell on Europe in the 14th century was distinguished by its ferocity and its longevity. From its origins in central Asia, it was carried by rats aboard ships, reaching Italy at the fall of 1347 and quickly spreading as far as Britain and Scandinavia. The Black Death killed about a quarter of Europe's population and recurred periodically over the next three centuries...

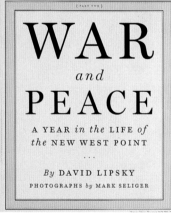

PUBLICATION Rolling Stone

ART DIRECTOR Fred Woodward

DESIGNERS Fred Woodward, Gail Anderson, Siung Tjia, Ken DeLago, Andy Omel, Lee Berresford

ILLUSTRATOR Steve Brodner

PHOTO EDITORS Rachel Knepfer, Fiona McDonagh, Audrey Landreth

PHOTOGRAPHERS Mark Seliger, David LaChapelle, Kurt Markus, Peter Lindbergh

PUBLISHER Straight Arrow Publishers

ISSUES November 11, 1999, December 16, 1999, December 30, 1999

CATEGORY Magazine of the Year

    A **MERIT** Cover

    B **MERIT** Feature Spread

ELVIS COSTELLO WITH
HIS FATHER, ROSS MACMANUS

the Costellos

"THE FAMOUS
STORY ABOUT
ELVIS IS THAT
HIS VERY FIRST
WORDS WERE,
'SKIN, MOMMY.'
HE WANTED
'I'VE GOT YOU
UNDER MY SKIN,'
BY SINATRA."
—ROSS
MacMANUS

DECLAN MACMANUS TOOK TO
the stage in 1977, an angry young
man sporting Buddy Holly glasses
and a strange name: Elvis Costello. But he wasn't the first
MacManus to use Costello as his
stage name – that was his dad,
Ross, a jazz trumpeter and pop
vocalist since the early Fifties. "He
had a ska/blue beat hit in Germany," says Elvis with pride, "and

Photographs by PETER LINDBERGH

✠ THE ✠✠

THE OSCAR-WINNING ACTOR WHO

PASSION

SAYS HE BUILT A CAREER ON BEING

✠✠ OF ✠✠

"UNPREDICTABLE AND FRIGHTENING"

NICOLAS

REVEALS A SIDE NOBODY KNOWS

✠✠ CAGE

BY FRED SCHRUERS

· 95 ·

The New York Times Magazine

JANUARY 17, 1999 / SECTION 6

**Bill Clinton's
Legacy
(First Draft)**

By Jacob Weisberg

6
PUBLICATION The New York Times Magazine
ART DIRECTOR Janet Froelich
DESIGNER Jennifer Gilman
PUBLISHER The New York Times
ISSUES January 17, 1999
CATEGORY Cover

Ss Hh Oo Ww Aa Nn Dd Tt Ee Ll Ll

It's never too early for kids to start questioning the meaning of fashion. The ABC's of spring children's wear.

Photographs by Robert Trachtenberg | Styled by Elizabeth Stewart

The "teacher" Pamela Gordon in a wool suit by Oscar de la Renta. Shoes by Jimmy Choo. Eyeglass frames by Morgenthal-Frederics. Steel furniture[2] from Sonrisa, New York and Los Angeles.

Marisa Ruiz wears a pink cotton dress, $20, from the Children's Place, 22 West 34th Street. Socks by Tic Tac Toe. Mary Janes by Stride Rite. Verena Wildstaetten[3] is wearing a cutaway coat and muslin dress by Comme des Garçons.

Manon Troncin in a cotton waffle-print jumper, $25, from Oshkosh B'Gosh. Call (800) 692-4674. Cashmere sweater, $128, from M.A.G. At Natalie and Friends, 131 West 33d Street. Barneys New York. Jimmy Choo shoes for Tristan Webber. Prop stylist[3]: Melanie Paisis. Market editor: George Kotsiopoulos. Children's grooming: Mitzi Spallas at Cloutier. Makeup: Troy Jensen at the Artist Group. Hair: Robert Vetica at the Artist Group.

■ 7
PUBLICATION The New York Times Magazine
ART DIRECTOR Janet Froelich
DESIGNER Claude Martel
PHOTOGRAPHER Robert Trachtenberg
STYLIST Elizabeth Stewart
PUBLISHER The New York Times
ISSUES February 28, 1999
CATEGORY Feature Story

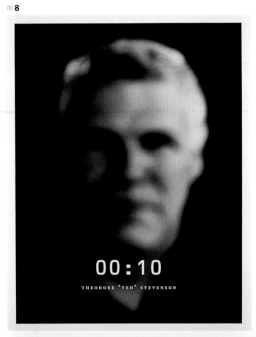

00:10

THEODORE "TED" STEVENSON

00:01

SAMUEL G. WASHINGTON

00:00

DOLORES L. GREENFIELD

08:30 A.M.

09:30 A.M.

PUBLICATION Collateral Therapeutics 1998 Annual Report
CREATIVE DIRECTOR Bill Cahan
DESIGNER Kevin Roberson
PHOTOGRAPHERS Christine Alicino, Bill Phelps,
Robert Schlatter, Ken Probst
STUDIO Cahan & Associates
ISSUE April 1999
CATEGORY Entire Issue

EVERY DAY THE U.S. SPENDS APPROXIMATELY		\$460 MILLION ON CARDIOVASCULAR CARE	
\$19,500,000	\$19,500,000	12:00 A.M.	12:00 P.M.
\$19,500,000	\$19,500,000	01:00 A.M.	01:00 P.M.
\$19,500,000	\$19,500,000	02:00 A.M.	02:00 P.M.
\$19,500,000	\$19,500,000	03:00 A.M.	03:00 P.M.
\$19,500,000	\$19,500,000	04:00 A.M.	04:00 P.M.
\$19,500,000	\$19,500,000	05:00 A.M.	05:00 P.M.
\$19,500,000	\$19,500,000	06:00 A.M.	06:00 P.M.
\$19,500,000	\$19,500,000	07:00 A.M.	07:00 P.M.
\$19,500,000	\$19,500,000	08:00 A.M.	08:00 P.M.
\$19,500,000	\$19,500,000	09:00 A.M.	09:00 P.M.
\$19,500,000	\$19,500,000	10:00 A.M.	10:00 P.M.
\$19,500,000	\$19,500,000	11:00 A.M.	11:00 P.M.

\$468,000,000

24 HOURS

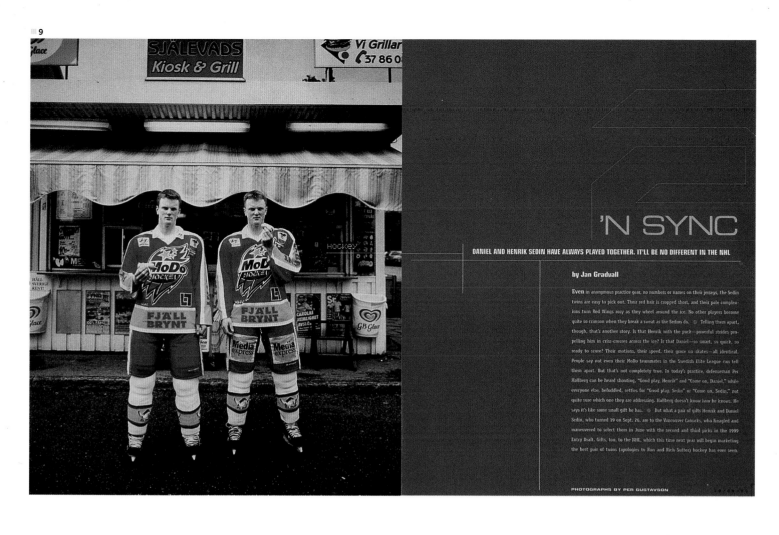

'N SYNC

DANIEL AND HENRIK SEDIN HAVE ALWAYS PLAYED TOGETHER. IT'LL BE NO DIFFERENT IN THE NHL

by Jan Gradvall

Even in anonymous practice gear, no numbers or names on their jerseys, the Sedin twins are easy to pick out. Their red hair is cropped short, and their pale complexions turn Red Wings rosy as they wheel around the ice. No other players become quite so crimson when they break a sweat as the Sedins do. ⊙ Telling them apart, though, that's another story. Is that Henrik with the puck—powerful strides propelling him in criss-crosses across the ice? Is that Daniel—so smart, so quick, so ready to score? Their motions, their speed, their grace on skates—all identical. People say not even their MoDo teammates in the Swedish Elite League can tell them apart. But that's not completely true. In today's practice, defenseman Per Hallberg can be heard shouting, "Good play, Henrik" and "Come on, Daniel," while everyone else, befuddled, settles for "Good play, Sedin" or "Come on, Sedin," not quite sure which one they are addressing. Hallberg doesn't know how he knows. He says it's like some small gift he has. ⊙ But what a pair of gifts Henrik and Daniel Sedin, who turned 19 on Sept. 26, are to the Vancouver Canucks, who finagled and maneuvered to select them in June with the second and third picks in the 1999 Entry Draft. Gifts, too, to the NHL, which this time next year will begin marketing the best pair of twins (apologies to Ron and Rich Sutter) hockey has ever seen.

PHOTOGRAPHS BY PER GUSTAVSON

9
PUBLICATION ESPN
DESIGN DIRECTOR Peter Yates
DESIGNER Reyes Meléndez
PHOTO EDITOR Nik Kleinberg
PHOTOGRAPHER Per Gustavson
PUBLISHER Disney Publishing Worldwide
ISSUE October 4, 1999
CATEGORY Feature Spread

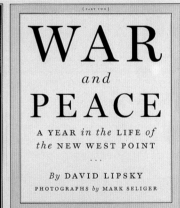

■ 10
PUBLICATION Rolling Stone
ART DIRECTOR Fred Woodward
DESIGNERS Siung Tjia, Fred Woodward, Gail Anderson,
Ken DeLago, Andy Omel, Lee Berresford
PHOTO EDITORS Rachel Knepfer, Audrey Landreth
PHOTOGRAPHERS Mark Seliger, Linda McCartney, Jim Marshall
PUBLISHER Straight Arrow Publishers
ISSUE December 16, 1999
CATEGORY Entire Issue

■ 11
PUBLICATION Rolling Stone
ART DIRECTOR Fred Woodward
DESIGNERS Fred Woodward, Siung Tjia
PHOTO EDITORS Rachel Knepfer, Audrey Landreth
PHOTOGRAPHERS Annie Leibovitz, Anton Corbijn, David LaChapelle, Albert Watson,
Mark Seliger, Mick Rock, Lynn Goldsmith, Kevin Mazur, Peter Beard,
James Schnepf, Linda McCartney, Norman Seef, John Marshall, M. Renard
PUBLISHER Straight Arrow Publishers
ISSUE December 16, 1999
CATEGORY Cover

BEHIND THE SCENES

RollingStone

design ■ SILVER

SPECIAL PHOTO ISSUE

Mick Jagger

credit; jim marshall

JOHN LENNON

Annie Leibovitz

MADE IN U.S.A.

ANNIE   1980

David Bowie

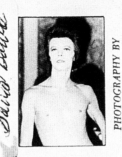

PHOTOGRAPHY BY MICK ROCK

Britney Spears

© 1999

DAVID LACHAPELLE

1975

© NORMAN SEEFF

Joni Mitchell
CR: Norman Seeff

796 96dd 94#

X Lou Reed

Andy Warhol

MADONNA

HERB RITTS 1990

R829Y11A

1282

M. RENARD

DYLAN, B.

ALBERT WATSON

Jack Nicholson

© Kevin Mazur
All Rights Reserved

Kurt, courtney + Frances Bean

aretha

Aretha Franklin

1969

PHOTOGRAPH BY LINDA McCARTNEY

BRUCE SPRINGSTEEN

LYNN GOLDSMITH

Bono

MARK SELIGER

DREW BARRYMORE
NYC

View from this side

JAMES SCHNEPF

P- 135575

L.L. COOL J

Peter Beard

Keith Richards!

CORBIJN

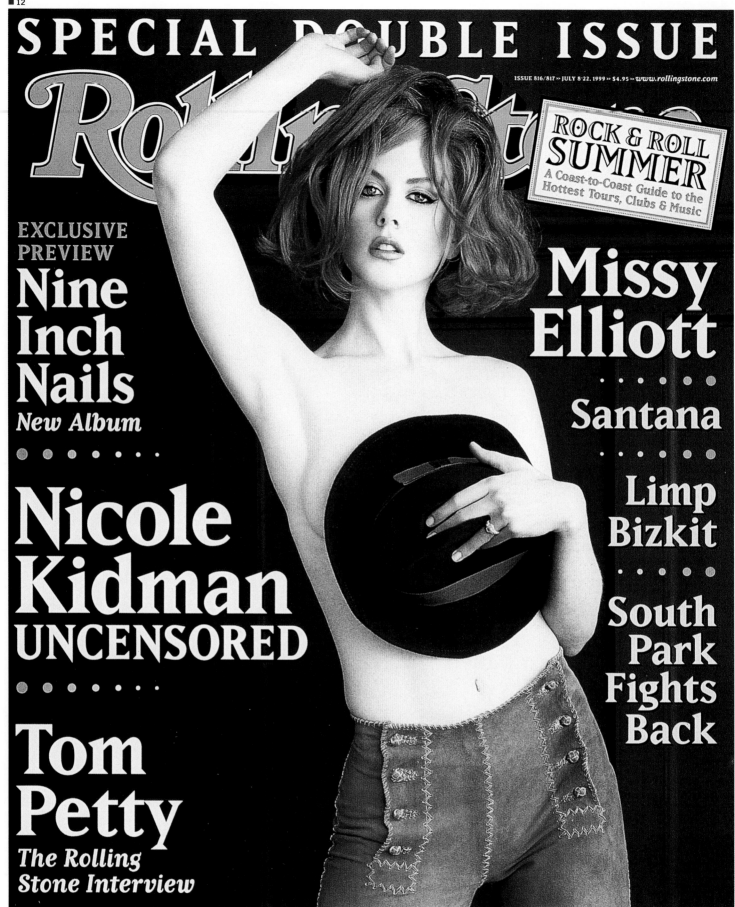

SPECIAL DOUBLE ISSUE

Rolling Stone

ISSUE 816/817 » JULY 8-22, 1999 » $4.95 » *www.rollingstone.com*

ROCK & ROLL SUMMER
A Coast-to-Coast Guide to the Hottest Tours, Clubs & Music

EXCLUSIVE PREVIEW
Nine Inch Nails
New Album

• • • • • •

Nicole Kidman UNCENSORED

• • • • • •

Tom Petty
The Rolling Stone Interview

Missy Elliott

• • • • • •

Santana

• • • • •

Limp Bizkit

• • • • •

South Park Fights Back

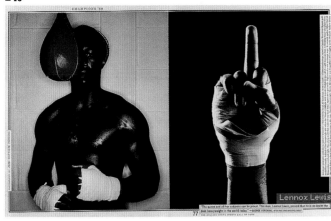

■12
PUBLICATION Rolling Stone
ART DIRECTOR Fred Woodward
DESIGNER Fred Woodward
PHOTO EDITOR Rachel Knepfer
PHOTOGRAPHER Herb Ritts
PUBLISHER Straight Arrow Publishers
ISSUE July 8, 1999
CATEGORY Cover

■13
PUBLICATION Rolling Stone
ART DIRECTOR Fred Woodward
DESIGNER Fred Woodward
PHOTO EDITORS Rachel Knepfer, Fiona McDonagh
PHOTOGRAPHERS Jean-Baptiste Mondino,
Fred Woodward, Martin Schoeller, Mark Seliger
PUBLISHER Straight Arrow Publishers
CATEGORY Feature Story

```
E R G I N D I A C N V U E L V E
N P I E C O D V I D H G J A B B
R U C C N G C H C M A D O N N A
I E A R K S M A R T I N S J A L
Q R L I O Y L R O C O G H U N K
U T A C U A H A L L A B H Q D F
E O T O R N O T L D V E Y K S C
A R I E C Q S A I E I L C N P O
S F N T H E P Y N G D O C A I L
C E O R L J I O G O A C U N D L
G D X O I N T Q Y K B A P C O I
R O B I L S A M Z I C E O Y L N
O W O C V R L P A K L I F E P S
S X A I N T E R V I E W P F S L
A M E N U D O D T G R A M M Y S
```

PHOTOGRAPHS BY DAVID LACHAPELLE

sony style

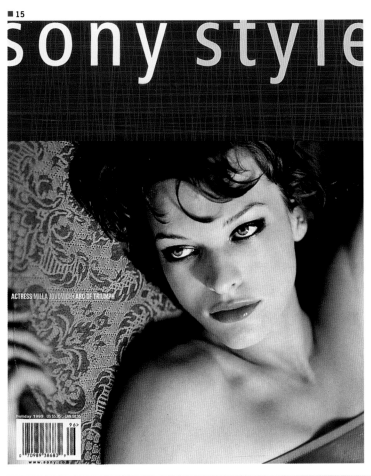

ACTRESS MILLA JOVOVICH ■ ARC OF TRIUMPH

holiday 1999 US $5.95 / CAN $8.95

www.sony.com

sony style

individuality
Expressions of digital creativity

manual for digital living

contents

originality

essentials 11.99

ROUGH RIDER

jennifer lopez

The drive to excel is key for this multi-talented artist

Jennifer Lopez has recently become accustomed to stealing the show. Her smoldering performance opposite George Clooney in 1998's Oscar-nominated *Out of Sight* made her a household name. Her elegant appearance at the Academy Awards in March wearing a princess-like Badgley Mischka gown put her on many best-dressed lists. And when she served as

BY WENDY MITCHELL

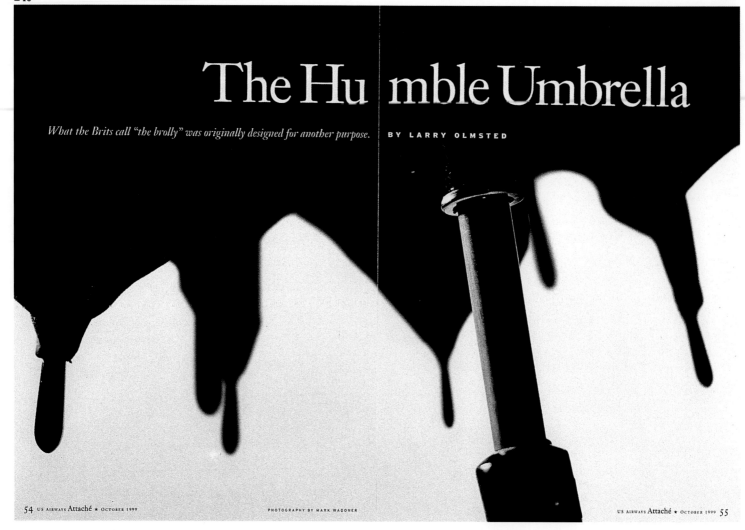

The Hu mble Umbrella

What the Brits call "the brolly" was originally designed for another purpose. BY LARRY OLMSTED

54 US AIRWAYS Attaché ★ OCTOBER 1999   PHOTOGRAPHY BY MARK WAGONER   US AIRWAYS Attaché ★ OCTOBER 1999 55

■ 16
PUBLICATION Attaché
ART DIRECTOR Paul Carstensen
DESIGNER Paul Carstensen
PHOTOGRAPHER Mark Wagoner
PUBLISHER Pace Communications
CLIENT US Airways
ISSUE October 1999
CATEGORY Feature Spread

■ 17
PUBLICATION Esquire
DESIGN DIRECTOR Robert Priest
ART DIRECTOR Rockwell Harwood
PHOTO EDITOR Simon Barnett
PHOTOGRAPHER Gregory Heisler
PUBLISHER The Hearst Corporation-Magazines Division
ISSUE June 1999
CATEGORY Cover

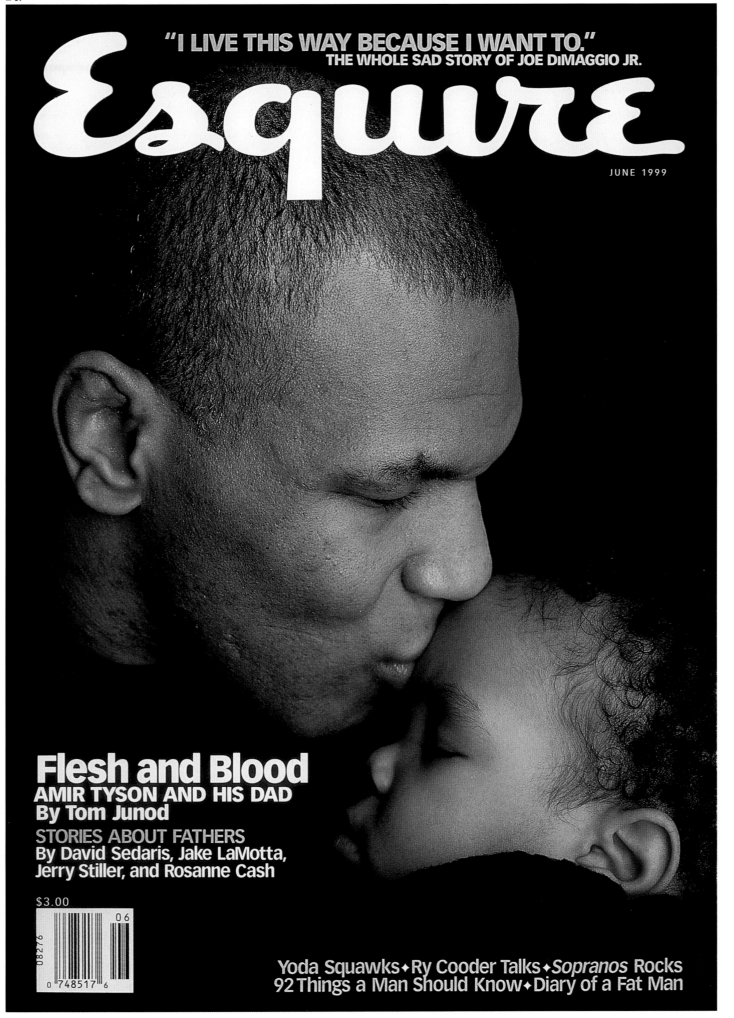

"I LIVE THIS WAY BECAUSE I WANT TO."
THE WHOLE SAD STORY OF JOE DiMAGGIO JR.

Esquire

JUNE 1999

Flesh and Blood
AMIR TYSON AND HIS DAD
By Tom Junod
STORIES ABOUT FATHERS
By David Sedaris, Jake LaMotta,
Jerry Stiller, and Rosanne Cash

$3.00

06

08276

0 748517 6

Yoda Squawks✦Ry Cooder Talks✦*Sopranos* Rocks
92 Things a Man Should Know✦Diary of a Fat Man

Helen Wilkinson

"If feminism doesn't address
what's happening to men today,
it's not going to move forward."

Article by Keith H. Hammonds   Photographs by Harry Borden

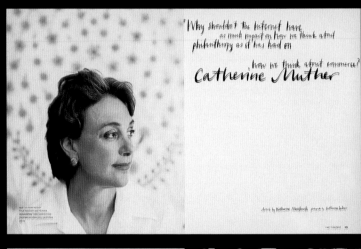

I've organize people not just around issues
but around their values.

Ernesto Cortés Jr.

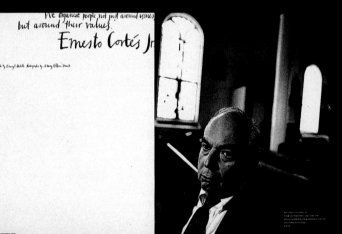

"Why shouldn't the Internet have
as much impact on how we think about
philanthropy as it has had on

how we think about commerce?

Catherine Muther

Article by Chuck Salter

"When you learn how to die,
you learn how to live."

Morrie Schwartz

#18

PUBLICATION Fast Company
ART DIRECTOR Patrick Mitchell
DESIGNERS Patrick Mitchell, Emily Crawford
ILLUSTRATOR Susy Pilgrim Waters
PHOTO EDITOR Alicia Jylkka
PHOTOGRAPHERS Mary Ellen Mark, Antonin Kratochvil,
Peter Ross, Kate Swan, Fredrik Brodén, Harry Borden,
PUBLISHER Fast Company

■ 19

■ 19
PUBLICATION Entertainment Weekly
DESIGN DIRECTOR John Korpics
DESIGNERS Geraldine Hessler, John Walker, Erin Whelan, Jennifer Procopio, Ellene Standke, Liliane Vilmenay, Joe Kimberling, Edith Gutierrez
PHOTO EDITOR Sarah Rozen
PHOTOGRAPHERS Matthew Rolston, Michael O'Neill
PUBLISHER Time Inc.
ISSUE June 25, 1999
CATEGORY Entire Issue

September 1999
US $7.00 | CAN $9.00

interiors

BARBARA BARRY
AYSE BIRSEL
ALEXA HAMPTON
STEPHANIE ODEGARD
COURTNEY SLOANE
LAURINDA SPEAR
MARGO GRANT WALSH
EVA ZEISEL

FEMALE LEADS

120° OF SEPARATION

ALL ABOUT EVA

URBAN LEGEND

FOR LAURINDA SPEAR, partner of Arquitectonica in Miami, being noted for her sex in a mostly male profession is a non-issue. Her C.V. lists a 1998 lecture titled "The Challenges Facing a Contemporary Woman Architect," yet she insists that the talk had only to do with her buildings. The notion of a "female architect" is a false construct, she claims. "Isn't it really more about the designer's character?" When Spear enrolled in Columbia's graduate school of architecture in the '70s, after receiving a B.F.A. from Brown, so few women were in attendance that "doors were opened," she says. She was there, she explains, because "I liked the functional and civic aspects of the field. And I wanted to work with other people." In 1977, she founded Arquitectonica (a variation on the Spanish word for "architectural") in her home-town, Miami, with her husband, Peruvian-born Bernardo Fort-Brescia, whom she had met as a grad student. Today, the firm has more than 200 employees and additional offices in New York, L.A., Paris, Manila, Lima, Buenos Aires, São Paulo, Hong Kong, and Shanghai. Early in the design world continuum, Arquitectonica's work with color for which the firm pioneered its signature style. Art Deco–inspired lines, a description that makes Spear cringe. "We never thought we were doing a 'style,'" she says. "We enjoyed working with color, but we didn't—and don't—do it to brighten things up. We think about what would be appropriate architecture for its place and purpose." Nor does she embrace the word "postmodern," though even today, the firm is often known for "that building with the hole in the middle of it," a.k.a. the Atlantis condominium in downtown Miami. | For Spear, the firm's reliance on simple, evocative forms that are easy to relate to isn't postmodernism, but accessible modernism. Two elementary schools in Miami make her case. White, block-like structures accented with geometric patterns, wave-shaped rooflines (acknowledging the ocean's ubiquity), and bright colors, they cater to children both visually and physically without a hint of condescension. On a vastly different site is E Walk, the 45-story Westin hotel/retail complex rising at Eighth Avenue and 42nd Street in New York, a prized location within the transformed Times Square district. The aesthetic guidelines developed by architect Robert A.M. Stern for this gaudy neighborhood seemed adventurous even to Spear. "We considered toning things down a bit, but Bob said, 'This is no time to get tasteful on me,'" she recalls. Arquitectonica's competition-winning solution is a sleek tower whose base will be a cacophony of images and colorful lights vying for attention along the neon-drenched streets. |

ARCHITECT LAURINDA SPEAR HELPED TO TRANSFORM MIAMI'S LOOK IN THE 80S. LATELY SHE'S BEEN SPREADING HER PALETTE AND PLAYFULNESS TO OTHER CITIES.

BY KIRA L. GOULD

■ 21

TIB R
KALMAN, DEVIL.

His work is subversive. He was a fire starter. Tibor Kalman designed his way through the worlds of magazines, advertising, and film, up until his death, at 49, in May. He was a provocateur, a protester, a prankster. *Tiborocity: Design and Undesign* – an exhibit of his troublemaking works at the San Francisco Museum of Modern Art through October 26 – celebrates Tibor's work and his spirit, capturing both his uncommon sense and his sense of humor. He collected onion rings, eggbeaters, product packaging, and an enormous following of disciples who wanted design to be more than merely style. For Tibor, the best design moved people to action rather than consumption (a fact that irritated many of his clients). He was determined to make every-one look and question, even if he had to be a devil to do it. One Christmas, Tibor's design firm, M&Co, sent clients a box containing a can of apple juice, a sandwich, and a slice of pound cake – the same meal being handed out on the streets of New York by the Coalition for the Homeless (included was a $20 bill with the suggestion that it would buy a burger at the 21 Club – or Christmas dinner for 18 homeless people). As the editor of *Colors* magazine, he repeatedly asked us "What if ...?" His depiction of Ronald Reagan with AIDS forced us to ask how policies might have been different ... if. Often Tibor was devilish with a wink. An M&Co watch placed the hours in the wrong order. He was a big believer in turning things upside down, as he did to the A's in TALKING HEADS on the cover of the *Remain in Light* album. And he turned all of modern design on its head along the way. – *Richard Pandiscio*

This story, created by Richard Pandiscio, longtime friend of Tibor Kalman, combines Tiborisms with sketches of *Tiborocity*'s floor plan by Tibor's wife, Maira, an artist and children's book author.

WIRED AUGUST 1999   164

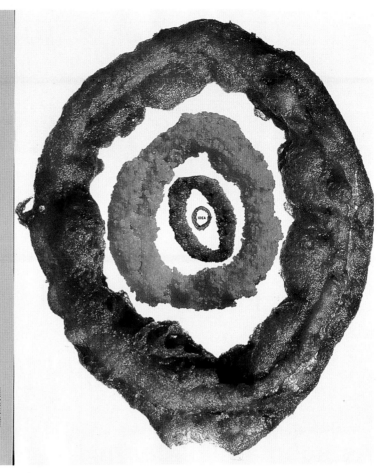

■ 20
PUBLICATION Interiors
ART DIRECTOR Paul Carlos
DESIGNERS Paul Carlos, Heather Buckley
PHOTO EDITOR Mackenzie Green
PHOTOGRAPHERS Brigitte LaCombe, Graham MacIndoe
PUBLISHER BPI Communications
ISSUE September 1999
CATEGORY Redesign

■ 21
PUBLICATION Wired
DESIGN DIRECTOR Daniel Carter
DESIGNER Richard Pandiscio
ILLUSTRATORS Richard Pandiscio, Maira Kalman
PHOTO EDITOR Christa Aboitiz
PHOTOGRAPHER Davies + Starr
PUBLISHER Condé Nast Publications, Inc.
ISSUE August 1999
CATEGORY Feature Spread

family tree *retrace the lines of your family history to discover the names of the remarkable people who came before you*

Family is a powerful word, evocative of love and belonging, of a safe place in an uncertain world. It's also an astonishing concept: Each of us is a link in an unbroken chain stretching back beyond the memory of our most elderly relative. We exist today because countless generations of people met, married, and had children, yet we know little or nothing about them. What were their names? Where did they live? When did they come to this country, and from where?

The moment you begin to answer these questions, you embark on an adventure—one that may take you down the narrow, winding streets of a foreign city or just up the stairs to the attic. You may discover an ethnic or a national heritage you never knew about, find a family name to give to a new baby, or just explore how your own story fits into the American epic. It's not always easy to unravel the skeins of time, but no other sleuthing job will ever be so satisfying.

Begin the information-gathering process close to home: List your name, and your siblings' names and birth dates, then your parents' and grandparents' names along with the places and dates of their births, and their marriage dates. The next step is to conduct genealogical interviews with your family, speaking with your oldest, frailest relations first. Ask the basics—names, dates, marriages—recording everything anyone remembers: what your great-uncle used to say about the old country, the location of the cabin where the family summered in the twenties. Use any prop that might jog a fading memory. Haul out the photo albums, and check the family Bible. Keep careful, organized notes, and pay careful attention to any place-names.

At this point you may want to think about limiting the scope of your research. Some people find that it's more practical to trace a single family line (a paternal or maternal one) rather than going off in all directions at once. To continue your search, you must know—fairly exactly—where your ancestors lived. As Brian G. Andersson of Ellis Island and Castle Garden Research, in New York City, says, "Place is your key starting point, not only for census data but also vital records: birth, marriage, and death certificates, not to mention wills and property records, all of which are filed by location." One good source for these documents is the National Archives and Records Administration—there are thirteen branches across the country—which keeps records of census data from 1790 to 1920, as well as things like death certificates and property records. It's a treasure trove of information, but to use it you must know that your great-great-grandfather lived

Family trees are often beautiful works of art in their own right, as well as informative records of genealogy. OPPOSITE: The calligrapher who designed this Victorian family tree in 1884 inked in the names of the earliest ancestors in the Carpenter family just above the trunk; each subsequent generation branches farther out along the spreading boughs.

PHOTOGRAPHS BY WILLIAM ABRANOWICZ TEXT BY ANN E. BERMAN

MARTHA STEWART Living

FOUNTAIN TREATS LAVENDER
FRIED CHICKEN 101 **FLAGS**
5&10¢ STORES CANVAS

JULY/AUGUST 1999 $4.50 USA (CAN. $5.50)
www.marthastewart.com

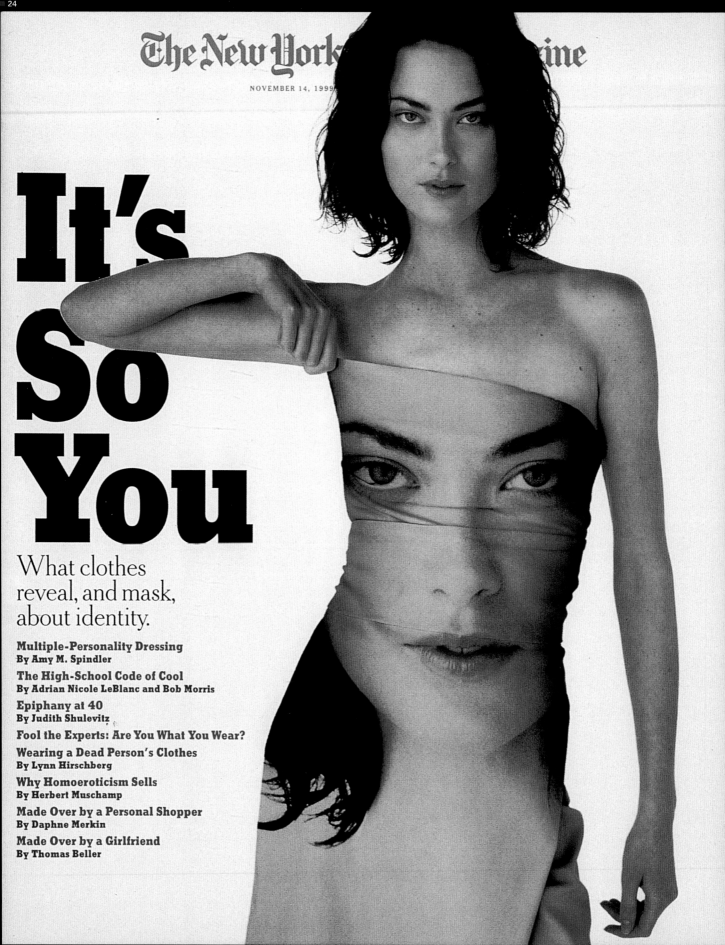

The New York Magazine

NOVEMBER 14, 1999

It's So You

What clothes reveal, and mask, about identity.

Multiple-Personality Dressing
By Amy M. Spindler

The High-School Code of Cool
By Adrian Nicole LeBlanc and Bob Morris

Epiphany at 40
By Judith Shulevitz

Fool the Experts: Are You What You Wear?

Wearing a Dead Person's Clothes
By Lynn Hirschberg

Why Homoeroticism Sells
By Herbert Muschamp

Made Over by a Personal Shopper
By Daphne Merkin

Made Over by a Girlfriend
By Thomas Beller

Eyes

Wide Open
When an obscure Arab scientist solved the riddle of light, the universe no longer belonged to God.

By Richard Powers

y any human measure, a millennium is a considerable chunk of time. It is the longest fixed unit of time with a distinct name in common usage. At the beginning of our spent millennium and at frequent intervals throughout it, vexed to nightmare by the calendar, believers have awaited Christ's imminent return to rule over a new heaven and earth in a kingdom that was to run for the unthinkable span of a thousand years. Near the millennium's end, the Nazis, refiners of another one of the period's most persistent concepts, predicted their own third kingdom would last for a thousand years. They were off by 988.

At the start of this millennium, nothing resembling an accurate map of any continent existed. Now a hand-held Global Positioning System satellite receiver can pinpoint its owner's location anywhere on the face of the globe. Trade and enterprise have expanded beyond all reckoning. More volumes are printed each year than existed in the year 1000. The last 10 centuries have also seen global deforestation, a steep falling off in spoken languages and mass extinction on a scale beyond anything since the Cretaceous.

Any search for the millennium's most important concept already dooms itself to myopia. Consider the candidates that spring to mind: parliamentary democracy, the nation-state, free markets, due proc-

Photograph by Tom Schierlitz. Concept by Stefan Sagmeister.

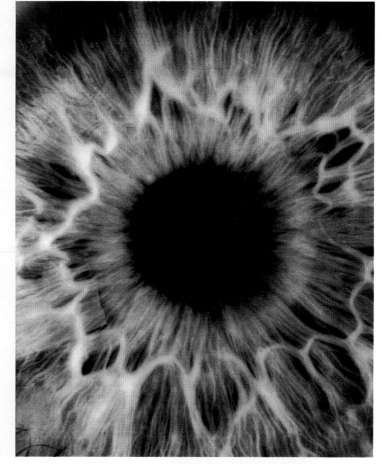

When Tristram Met Isolde
True love may last forever, but it hasn't been around that long.

By Joyce Carol Oates

A Pilgrim's Progress
The Bible as civic blueprint.

The Book That Killed
Colonialism
As the West clamored for spices, the novelist 'Multatuli' cried for justice.

By Pramoedya Ananta Toer

Everything
Place in Its
One man's love affair with the periodic table.

By Oliver Sacks

■ 24
PUBLICATION The New York Times Magazine
ART DIRECTOR Janet Froelich
DESIGNER Claude Martel
PHOTO EDITOR Kathy Ryan
PHOTOGRAPHER Andrew Eccles
PUBLISHER The New York Times
ISSUE November 14, 1999
CATEGORY Cover

■ 25
PUBLICATION The New York Times Magazine
ART DIRECTORS Janet Froelich, Joele Cuyler
DESIGNERS Joele Cuyler, Ignacio Rodriguez
PHOTO EDITORS Kathy Ryan, Sarah Harbutt
PHOTOGRAPHERS Tom Schierlitz, Dan Winters, Amy Guip
PUBLISHER The New York Times
ISSUE April 18, 1999
CATEGORY Feature Story

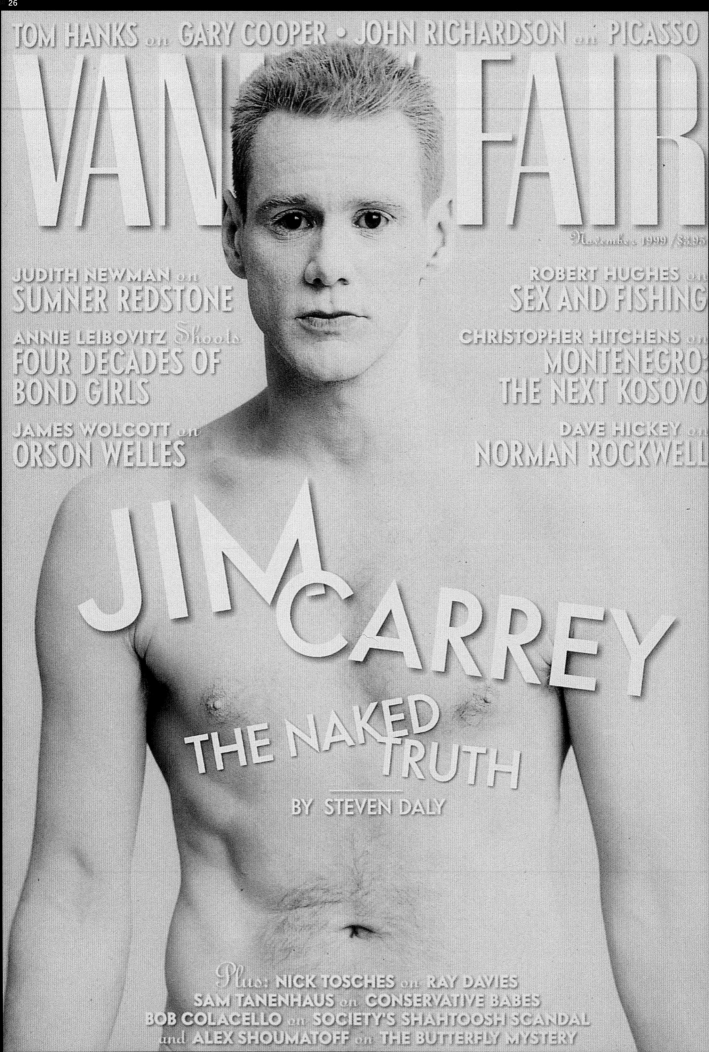

TOM HANKS on GARY COOPER • JOHN RICHARDSON on PICASSO

VANITY FAIR

November 1999 / $3.95

JUDITH NEWMAN on
SUMNER REDSTONE

ANNIE LEIBOVITZ *Shoots*
**FOUR DECADES OF
BOND GIRLS**

JAMES WOLCOTT on
ORSON WELLES

ROBERT HUGHES on
SEX AND FISHING

CHRISTOPHER HITCHENS on
**MONTENEGRO:
THE NEXT KOSOVO**

DAVE HICKEY on
NORMAN ROCKWELL

JIM McCARREY

THE NAKED TRUTH

BY STEVEN DALY

Plus: **NICK TOSCHES** on **RAY DAVIES**
SAM TANENHAUS on **CONSERVATIVE BABES**
BOB COLACELLO on **SOCIETY'S SHAHTOOSH SCANDAL**
and **ALEX SHOUMATOFF** on **THE BUTTERFLY MYSTERY**

THREE TIMES A NAUGHTY (from left):
Kay Gee, Treach, and Vin Rock

PHOTOGRAPHED BY ANDREW SOUTHAM MARCH 16, 1999, CHELSEA, NEW YORK CITY

TREACHEROUS

*Wake up, sleepyheads: **Naughty by Nature's** Fury is much more than a blast from the past. By Matt Diehl*

TRIO

VIBE 111

■ 26

PUBLICATION Vanity Fair
DESIGN DIRECTOR David Harris
ART DIRECTOR Gregory Mastrianni
PHOTO EDITORS Susan White, Lisa Berman,
SunHee Grinnell, Kathryn MacLeod,
PHOTOGRAPHER Annie Leibovitz
PUBLISHER Condé Nast Publications, Inc.
ISSUE November 1999
CATEGORY Cover

■ 27

PUBLICATION Vibe
DESIGN DIRECTOR Dwayne Shaw
DESIGNER Brandon Kavulla
PHOTO EDITOR George Pitts
PHOTOGRAPHER Andrew Southam
PUBLISHER Miller Publishing Group
ISSUE June 1999
CATEGORY Feature Spread

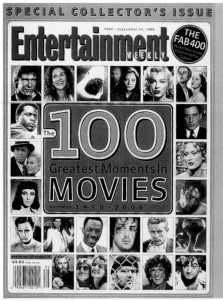

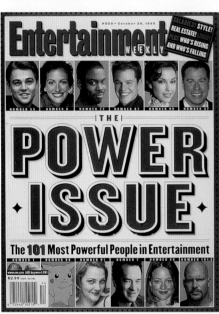

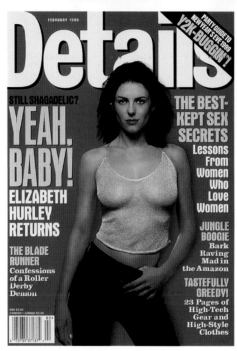

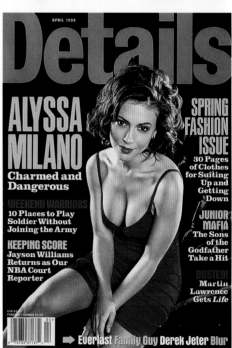

■ 28
PUBLICATION Entertainment Weekly
DESIGN DIRECTOR Geraldine Hessler
ART DIRECTOR John Walker
DESIGNERS Geraldine Hessler, John Walker, Joe Kimberling, Jennifer Procopio, Ellene Standke, Liliane Vilmenay, Jennie Chang, Edith Gutierrez, Erin Whelan, George McCalman
PHOTO EDITORS Sarah Rozen, Denise Sfraga, Deborah Dragon
PHOTOGRAPHERS Armando Gallo, Sante D'Orazio, Norman Jean Roy, Andrew Eccles, Mirek Towski, Mitch Gerber, Andrea Renault, Catherine Ledner, Timothy Greenfield-Sanders, Darryl Estrine, Ron Batzdorff, Ken Regan, Richard Miller, Jim Wright, Stephen Wayda, Robert Fleischauer, Brigitte LaCombe, Albert Sanchez, Jon Ragel, Mary Grandpré
PUBLISHER Time Inc.
ISSUES October 29, 1999, September 4, 1999, December 24-31, 1999
CATEGORY Magazine of the Year

■ 29
PUBLICATION Details
DESIGN DIRECTOR Robert Newman
DESIGNERS John Giordani, Alden Wallace, Ronda Thompson, Chad Tomlinson, Wyatt Mitchell, Marcus Burrowes
PHOTO EDITORS Greg Pond, Halla Timon
PUBLISHER Condé Nast Publications, Inc.
ISSUES February 1999, March 1999, April 1999
CATEGORY Magazine of the Year

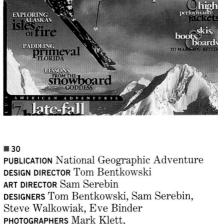

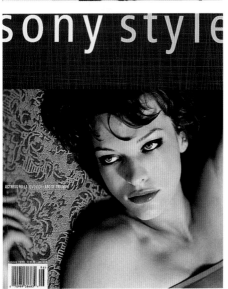

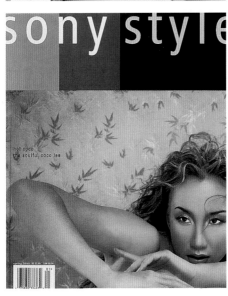

■ 30
PUBLICATION National Geographic Adventure
DESIGN DIRECTOR Tom Bentkowski
ART DIRECTOR Sam Serebin
DESIGNERS Tom Bentkowski, Sam Serebin,
Steve Walkowiak, Eve Binder
PHOTOGRAPHERS Mark Klett,
Lanny Johnson, Mark Gamba
PUBLISHER National Geographic Society
ISSUES Spring 1999, Fall 1999, Winter 1999
CATEGORY Magazine of the Year
    A MERIT Cover

■ 31
PUBLICATION Copenhagen Living
CREATIVE DIRECTOR Anders Peter Mejer
DESIGNER Anders Peter Mejer
PHOTO EDITOR Anders Peter Mejer
PHOTOGRAPHERS Lionel Guyou, Tor Jørgensen
STUDIO Embryo Design
PUBLISHER CPH Living Publishing
ISSUES June 10, 1999, November 12, 1999
CATEGORY Magazine of the Year

■ 32
PUBLICATION Sony Style
CREATIVE DIRECTOR Terry Ross Koppel
ART DIRECTOR Darcy Doyle
DESIGNERS Kristina DiMatteo, Jennifer Muller,
Jason Lancaster, Karen Yi
PHOTO EDITORS Julie Claire, Linda Fernbacher
PUBLISHER Time Inc. Custom Publishing
ISSUES Fall 1999, Holiday 1999, Spring 2000
CATEGORY Magazine of the Year

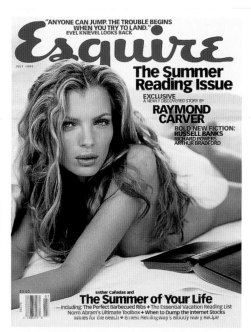

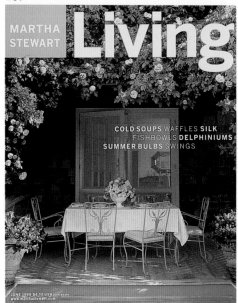

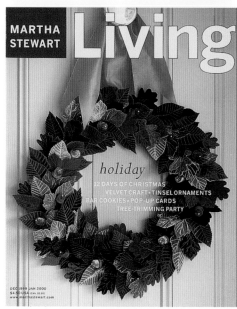

■ 33

PUBLICATION Esquire
DESIGN DIRECTOR Robert Priest
ART DIRECTOR Rockwell Harwood
DESIGNERS Paul Scirecalabrissotto, Joshua Liberson
ILLUSTRATOR Roberto Parada
PHOTO EDITORS Simon Barnett, Patti Wilson
PHOTOGRAPHERS Sam Jones, Patrick Demarchelier, Peggy Sirota
PUBLISHER The Hearst Corporation-Magazines Division
ISSUES May 1999, July 1999, August 1999
CATEGORY Magazine of the Year

■ 34

PUBLICATION Martha Stewart Living
DESIGN DIRECTOR Eric A. Pike
ART DIRECTORS James Dunlinson, Scot Schy, Susan Corral, Stacey Dietz, , Linda Kocur, Helen Sanematsu, Brooke Hellewell, Claudia Bruno
PHOTO EDITOR Heidi J. Posner
PHOTOGRAPHERS Gentl & Hyers, Minh & Wass, Christopher Baker, Beatriz Da Costa, David Sawyer, John Dugdale, Victor Schrager, Jason Schmidt, Dana Gallagher, Charles Maraia, Anna Williams, Reed Davis, Anita Calero, Matthew Septimus, Simon Watson, Raymond Meeks, Tim Street-Porter
PUBLISHER Martha Stewart Living Omnimedia
ISSUES March 1999, June 1999, December 1999/January 2000
CATEGORY Magazine of the Year

Graphis 322

A

A

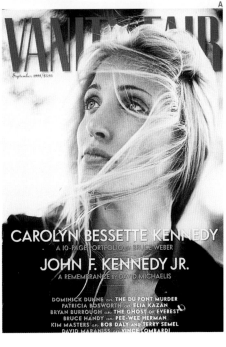

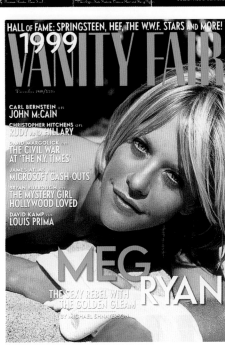

Graphis 324

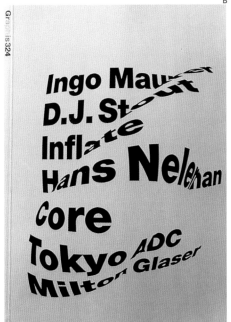

B

Graphis 323

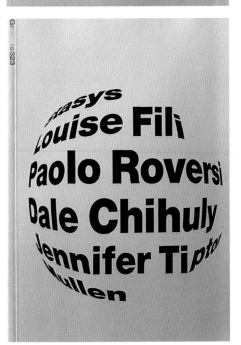

■ 35
PUBLICATION Graphis
CREATIVE DIRECTOR B. Martin Pedersen
ART DIRECTOR Massimo Acanfora
DESIGNERS B. Martin Pedersen, Massimo Acanfora
PUBLISHER Graphis
ISSUES July/August, September/October, November/December 1999
CATEGORY Magazine of the Year
    A **MERIT** Cover
    B **MERIT** Cover and Entire Issue

■ 36
PUBLICATION Vanity Fair
DESIGN DIRECTOR David Harris
ART DIRECTORS Gregory Mastrianni, Julie Weiss, Mimi Dutta
DESIGNERS Lee Ruelle, Lisa Kennedy
PHOTO EDITORS Susan White, Lisa Berman, Jeannie Rhodes
PHOTOGRAPHERS Annie Leibovitz, Bruce Weber, Mario Testino
PUBLISHER Condé Nast Publications, Inc.
ISSUES April 1999, September 1999, December 1999
CATEGORY Magazine of the Year
    A **MERIT** Cover

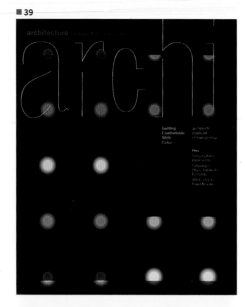

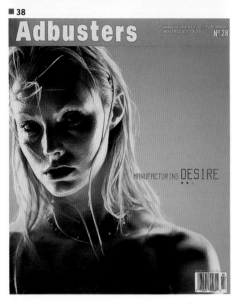

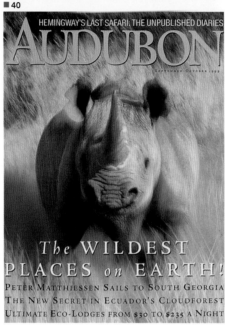

■ 43

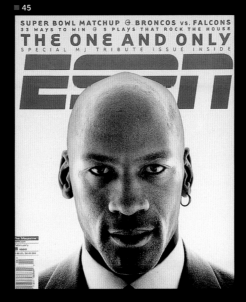

■ 45

■ 47

■ 44

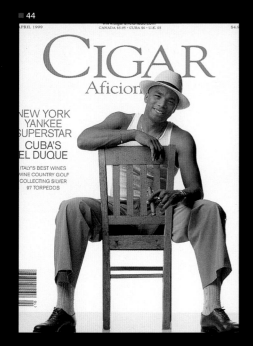

■ 46

■ 48

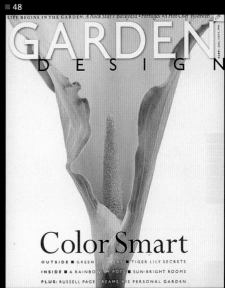

■ 43
PUBLICATION The Business
ART DIRECTOR Gary Cook
DESIGNER Gary Cook
ILLUSTRATOR Andy Bridge
PHOTOGRAPHER Mathew Donaldson
PUBLISHER The Financial Times Ltd.
ISSUE November 6, 1999
CATEGORY Cover

■ 44
PUBLICATION Cigar Aficionado
CREATIVE DIRECTOR Martin Leeds
ART DIRECTOR Lori Ende
PHOTOGRAPHER Michael O'Neill
PUBLISHER M. Shanken Communications Inc.
ISSUE April 1999
CATEGORY Cover

■ 45
PUBLICATION ESPN
DESIGN DIRECTOR F. Darrin Perry
ART DIRECTOR Peter Yates
DESIGNERS Yvette L. Francis,
Bruce Glase, Chris Rudzik
PHOTO EDITOR Nik Kleinberg
PHOTOGRAPHER Darryl Estrine
PUBLISHER Disney Publishing Worldwide
ISSUE February 8, 1999
CATEGORY Cover

■ 46
PUBLICATION Esquire
DESIGN DIRECTOR John Korpics
PHOTO EDITOR Simon Barnett
PHOTOGRAPHER Matthew Rolston
PUBLISHER The Hearst Corporation-
Magazines Division
ISSUE November 1999
CATEGORY Cover

■ 47
PUBLICATION Garden Design
CREATIVE DIRECTOR Michael Grossman
ART DIRECTOR Toby Fox
DESIGNERS Michael Grossman, Toby Fox
PHOTO EDITOR Stella Kramer
PHOTOGRAPHER André Baranowski
PUBLISHER Meigher Communications
ISSUE June/July 1999
CATEGORY Cover

■ 48
PUBLICATION Garden Design
CREATIVE DIRECTOR Michael Grossman
ART DIRECTOR Toby Fox
DESIGNERS Michael Grossman, Toby Fox
PHOTO EDITOR Heidi Yockey
PHOTOGRAPHER André Baranowski
PUBLISHER Meigher Communications
ISSUE August/September 1999
CATEGORY Cover

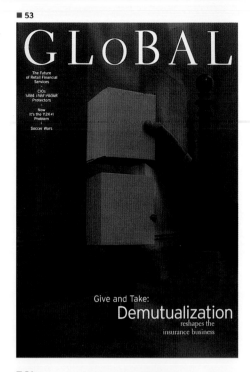

■ 49
PUBLICATION Fast Company
ART DIRECTOR Patrick Mitchell
DESIGNER Patrick Mitchell
ILLUSTRATOR John Hersey
PUBLISHER Fast Company
ISSUE November 1999
CATEGORY Cover

■ 50
PUBLICATION Fast Company
ART DIRECTOR Patrick Mitchell
DESIGNER Patrick Mitchell
ILLUSTRATOR John Hersey
PUBLISHER Fast Company
ISSUE November 1999
CATEGORY Cover

■ 51
PUBLICATION Fast Company
ART DIRECTOR Patrick Mitchell
DESIGNER Patrick Mitchell
ILLUSTRATOR Steve Wacksman
PUBLISHER Fast Company
ISSUE October 1999
CATEGORY Cover

■ 52
PUBLICATION Form
CREATIVE DIRECTOR John Bark
ART DIRECTOR Christoffer Wessel
STUDIO Bark Design
PUBLISHER The Swedish Society
of Crafts and Design
ISSUE April 1999
CATEGORY Cover

■ 53
PUBLICATION Global
ART DIRECTOR Tom Brown
DESIGNER Tom Brown
PHOTOGRAPHER Fredrik Brodén
STUDIO Tom Brown Art & Design
PUBLISHER Deloitte & Touche, LLP
ISSUE March/April 1999
CATEGORY Cover

■ 54
PUBLICATION Guardian Weekend
ART DIRECTOR Mark Porter
DESIGNERS Balwant Ahira, Maggie Murphy
PHOTO EDITOR Jane Greening
PUBLISHER Guardian Media Group
ISSUE May 22, 1999
CATEGORY Cover

■ 55

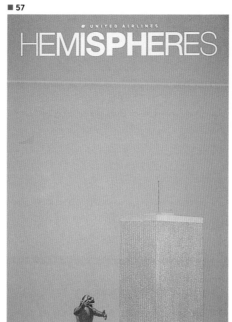

■ 57

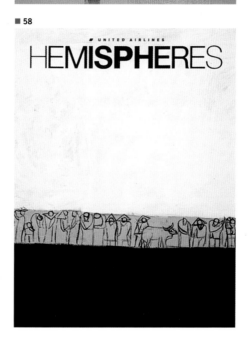

■ 59

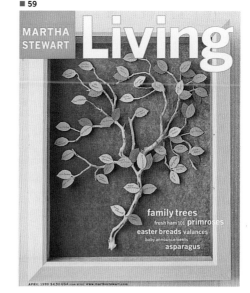

■ 56

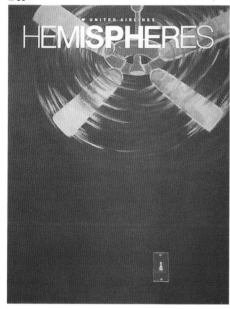

■ 58

■ 60

■ 55
PUBLICATION GW
CREATIVE DIRECTOR Jim Gray
ART DIRECTOR Jim Gray
DESIGNER Jim Gray
ILLUSTRATOR Brian Cronin
STUDIO Concept Foundry
PUBLISHER George Washington University
ISSUE Spring 1999
CATEGORY Cover

■ 56
PUBLICATION Hemispheres
DESIGN DIRECTOR Jaimey Easler
ART DIRECTORS Jaimey Easler,
Jody Mustain, Kevin de Miranda
ILLUSTRATOR Joan Brown
PUBLISHER Pace Communications
CLIENT United Airlines
ISSUE February 1999
CATEGORY Cover

■ 57
PUBLICATION Hemispheres
DESIGN DIRECTOR Jaimey Easler
ART DIRECTORS Jaimey Easler,
Jody Mustain, Kevin de Miranda
ILLUSTRATOR Tom LaDuke
PUBLISHER Pace Communications
CLIENT United Airlines
ISSUE August 1999
CATEGORY Cover

■ 58
PUBLICATION Hemispheres
DESIGN DIRECTOR Jaimey Easler
ART DIRECTORS Jaimey Easler,
Jody Mustain, Kevin de Miranda
ILLUSTRATOR Lan Nguyen
PUBLISHER Pace Communications
CLIENT United Airlines
ISSUE November 1999
CATEGORY Cover

■ 59
PUBLICATION Martha Stewart Living
DESIGN DIRECTOR Eric A. Pike
DESIGNERS Eric A. Pike,
Anthony Cochran, Kerin Brooks
PHOTO EDITOR Heidi J. Posner
PHOTOGRAPHER William Abranowicz
PUBLISHER Martha Stewart Living Omnimedia
ISSUE April 1999
CATEGORY Cover

■ 60
PUBLICATION Martha Stewart Weddings
ART DIRECTOR Ellen Burnie
DESIGNERS Ellen Burnie,
Lindsey Taylor, Rebecca Thuss
PHOTO EDITOR Heidi J. Posner
PHOTOGRAPHER Carlton Davis
PUBLISHER Martha Stewart Living Omnimedia
ISSUE Summer 1999
CATEGORY Cover

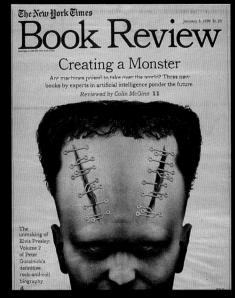

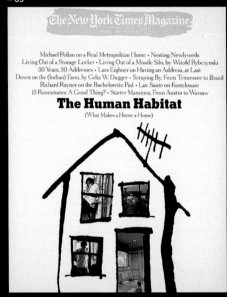

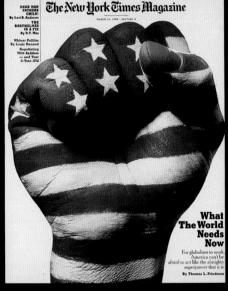

61
PUBLICATION The New York Times Book Review
ART DIRECTOR Steven Heller
ILLUSTRATOR Mirko Ilíc
PUBLISHER The New York Times
ISSUE January 3, 1999
CATEGORY Cover

62
PUBLICATION The New York Times Book Review
ART DIRECTOR Steven Heller
ILLUSTRATOR Richard McGuire
PUBLISHER The New York Times
ISSUE January 31, 1999
CATEGORY Cover

63
PUBLICATION The New York Times Magazine
ART DIRECTOR Janet Froelich
DESIGNER Catherine Gilmore-Barnes
ILLUSTRATOR Christoph Niemann
PUBLISHER The New York Times
ISSUE March 7, 1999
CATEGORY Cover

64
PUBLICATION The New York Times Magazine
ART DIRECTOR Janet Froelich
DESIGNER Nancy Harris
ILLUSTRATOR John Kascht
PUBLISHER The New York Times
ISSUE January 3, 1999
CATEGORY Cover

65
PUBLICATION The New York Times Magazine
ART DIRECTOR Janet Froelich
DESIGNER Nancy Harris
PUBLISHER The New York Times
ISSUE March 14, 1999
CATEGORY Cover

66
PUBLICATION The New York Times Magazine
ART DIRECTOR Janet Froelich
PHOTO EDITOR Kathy Ryan
PHOTOGRAPHER Craig Cutler
PUBLISHER The New York Times
ISSUE March 28, 1999
CATEGORY Cover

67
PUBLICATION The New York Times Magazine
ART DIRECTOR Janet Froelich
DESIGNER Claude Martel
PHOTO EDITOR Kathy Ryan
PHOTOGRAPHER Tom Schierlitz
PUBLISHER The New York Times
ISSUE September 26, 1999
CATEGORY Cover

68
PUBLICATION The New York Times Magazine
ART DIRECTOR Janet Froelich
DESIGNER Janet Froelich
ILLUSTRATOR John Maeda
PUBLISHER The New York Times
ISSUE October 10, 1999
CATEGORY Cover

69
PUBLICATION The New York Times Magazine
ART DIRECTORS Janet Froelich, Joele Cuyler
DESIGNERS Joele Cuyler, Ignacio Rodriguez
ILLUSTRATOR Christoph Niemann
PHOTO EDITORS Kathy Ryan, Sarah Harbutt
PHOTOGRAPHER Albert Watson
PUBLISHER The New York Times
ISSUE October 17, 1999
CATEGORY Cover

The New York Times Magazine

MARCH 14, 1999 / SECTION 6

SECRETS
AND LIES:
AN ADOPTION
TRAGEDY
By Lisa Belkin

THE MICHAEL
JORDAN
OF FRANCE
By John Vinocur

WIFE POWER
By Margaret Talbot

NED ROREM
ON MOURNING

amazon.com

Earth's Biggest What, Exactly?

*A virtual success story,
by Peter de Jonge*

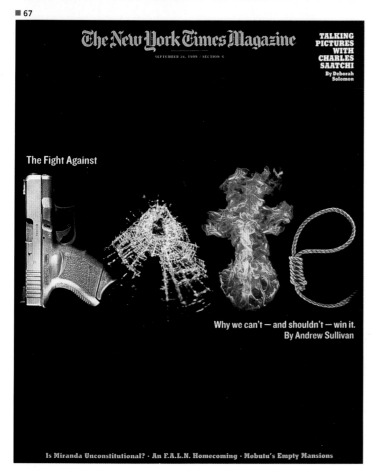

The New York Times Magazine

SEPTEMBER 26, 1999 / SECTION 6

TALKING
PICTURES
WITH
CHARLES
SAATCHI
By Deborah
Solomon

The Fight Against

HATE

Why we can't — and shouldn't — win it.
By Andrew Sullivan

Is Miranda Unconstitutional? · An F.A.L.N. Homecoming · Mobutu's Empty Mansions

The New York Times Magazine

OCTOBER 10, 1999 / SECTION 6

THE NEW NEW THING

How Jim Clark taught America what the techno-economy was all about. By Michael Lewis

Plus: Why Matthew Barney Matters, by Michael Kimmelman

The New York Times Magazine

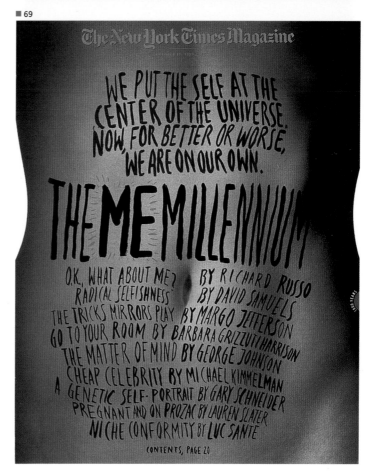

WE PUT THE SELF AT THE
CENTER OF THE UNIVERSE.
NOW, FOR BETTER OR WORSE,
WE ARE ON OUR OWN.

THE ME MILLENNIUM

O.K., WHAT ABOUT ME? BY RICHARD RUSSO
RADICAL SELFISHNESS BY DAVID SAMUELS
THE TRICKS MIRRORS PLAY BY MARGO JEFFERSON
GO TO YOUR ROOM BY BARBARA GRIZZUTI HARRISON
THE MATTER OF MIND BY GEORGE JOHNSON
CHEAP CELEBRITY BY MICHAEL KIMMELMAN
A GENETIC SELF-PORTRAIT BY GARY SCHNEIDER
PREGNANT AND ON PROZAC BY LAUREN SLATER
NICHE CONFORMITY BY LUC SANTE

CONTENTS, PAGE 20

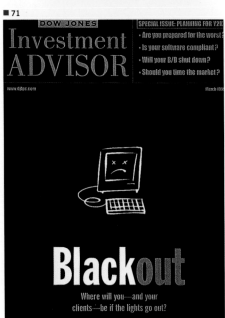

■ 70
PUBLICATION Interiors
ART DIRECTOR Paul Carlos
DESIGNERS Paul Carlos, Heather Buckley
PHOTO EDITOR Mackenzie Green
PHOTOGRAPHER Brigitte LaCombe
PUBLISHER BPI Communications
ISSUE September 1999
CATEGORY Cover

■ 71
PUBLICATION Investment Advisor
CREATIVE DIRECTOR Dorothy A. Jones
ILLUSTRATOR Christoph Hitz
PUBLISHER Investment Advisor Group
ISSUE March 1999
CATEGORY Cover

■ 72
PUBLICATION Jane
ART DIRECTOR Johan Svensson
DESIGNER Amy Demas
PHOTO EDITOR Cary Estes Leitzes
PHOTOGRAPHER Matthew Rolston
PUBLISHER Fairchild Publications
ISSUE December 1999
CATEGORY Cover

■ 73
PUBLICATION Metropolitan Home
ART DIRECTOR Keith G. D'Mello
DESIGNER Keith G. D'Mello
PHOTO EDITOR Hilary E. Clark
PHOTOGRAPHER Tim Street-Porter
PUBLISHER Hachette Filipacchi Magazines, Inc.
ISSUE September/October 1999
CATEGORY Cover

■ 74
PUBLICATION MIX
ART DIRECTORS Matthew P. Beckerle, Terry Lau
DESIGNERS Matthew P. Beckerle, Terry Lau
STUDIO creative activity design company
PUBLISHER Parallélogramme Artist-Run Culture
and Publishing Inc.
ISSUE September 5, 1999
CATEGORY Cover

∎ 75

∎ 77

∎ 78

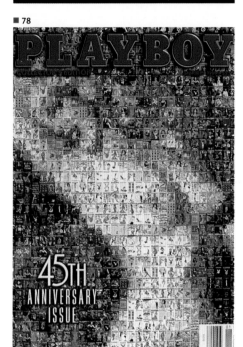

∎ 79

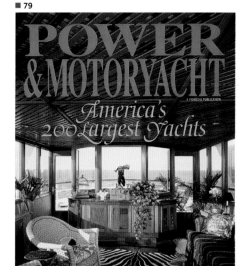

∎ 80

∎ 75
PUBLICATION National Geographic
ART DIRECTOR Constance H. Phelps
PHOTOGRAPHER Joe McNally
PUBLISHER National Geographic Society
ISSUE August 1999
CATEGORY Cover

∎ 76
PUBLICATION The Observer Life
ART DIRECTOR Wayne Ford
DESIGNER Wayne Ford
PHOTO EDITOR Jennie Ricketts
PHOTOGRAPHER Michael O'Neill
PUBLISHER Guardian Newspapers Limited
ISSUE December 26, 1999
CATEGORY Cover

∎ 77
PUBLICATION Orion
CREATIVE DIRECTOR Hans Teensma
DESIGN DIRECTOR Katie Craig
PHOTO EDITOR Hadas Dembo
PHOTOGRAPHER Adam Fuss
STUDIO Impress, Inc.
PUBLISHER Orion Society
ISSUE Autumn 1999
CATEGORY Cover

∎ 78
PUBLICATION Playboy
ART DIRECTOR Tom Staebler
DESIGNER Rob Silvers
ILLUSTRATOR Rob Silvers
PUBLISHER Playboy Enterprises International, Inc.
ISSUE January 1999
CATEGORY Cover

∎ 79
PUBLICATION Power & Motor Yacht
ART DIRECTOR Sara Hylan
DESIGNER Rebecca Perez
PHOTOGRAPHER Neil Alexander
PUBLISHER Primedia Magazines Inc.
ISSUE November 1999
CATEGORY Cover

∎ 80
PUBLICATION Premiere
ART DIRECTOR Richard Baker
DESIGNER Richard Baker
PHOTO EDITOR Nancy Jo Iacoi
PHOTOGRAPHER Brigitte LaCombe
PUBLISHER Hachette Filipacchi Magazines, Inc.
ISSUE September 1999
CATEGORY Cover

■ 81

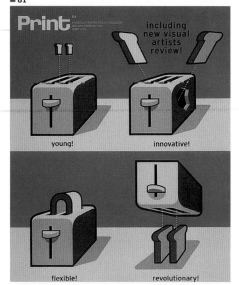

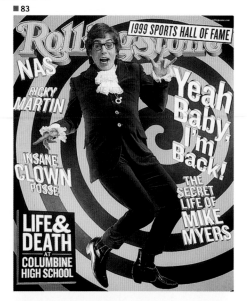

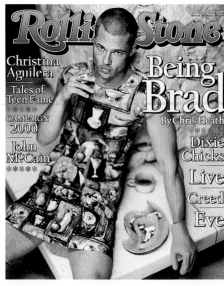

■ 82

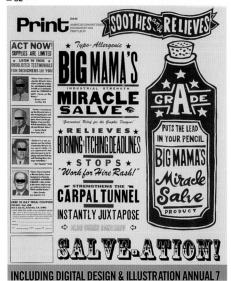

■ 81
PUBLICATION Print
ART DIRECTOR Andrew Kner
DESIGNER Christoph Niemann
ILLUSTRATOR Christoph Niemann
PUBLISHER RC Publications
ISSUE January 1999
CATEGORY Cover

■ 83
PUBLICATION Rolling Stone
ART DIRECTOR Fred Woodward
DESIGNER Fred Woodward
PHOTO EDITOR Rachel Knepfer
PHOTOGRAPHER Mark Seliger
PUBLISHER Straight Arrow Publishers
ISSUE June 10, 1999
CATEGORY Cover

■ 85
PUBLICATION Rolling Stone
ART DIRECTOR Fred Woodward
DESIGNER Fred Woodward
PHOTO EDITOR Rachel Knepfer
PHOTOGRAPHER Mark Seliger
PUBLISHER Straight Arrow Publishers
ISSUE October 16, 1999
CATEGORY Cover

■ 82
PUBLICATION Print
ART DIRECTOR Andrew Kner
DESIGNERS Julie Belcher, Kevin Bradley
ILLUSTRATOR Julie Belcher
PHOTOGRAPHER Kevin Bradley
STUDIO Yee-Haw Industries
PUBLISHER RC Publications
ISSUE July 1999
CATEGORY Cover

■ 84
PUBLICATION Rolling Stone
ART DIRECTOR Fred Woodward
DESIGNER Fred Woodward
PHOTO EDITOR Rachel Knepfer
PHOTOGRAPHER Mark Seliger
PUBLISHER Straight Arrow Publishers
ISSUE September 16, 1999
CATEGORY Cover

■ 86
PUBLICATION Saveur
CREATIVE DIRECTOR Michael Grossman
ART DIRECTOR Jill Armus
DESIGNERS Michael Grossman, Jill Armus
PHOTO EDITOR María Millán
PHOTOGRAPHER Martin Schreiber
PUBLISHER Meigher Communications
ISSUE May/June 1999
CATEGORY Cover

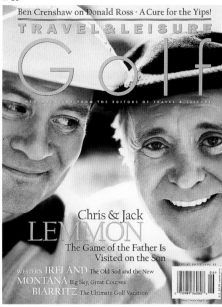

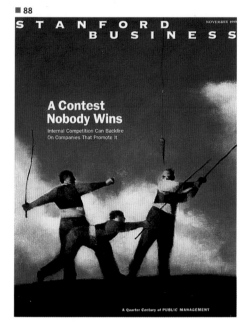

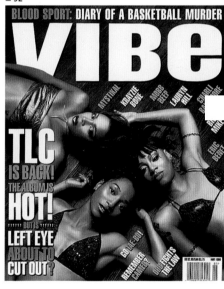

■ 87
PUBLICATION Selling Power
ART DIRECTOR Colleen McCudden
DESIGNER Colleen McCudden
ILLUSTRATOR Scott Matthews
PUBLISHER Personal Selling Power
ISSUE November/December 1999
CATEGORY Cover

■ 88
PUBLICATION Stanford Business
ART DIRECTOR Nan Christensen
DESIGNER Steven Powell
ILLUSTRATOR Brad Holland
PUBLISHER Stanford Business School
ISSUE November 1999
CATEGORY Cover

■ 89
PUBLICATION Travel & Leisure Golf
DESIGN DIRECTOR Tom Brown
ART DIRECTORS Dirk Barnett, Todd Albertson
DESIGNERS Tom Brown,
Dirk Barnett, Todd Albertson
PHOTO EDITOR Maisie Todd
PHOTOGRAPHER Sam Jones
PUBLISHER American Express Publishing Co.
ISSUE May/June 1999
CATEGORY Cover

■ 90
PUBLICATION Texas Monthly
CREATIVE DIRECTOR D. J. Stout
DESIGNER D. J. Stout
ILLUSTRATOR Steve Pietzch
PHOTO EDITOR D. J. Stout
PHOTOGRAPHER Rick Patrick
PUBLISHER Emmis Communications Corp.
ISSUE November 1999
CATEGORY Cover

■ 91
PUBLICATION U&lc
CREATIVE DIRECTOR Clive Chiu
ART DIRECTOR Deanna Lowe
DESIGNER Deanna Lowe
PUBLISHER International Typeface Corp.
ISSUE Fall 1999
CATEGORY Cover

■ 92
PUBLICATION Vibe
DESIGN DIRECTOR Dwayne Shaw
PHOTO EDITOR George Pitts
PHOTOGRAPHER Seb Janiak
PUBLISHER Miller Publishing Group
ISSUE May 1999
CATEGORY Cover

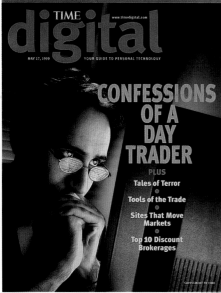

■ 93

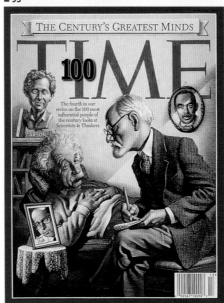

■ 94

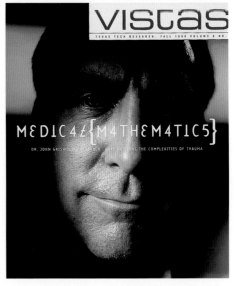

■ 96

■ 97

■ 95

■ 93
PUBLICATION Time Digital
ART DIRECTOR Susan Langholz
PHOTOGRAPHER Aaron Goodman
ISSUE May 17, 1999
CATEGORY Cover

■ 94
PUBLICATION Time
ART DIRECTOR Arthur Hochstein
ILLUSTRATOR Arthur Hochstein
PHOTOGRAPHERS Terry Ashe, Dirck Halstead,
David Burnett, Cynthia Johnson, Martin Simon
PUBLISHER Time Inc.
ISSUE February 22, 1999
CATEGORY Cover

■ 95
PUBLICATION Time
ART DIRECTOR Arthur Hochstein
ILLUSTRATOR Mark Summers
PUBLISHER Time Inc.
ISSUE March 29, 1999
CATEGORY Cover

■ 96
PUBLICATION USA Weekend Magazine
CREATIVE DIRECTOR Casey Shaw
ART DIRECTOR Pamela Smith
PHOTOGRAPHER Renée Comet
ISSUE July 2-4, 1999
CATEGORY Cover

■ 97
PUBLICATION Vistas: Texas Tech Research
CREATIVE DIRECTORS Scott C. Dadich,
Artie D. Limmer
ART DIRECTOR Scott C. Dadich
DESIGNERS Scott C. Dadich, Alyson Keeling
PHOTO EDITOR Artie D. Limmer
PHOTOGRAPHER Artie D. Limmer
PUBLISHER Texas Tech University
ISSUE Fall 1999
CATEGORY Cover

■ 98
PUBLICATION Metropoli
DESIGN DIRECTOR Carmelo Caderot
ART DIRECTOR Rodrigo Sanchez
DESIGNER Rodrigo Sanchez
PHOTO EDITOR Rodrigo Sanchez
PHOTOGRAPHER Trevor Ray Hart
PUBLISHER Unidad Editorial S.A.
ISSUE July 16, 1999
CATEGORY Cover

■ 99
PUBLICATION Inspired
CREATIVE DIRECTORS Walter Bernard,
Milton Glaser
ART DIRECTOR Nancy Eising
PHOTO EDITOR Laurie Kratochvil
PHOTOGRAPHER Herb Ritts
STUDIO WBMG, Inc.
PUBLISHER Knowledge Universe
ISSUE Fall 1999
CATEGORY Cover

■ 100
PUBLICATION Metropoli
DESIGN DIRECTOR Carmelo Caderot
ART DIRECTOR Rodrigo Sanchez
DESIGNER Rodrigo Sanchez
PHOTO EDITOR Rodrigo Sanchez
PUBLISHER Unidad Editorial S.A.
ISSUE January 29, 1999
CATEGORY Cover

■ 101
PUBLICATION Inspired
CREATIVE DIRECTORS Walter Bernard,
Milton Glaser
ART DIRECTOR Nancy Eising
PHOTO EDITOR Laurie Kratochvil
PHOTOGRAPHER Albert Watson
STUDIO WBMG, Inc.
PUBLISHER Knowledge Universe
ISSUE Fall 1999
CATEGORY Cover

■ 98

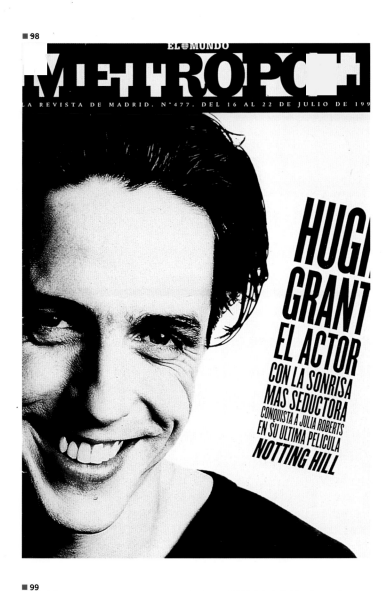

EL MUNDO
METROPOLI
LA REVISTA DE MADRID. N°477. DEL 16 AL 22 DE JULIO DE 199

HUGH
GRANT
EL ACTOR
CON LA SONRISA
MAS SEDUCTORA
CONQUISTA A JULIA ROBERTS
EN SU ULTIMA PELICULA
NOTTING HILL

■ 100

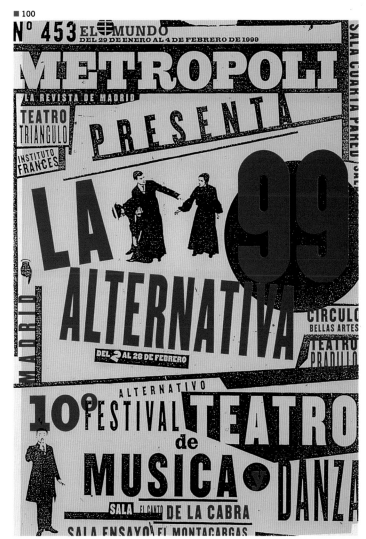

N° 453 EL MUNDO
DEL 29 DE ENERO AL 4 DE FEBRERO DE 1999
METROPOLI
LA REVISTA DE MADRID
TEATRO TRIANGULO
INSTITUTO FRANCES
PRESENTA
LA ALTERNATIVA 99
DEL 2 AL 28 DE FEBRERO
MADRID
CIRCULO BELLAS ARTES
TEATRO PRADILLO
ALTERNATIVO
10° FESTIVAL TEATRO
de
MUSICA ● DANZA
SALA EL CANTO DE LA CABRA
SALA ENSAYO EL MONTACARGAS

■ 99

inspired
No.0 $5.00

An Encounter
With Cirque
du Soleil

Catching
Lauryn Hill

The Starry
Nights of
Wu Xia Liu

DALE CHIHULY
The Glass Alchemist

■ 101

inspired
No.0 $5.00

Catching
Lauryn
Hill

Dale Chihuly Wu Xia Liu
CIRQUE DU SOLEIL

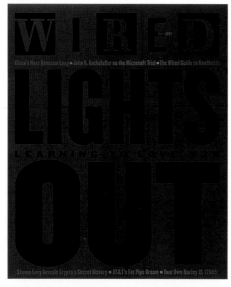

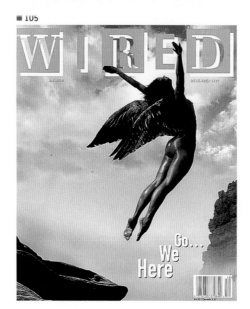

■ 102
PUBLICATION Worth
ART DIRECTOR Philip Bratter
DESIGNER Philip Bratter
PHOTO EDITOR Marianne Butler
PHOTOGRAPHER Davies + Starr
PUBLISHER Worth Media
ISSUE Winter 1999
CATEGORY Cover

■ 103
PUBLICATION Wired
DESIGN DIRECTOR Thomas Schneider
DESIGNER Thomas Schneider
ILLUSTRATOR Matt Groening
PUBLISHER Condé Nast Publications, Inc.
ISSUE February 1999
CATEGORY Cover

■ 104
PUBLICATION Wired
DESIGN DIRECTOR Thomas Schneider
DESIGNER Thomas Schneider
PUBLISHER Condé Nast Publications, Inc.
ISSUE April 1999
CATEGORY Cover

■ 105
PUBLICATION Wired
DESIGN DIRECTOR Daniel Carter
PHOTO EDITOR Christa Aboitiz
PHOTOGRAPHER James Porto
PUBLISHER Condé Nast Publications, Inc.
ISSUE December 1999
CATEGORY Cover

■ 106
PUBLICATION Viva
DESIGN DIRECTOR Iñaki Palacios
ART DIRECTORS Gustavo Lo Valvo, Serfio Juan
PUBLISHER Clarin Newspaper
ISSUE July 11, 1999
CATEGORY Cover

■ 107
PUBLICATION Crain's New York Business
ART DIRECTOR Steven Krupinski
PUBLISHER Crain Communications Inc.
ISSUE July 5, 1999
CATEGORY Front Page

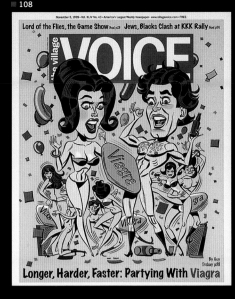

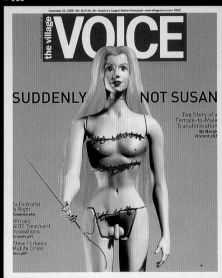

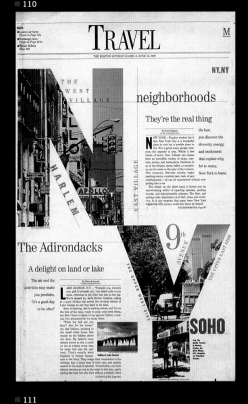

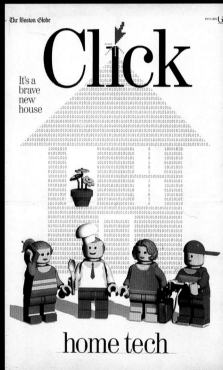

108
PUBLICATION The Village Voice
DESIGN DIRECTOR Ted Keller
ART DIRECTOR Minh Uong
DESIGNER Stacy Wakefield
ILLUSTRATOR Mitch O'Connell
PUBLISHER VV Publishing Corp.
ISSUE November 2, 1999
CATEGORY Front Page

109
PUBLICATION The Village Voice
DESIGN DIRECTOR Ted Keller
ART DIRECTOR Minh Uong
DESIGNER Stacy Wakefield
ILLUSTRATOR Mirko Ilíc
PUBLISHER VV Publishing Corp.
ISSUE November 11, 1999
CATEGORY Front Page

110
PUBLICATION The Boston Globe
DESIGN DIRECTOR Dan Zedek
ART DIRECTOR Keith A. Webb
DESIGNER Keith A. Webb
PUBLISHER The Globe Newspaper Co.
ISSUE June 13, 1999
CATEGORY Front Page

111
PUBLICATION The Boston Globe
DESIGN DIRECTOR Dan Zedek
ART DIRECTOR Keith A. Webb
DESIGNER Keith A. Webb
ILLUSTRATOR Sean McNaughton
PUBLISHER The Globe Newspaper Co.
ISSUE June 13, 1999
CATEGORY Front Page

112
PUBLICATION The Boston Globe
DESIGN DIRECTOR Dan Zedek
ART DIRECTOR Keith A. Webb
DESIGNER Keith A. Webb
ILLUSTRATOR Sean McNaughton
PUBLISHER The Globe Newspaper Co.
ISSUE June 13, 1999
CATEGORY Front Page

113
PUBLICATION Chicago Tribune
ART DIRECTOR Joe Darrow
PUBLISHER Chicago Tribune Company
ISSUE February 21, 1999
CATEGORY Front Page

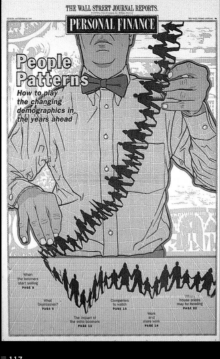

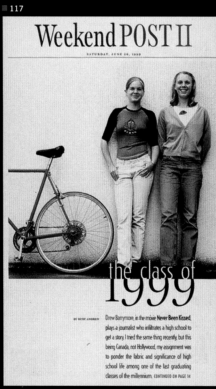

Picture This

At a time when print communicators are lamenting that broadcast and electronic media have carved deep inroads into their market, British publisher DK Eyewitness Books is selling millions of visually lavish travel guides and reference books worldwide by making words and pictures work together on the printed page.

THE PARKS

Until recently the San Francisco Bay Area boasted what was arguably America's best-loved, most-visited anonymous national park. Some 20 million people visit it each year. Local residents treat it like an extension of their own back-yards. But it took a branding program to make people fully appreciate how impressive the Golden Gate National Parks is and clamor for products bearing its name.

@issue:

The Human Touch

The trademark "face" is a carry over from yesteryear when goods were produced locally and consumers knew the people who made the products they bought – if not personally, then certainly by word-of-mouth reputation. A portrait logo of the company founder was a natural extension of this relationship. It connected the product to a friendly and trustworthy face and suggested the maker proudly vouched for its quality. Still, few images are more memorable than a human face, and companies have adopted cultural heroes, fictitious professional experts, cartoon mascots and composite satisfied customers as branding devices. These days new people trademarks are rare, however. Cultural diversity, sensitivity to ethnic stereotypes and the nature of modern products have made it difficult to represent a company in the form of a single person, real or imagined. Still most of us think of classic trademark faces fondly, recognizing them on sight and viewing them as old friends. See if you can connect these people with their brand names.

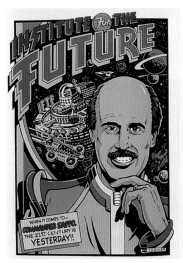

Futurist Paul Saffo on Design

What will the future hold for business and design? Paul Saffo, director of the Institute for the Future in Silicon Valley, talks about the impact of new information technologies with Peter Lawrence, chairman of Corporate Design Foundation.

Tupperware Shows Its Colors

For decades, many people lumped Tupperware into the same category as meatloaf and tuna casseroles – functional, sensible and not a whole lot of style. Your mother loved it; you found it bo-r-i-n-g! Look again. With their pure geometric shapes and spirited contemporary colors, Tupperware products are now valued for their aesthetic qualities and appreciated even by people who rarely step foot into a kitchen.

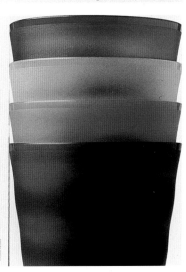

Few things are more maddening – or effective, depending on how you look at it – than having a silly advertising jingle stuck in your head. Ask practically anyone to repeat some that come to mind, and you'll be bombarded with taglines and slogans, often for products that haven't been produced in decades. Like children's rhymes, these marketing slogans are part of our cultural vocabulary. We love them because they're approachable, friendly, to the point. They speak to who we are as individuals and what we want. They humanize the brand and give it personality as well as an identity. Try matching these slogans to their products.

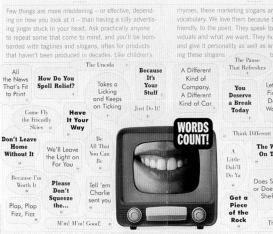

■ 120
PUBLICATION @issue
ART DIRECTOR Kit Hinrichs
DESIGNER Amy Crari
ILLUSTRATOR George Toomer
PHOTOGRAPHERS John Casado, Bob Esporza
STUDIO Pentagram Design, Inc.
PUBLISHER Corporate Design Foundation
CLIENT Potlatch Corporation
ISSUE 1999
CATEGORY Entire Issue

■ 121
PUBLICATION @issue
ART DIRECTOR Kit Hinrichs
DESIGNER Amy Chan
ILLUSTRATORS Woody Pirtle, Barron Storey, Regan Dunnick
PHOTOGRAPHERS John Blaustein, Bob Esparza
STUDIO Pentagram Design, Inc.
PUBLISHER Corporate Design Foundation
CLIENT Potlatch Corporation
ISSUE 1999
CATEGORY Entire Issue

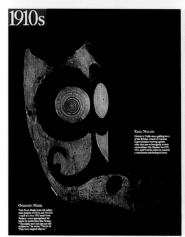

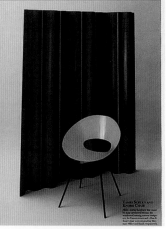

architecture

Architecture is inseparable from color. All architects—from vernacular regionalists to technophiles—are color experts, ready to discuss the implications of the most subtle nuances of hue and value. Studios are filled with color charts; computers eagerly offer millions of tonal variations. But color is also a threat. It might run amok, blurring or dissolving a project's carefully planned logic. For centuries, color has been associated with the illicit pleasures of seductive surfaces: sensuality, sexuality, femininity. Architects find their intense love of color embarrassing. Reluctant to admit that they are fetishists, they pretend to be heroic figures that tame the earthy dangers of color in the name of abstract virtues like order, structure, form, or space. They insist that color is only a secondary element—in the face of glaringly contradictory evidence. The history of the discipline is a history of stubborn denials. The remarkable myth that Modern architecture was white is but the latest in a long line of fallacies. Whole systems of drawing technique, formal analysis, criticism, and training have been developed to keep color in its place. But behind this resilient facade, architecture is awash with unspeakable pleasure. *Mark Wigley*

Mark Wigley is associate professor of Architecture at Princeton University, and author of White Walls, Designer Dresses.

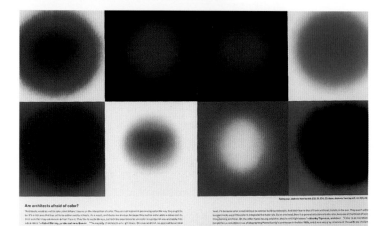

■ 122
PUBLICATION Architecutural Digest
ART DIRECTOR Jeffrey M. Nemeroff
DESIGNERS Jeffrey M. Nemeroff, Brett D. Hodges,
John O'Brien, Isaac Norton
PHOTOGRAPHERS Allen V. Green, Alan Weintraub,
Dennis Anderson, Erwin Blumenfeld
PUBLISHER Condé Nast Publications, Inc.
ISSUE April 1999
CATEGORY Entire Issue

■ 123
PUBLICATION Architecture
ART DIRECTOR Lisa Naftolin
DESIGNER Lisa Naftolin
PHOTOGRAPHER Anne Katrine Senstad
PUBLISHER BPI Communications
ISSUE February 1999
CATEGORY Feature Story

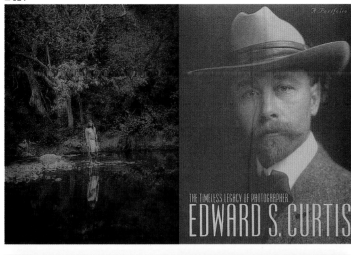

■ 124
PUBLICATION Arizona Highways
ART DIRECTORS Mary Winkelman Velgos, Barbara Glynn Denney
DESIGNER Barbara Glynn Denney
PHOTO EDITOR Richard Maack
PHOTOGRAPHER Edward S. Curtis
PUBLISHER Arizona Department of Transportation
ISSUE November 1999
CATEGORY Feature Story

■ 125
PUBLICATION B. Smith Style
ART DIRECTOR Dan Josephs
DESIGNER Dan Josephs
PHOTO EDITOR James Franco
PHOTOGRAPHER Stephanie Pfriender
PUBLISHER American Express Publishing Co.
ISSUE November/December 1999
CATEGORY Feature Story

■ 126
PUBLICATION Attaché
ART DIRECTOR Paul Carstensen
DESIGNER Paul Carstensen
PHOTOGRAPHER Doug Mindell
PUBLISHER Pace Communications
CLIENT US Airways
ISSUE September 1999
CATEGORY Feature Story

■ 127
PUBLICATION Attaché
ART DIRECTOR Paul Carstensen
DESIGNER Paul Carstensen
ILLUSTRATOR Tamara De Lempicka
PUBLISHER Pace Communications
CLIENT US Airways
ISSUE February 1999
CATEGORY Feature Spread

■ 128
PUBLICATION Attaché
ART DIRECTOR Paul Carstensen
DESIGNER Paul Carstensen
ILLUSTRATOR Michael Witte
PUBLISHER Pace Communications
CLIENT US Airways
ISSUE October 1999
CATEGORY Feature Story

■ 129
PUBLICATION Atomic
CREATIVE DIRECTOR Jeffrey R. Griffith
DESIGNER Jeffrey R. Griffith
PHOTOGRAPHER Brent Stirton
ISSUE September 20, 1999
CATEGORY Feature Spread

EXISTENZMINIMUM, THOUGH, HAD LESS TO DO WITH THE SLEEK MINIMALIST MOTTO "LESS IS MORE" THAN WITH THE IDEA OF PACKING AS MANY PEOPLE AS POSSIBLE IN A PHONE BOOTH.

BLONDE

a state of mind

FALL fashion finds
RED makes an impact
south beach shines

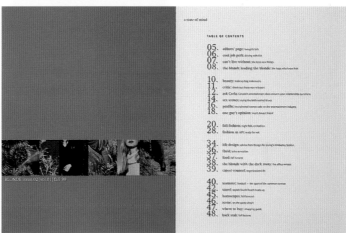

■ 130
PUBLICATION Big
CREATIVE DIRECTOR Marcelo Jünemann
ART DIRECTOR Doug Lloyd
DESIGNER Tin Ting Lee
PHOTOGRAPHERS Mario Sorrenti, John Akehurst, Cristophe Rihet, Doug Aitken, Taryn Simon, Jonathan DeVilliers
STUDIO Lloyd & Co.
PUBLISHER Big Magazine, Inc.
ISSUE August 1999
CATEGORY Entire Issue

■ 131
PUBLICATION Blonde
CREATIVE DIRECTOR Matthew P. Beckerle
ART DIRECTOR Matthew P. Beckerle
DESIGNER Matthew P. Beckerle
PHOTOGRAPHERS Ed Chin, Angela Brown
STUDIO creative activity design company
PUBLISHER Two Girls Publications
ISSUE September 15, 1999
CATEGORY Entire Issue

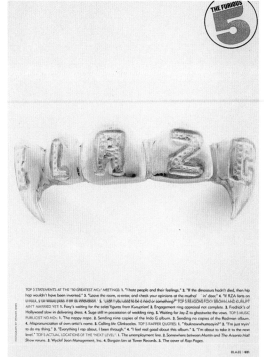

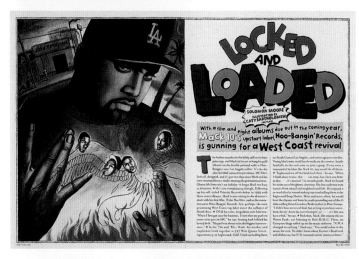

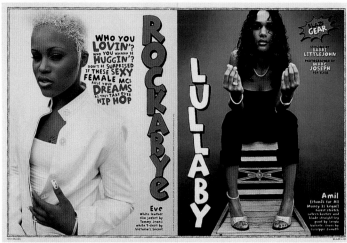

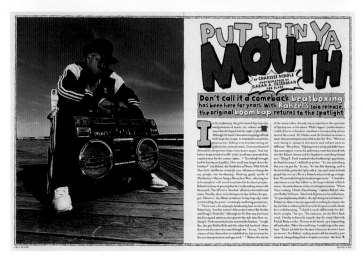

■ 132

PUBLICATION Blaze
ART DIRECTOR Mark Shaw
DESIGNER Wilbert G. Gutierrez
ILLUSTRATOR Caty Bartholomew
PHOTO EDITOR Janene Outlaw
PHOTOGRAPHERS Matt Mahurin, Marc Joseph,
Sarah A. Friedman
PUBLISHER Vibe/Spin Ventures
ISSUE September 1999
CATEGORY Entire Issue

■ 133

PUBLICATION Blaze
ART DIRECTOR Arem K. Duplessis
DESIGNER Arem K. Duplessis
PHOTO EDITOR Janene Outlaw
PHOTOGRAPHER Spencer Jones
PUBLISHER Vibe/Spin Ventures
ISSUE February 1999
CATEGORY Contents & Departments

■ 134

PUBLICATION Blaze
ART DIRECTOR Mark Shaw
DESIGNER Mark Shaw
PHOTO EDITOR Janene Outlaw
PHOTOGRAPHER Matt Mahurin
PUBLISHER Vibe/Spin Ventures
ISSUE September 1999
CATEGORY Feature Spread

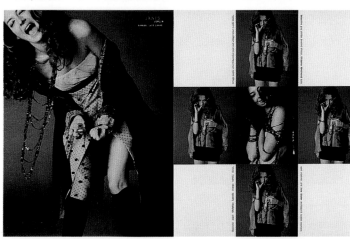

design ■ MERIT

■ 135
PUBLICATION Chicago Tribune Magazine
ART DIRECTOR David Syrek
PHOTOGRAPHER Peter Rosenbaum
PUBLISHER Chicago Tribune Company
ISSUE September 5, 1999
CATEGORY Feature Story

■ 136
PUBLICATION Clarity
CREATIVE DIRECTOR Greg Breeding
ART DIRECTOR Jeff Amstutz
DESIGNER Jeff Amstutz
ILLUSTRATOR Gary Kelley
STUDIO Journey Communications
PUBLISHER Guideposts
ISSUE June/July 1999
CATEGORY Feature Spread

■ 137
PUBLICATION Clarity
CREATIVE DIRECTOR Greg Breeding
ART DIRECTOR Jeff Amstutz
DESIGNER Adele Mulford
ILLUSTRATOR Mary Grandpré
STUDIO Journey Communications
PUBLISHER Guideposts
ISSUE August/September 1999
CATEGORY Feature Spread

■ 138
PUBLICATION Clark Memorandum
ART DIRECTOR David Eliason
DESIGNER Andy Goddard
PHOTOGRAPHER John Snyder
PUBLISHER BYU
Publications & Graphics
CLIENT BYU Law School
ISSUE Fall 1999
CATEGORY Feature Spread

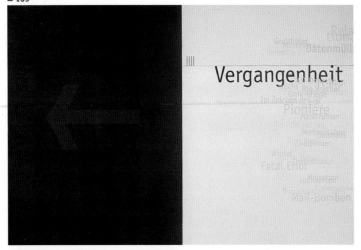

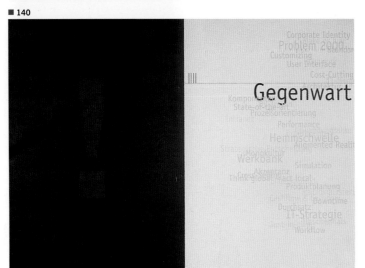

■ 139
PUBLICATION Computerwoche
CREATIVE DIRECTOR Horst Moser
DESIGNER Frank Gehrke
PHOTO EDITOR Horst Moser
STUDIO Independent Medien-Design
PUBLISHER Computerwoche Verlag
ISSUE November 12, 1999
CATEGORY Contents & Departments

■ 140
PUBLICATION Computerwoche
CREATIVE DIRECTOR Horst Moser
DESIGNER Frank Gehrke
PHOTO EDITOR Horst Moser
STUDIO Independent Medien-Design
PUBLISHER Computerwoche Verlag
ISSUE November 12, 1999
CATEGORY Contents & Departments

■ 141
PUBLICATION Computerwoche
CREATIVE DIRECTOR Horst Moser
DESIGNER Frank Gehrke
PHOTO EDITOR Horst Moser
STUDIO Independent Medien-Design
PUBLISHER Computerwoche Verlag
ISSUE November 12, 1999
CATEGORY Contents & Departments

■ 142
PUBLICATION Computerwoche
CREATIVE DIRECTOR Horst Moser
DESIGNER Frank Gehrke
PHOTO EDITOR Horst Moser
STUDIO Independent Medien-Design
PUBLISHER Computerwoche Verlag
ISSUE November 12, 1999
CATEGORY Contents & Departments

■ 143
PUBLICATION Computerwoche Young Professional
CREATIVE DIRECTOR Horst Moser
DESIGNER Nathalie Hummer
PHOTO EDITOR Horst Moser
STUDIO Independent Medien-Design
PUBLISHER Computerwoche Verlag
ISSUE February 1999
CATEGORY Feature Spread

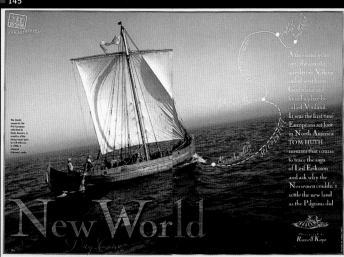

New World

CONTENTS

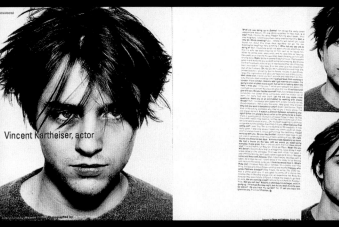

Vincent Kartheiser, actor

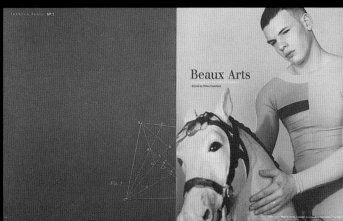

Beaux Arts

■ 144
PUBLICATION Condé Nast Traveler
DESIGN DIRECTOR Robert Best
DESIGNER Marc Whalen
ILLUSTRATOR David Butler
PHOTOGRAPHER Knut Bry
PUBLISHER Condé Nast Publications, Inc.
ISSUE February 1999
CATEGORY Feature Spread

■ 145
PUBLICATION Condé Nast Traveler
DESIGN DIRECTOR Robert Best
ILLUSTRATOR Anthony Sidwell
PHOTOGRAPHER Russell Kaye
PUBLISHER Condé Nast Publications, Inc.
ISSUE March 1999
CATEGORY Feature Spread

■ 146
PUBLICATION Contents
CREATIVE DIRECTOR Joseph Alferis
ART DIRECTORS Christopher Brooks, Joe Del Pesco
PHOTO EDITOR Jameson West
PHOTOGRAPHER Duane Michals
PUBLISHER Waxing Moon Communictaions, Inc.
ISSUE October 1999
CATEGORY Entire Issue

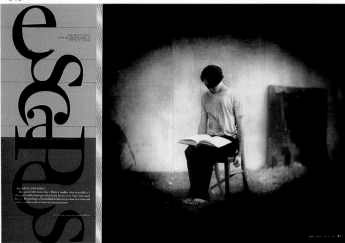

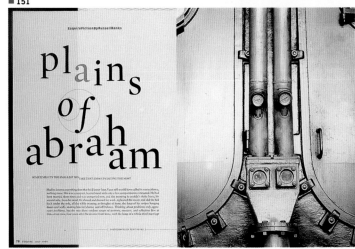

■ 147
PUBLICATION Esquire
DESIGN DIRECTOR Robert Priest
ART DIRECTOR Rockwell Harwood
DESIGNER Joshua Liberson
PHOTOGRAPHER Matt Mahurin
PUBLISHER The Hearst Corporation-Magazines Division
ISSUE May 1999
CATEGORY Feature Spread

■ 148
PUBLICATION Esquire
DESIGN DIRECTOR Robert Priest
ART DIRECTOR Rockwell Harwood
PHOTO EDITOR Simon Barnett
PHOTOGRAPHER Raymond Meeks
PUBLISHER The Hearst Corporation-Magazines Division
ISSUE July 1999
CATEGORY Feature Spread

■ 149
PUBLICATION Esquire
DESIGN DIRECTOR Robert Priest
ART DIRECTOR Rockwell Harwood
PHOTOGRAPHER Matt Mahurin
PUBLISHER The Hearst Corporation-Magazines Division
ISSUE July 1999
CATEGORY Feature Spread

■ 150
PUBLICATION Esquire
DESIGN DIRECTOR Robert Priest
ART DIRECTOR Rockwell Harwood
DESIGNERS Robert Priest, Rockwell Harwood
PHOTO EDITOR Patti Wilson
PHOTOGRAPHER Fredrik Brodën
PUBLISHER The Hearst Corporation-Magazines Division
ISSUE June 1999
CATEGORY Feature Spread

■ 151
PUBLICATION Esquire
DESIGN DIRECTOR Robert Priest
ART DIRECTOR Rockwell Harwood
PHOTO EDITOR Simon Barnett
PHOTOGRAPHER Ferit Kuyas
PUBLISHER The Hearst Corporation-Magazines Division
ISSUE July 1999
CATEGORY Feature Spread

the esquire twenty-one

2 1

WE ARE LUCKY, ON THE CUSP OF THE TWENTY-FIRST CENTURY, TO BE LIVING IN AN AGE OF GENIUS. In every field of human effort—from molecular biology to the color of music—the tools and rules are changing, generating startling innovations and then falling before them. Inspiration, arrogance, brilliance, stalk the land. So we present twenty-one innovators, creators, and thinkers whose work, in high fields and low, is transforming our civilization. Some you've heard of before, though probably not quite this way. Others you'll meet for the first time. There are a few who are so original we asked them to *show* what they do. And then there is one who is so full of invention, influence, and delight that he had to come first. . . .

NOVEMBER 1999 ESQUIRE **123**

Paul MacCready
By Phil Patton

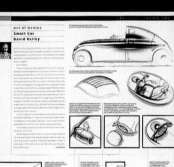

Act of Genius
Smart Car
David Kelley

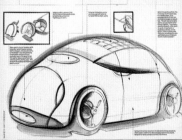

Iverson, Allen
By Charles P. Pierce

HE IS TOO QUICK FOR ANYONE STRONGER AND TOO STRONG FOR ANYONE AS QUICK, AND THERE IS NOBODY—LIVING OR DEAD—AS QUICK AS HE IS WITH THE BALL.

175 THINGS
A MAN SHOULD DO
BEFORE HE DIES

The Life List

1.

Date an older woman. **2.** Lose your virginity to an older woman. **3.** Have your young and tender heart carved into bite-sized pieces, lightly salted, and chewed by an older woman. **4.** Stand up to a bully. **5.** Fly in a Learjet. **6.** Jump out of a Cessna. **7.** Talk to God. **8.** Vote in anger. **9.** Run for office. **10.** Feel the recoil of a warm Kalashnikov. **11.** Save a life. **12.** Lend a hand, especially as concerns those hard-to-reach areas.

14. Take a Schvitz
Illustrator **Steve Brodner** goes behind the steams at New York's Russian and Turkish baths.

Go Around the World
By **Walter Russell Mead**
15.

16. Watch scrambled porn. **17.** Unplug your TV for a month. **18.** Climb a mountain—not Everest—without the slightest urge to write a book about it. **19.** Sail alone the ocean blue without the slightest urge to write a book about it. **20.** Write a brief autobiography without the slightest urge to publish it. **21.** Read all the books on your "Books to read before I die" list. **22.** Circumnavigate Corsica on a bright-red Ducati. **23.** Learn a useless language: Dutch, say. **24.** Learn a useless language: Dutch, say. **25.** Have a hero. **26.** Meet your hero. **27.** Be a hero. **28.** Gobble a meat-loaf sandwich at Graceland. **29.** Ride a burro through the agave fields of Oaxaca. **30.** Take a Greyhound from Portland, Oregon, to Portland, Maine—and if you think your ass hurts, imagine the suffering of the guy who's driving. **31.** Work for food. **32.** Assemble a rock band. Be the lead singer. Pleasure the groupies. **33.** Get booed (by the audience, not the groupies). **34.** Trash a hotel room, maybe one that belongs to an Schrager. **35.** Get fired, especially due not limited to's when you're getting fired because you want to get fired. **36.** Quit a job, loudly and righteously and with great streams of triumphant profanity. **37.** Build a valuable business. Sell it. Enjoy. **38.** Buy one spectacular loser of a stock—and never, ever forget it.

■ 152
PUBLICATION Esquire
DESIGN DIRECTOR John Korpics
ART DIRECTOR Rockwell Harwood
ILLUSTRATOR Mirko Ilic
PHOTO EDITOR Simon Barnett
PHOTOGRAPHERS Sam Jones, Butch Belair
PUBLISHER The Hearst Corporation-Magazines Division
ISSUE November 1999
CATEGORY Feature Story
A **MERIT** Single Page

■ 153
PUBLICATION Esquire
DESIGN DIRECTOR John Korpics
ART DIRECTOR Rockwell Harwood
PHOTO EDITOR Simon Barnett
PHOTOGRAPHER Butch Belair
PUBLISHER The Hearst Corporation-Magazines Division
ISSUE November 1999
CATEGORY Feature Spread

■ 154
PUBLICATION Esquire
DESIGN DIRECTOR John Korpics
ART DIRECTOR Rockwell Harwood
ILLUSTRATOR Matt Mahurin
PUBLISHER The Hearst Corporation-Magazines Division
ISSUE December 1999
CATEGORY Feature Spread

■ 155

PUBLICATION Entertainment Weekly
DESIGN DIRECTOR John Korpics
ART DIRECTOR Geraldine Hessler
DESIGNER Geraldine Hessler
ILLUSTRATOR Charles Burns
PHOTO EDITOR Richard Maltz
PUBLISHER Time Inc.
ISSUE April 30, 1999
CATEGORY Feature Story

■ 156

PUBLICATION Entertainment Weekly
DESIGN DIRECTOR Geraldine Hessler
ART DIRECTOR John Walker
DESIGNER Ellene Standke
ILLUSTRATOR Tavis Coburn
PUBLISHER Time Inc.
ISSUE October 29, 1999
CATEGORY Feature Spread

■ 157

PUBLICATION Entertainment Weekly
DESIGN DIRECTOR Geraldine Hessler
DESIGNER Edith Gutierrez
PHOTO EDITOR Sarah Rozen
PHOTOGRAPHER Mary Ellen Mark
PUBLISHER Time Inc.
ISSUE November 19, 1999
CATEGORY Contents & Departments

■ 158

PUBLICATION Entertainment Weekly
DESIGN DIRECTOR Geraldine Hessler
DESIGNERS Geraldine Hessler,
Ellene Standke
PHOTO EDITOR Denise Sfraga
PHOTOGRAPHER Mary Ellen Mark
PUBLISHER Time Inc.
ISSUE December 3, 1999
CATEGORY Feature Spread

design ■ MERIT

TWO SECONDS, MAYBE THREE. Michael Jackson glides backward on the balls of his feet. Two kids in Liverpool shake hands at a church social. Feedback fizz as Bob Dylon plugs his on amp. Dick dick dick dick. Dick dick. Dick dick dick. Dick dick—the first 11 notes of "Louie Louie," no mistoable bowl of dickouchery. A guy to the Bronx runs two turntobles through the same speakers and J-J-J likes what he hears. Some of the biggest seismic shifts in the history of pop culture can be traced in a tiny impulse, a blast of courage, a mistake. A moment, followed by a gasp, followed by a brand-new world. That is the essence of rock & roll. • Through all of its mutations and revolutions, pop music has always boiled down to the same 1961-sound manifestation of freekish whoretry. In this issue, EW strives to capture the beat of

these moments and—and as fleshal thinkers—rank them from 1 to 100. Some of these moments had a deep impact on the way we live now. Some didn't—they're just really funny or weird or fleeting, like pop itself. Scores of 19th-century pioneers blazed the way. Pop would be nowhere without the grace of Cole Porter and Duke Ellington and George Gershwin, the cool authority of Louis Armstrong and Hank Williams and Bill Monroe and Frank Sinatra, the fearless quartet of Robert Johnson and Bessie Smith and Billie Holiday and Charlie Parker, the freedom of Woody Guthrie. But we begin one sage after these, outside of traditional American gospers like jazz and country. We begin in the boom and glam of a new day, when everything could change in the blink of an eye, the shriek of a teenage girl, or the quiver of a pelvis...

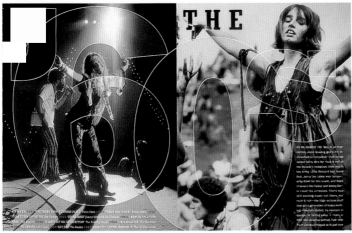

12/6/69

The Rolling Stones intended this first concert at a northern California racetrack to be a gesture of brotherly goodwill. It ended up being the ultimate bod trip, thanks to some out-of-control Hell's Angels, whom the organizers had magnificently hired to provide "security." One 18-year-old man, Meredith Hunter, was fatally stabbed, and countless others in the audience were beaten, clumped, and terrorized. The Jefferson Airplane's Marty Balin tried to stop a fight—and was knocked out cold. "I woke up with all these boot morks on me, like tattoos." Along with the Manson family's gristly Tate-LaBianca murders the previous summer, Altamont—coming only four months after Woodstock—presaged the ugly, discordant coda to the hippie dream of peace, love, and rock. **Rank 39**

IGGY POP Cuts His Chest on The First Stooges Tour

8/29/69

When proto-punk Iggy Pop stage-dived his flesh with two drumsticks at New York's State Pavilion on the Stooges' first national tour, it was a visceral foreshadowing of the violent onstage psychodramas that would characterize the performances up until the final implosion of the Stooges in 1974. The first nudist to make voluntary collabilee part of his act, Iggy would oul to broken glass, dive into concrete, and beat his local mid-microphone. What inspired such behavior? He dosh his on-performance euphoria, which included "a couple of hits of orange mescaline." **Rank 54**

APPALL IN THE FAMILY

More than any other style of art, rock culture brings out the beast in people. In concert and on record, these reprobates are on a mission to disgust, and—if they're today diabech. At right, a shock-rock rogues' gallery pays aprologies to Norman Rockwell. Clockwise from top: Alice Cooper, whose Grand Guignol theatrics on the stage included monster dragons; Marilyn Manson, bloody scary Iggy Pop; Wendy O. Williams, the Plasmatics' chainsaw-wielding dominatrix; and Sympo-antlent Ice Zazy Osbourne, about-of-the-time sedate Zara Schnando' Jay Hawkins, Alice dinner Zara Schnando; peep-shocking punk favorite GG Allin, and Chesky-hating mystical GG Pork—with 3/8 of the remaining thin-boys.
cheek Rockwell

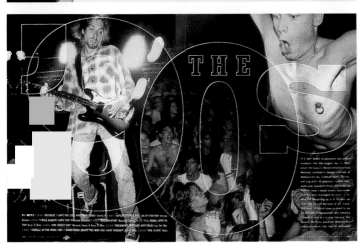

IT'S NOT HARD to pinpoint the exact moment the '80s began: Dec. 1, 1980, when the voter's Revered and Involued Method, suburban's long-at-hot star of Billboard's the Falliond Spot. He revealing shift of popular "alibis rap past pop positives from Garibaldo to Pollock, hate- related stesins have suite charits, was emerged for user. Y'in word EV Measuring on a in of them so that '80s in 2nd decade of all stess except the 10 point uses printed in in 15 effects, frequencent and cheery Maston in decide a pop history. No Guard. Kiv'ang universal delivery if a coharmd stesin that had 65 excluded...

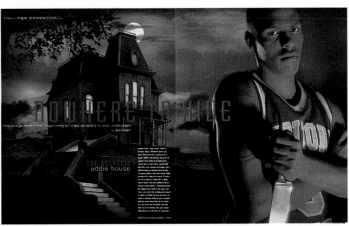

■159
PUBLICATION Entertainment Weekly
DESIGN DIRECTOR John Korpics
ART DIRECTOR Geraldine Hessler
DESIGNERS Geraldine Hessler, Jennifer Procopio
ILLUSTRATOR Mark Stutzman
PHOTO EDITOR Michele Romero
PUBLISHER Time Inc.
ISSUE May 28, 1999
CATEGORY Feature Story

■160
PUBLICATION ESPN
DESIGN DIRECTOR Peter Yates
ART DIRECTOR Yvette L. Francis
DESIGNER Yvette L. Francis
ILLUSTRATORS Aaron Goodman, George B. Fry III
PHOTO EDITOR Nik Kleinberg
PHOTOGRAPHER Eric Tucker
PUBLISHER Disney Publishing Worldwide
ISSUE November 29, 1999
CATEGORY Feature Story

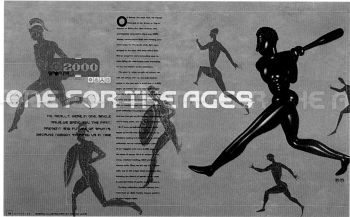

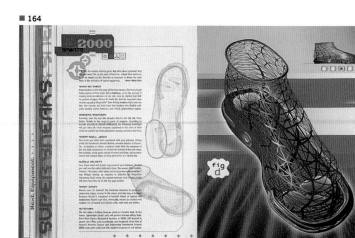

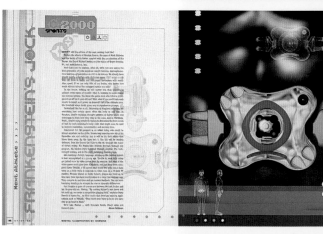

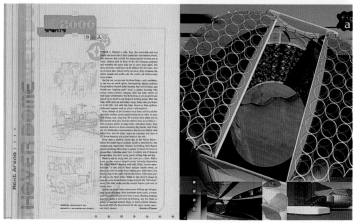

■ 161
PUBLICATION ESPN
DESIGN DIRECTOR F. Darrin Perry
ART DIRECTOR Peter Yates
DESIGNER F. Darrin Perry
ILLUSTRATOR Fayez Jafri
PUBLISHER Disney
Publishing Worldwide
ISSUE July 26, 1999
CATEGORY Feature Spread

■ 162
PUBLICATION ESPN
DESIGN DIRECTOR F. Darrin Perry
ART DIRECTOR Peter Yates
DESIGNER Yvette L. Francis
PHOTO EDITOR Nik Kleinberg
PHOTOGRAPHER Dan Campbell
PUBLISHER Disney
Publishing Worldwide
ISSUE August 9, 1999
CATEGORY Feature Spread

■ 163
PUBLICATION ESPN
DESIGN DIRECTOR Peter Yates
DESIGNER Yvette L. Francis
PHOTO EDITOR Nik Kleinberg
PHOTOGRAPHER Christopher Kolk
PUBLISHER Disney
Publishing Worldwide
ISSUE November 1, 1999
CATEGORY Feature Spread

■ 164
PUBLICATION ESPN
DESIGN DIRECTOR F. Darrin Perry
ART DIRECTOR Peter Yates
DESIGNERS F. Darrin Perry,
Bruce Glase
ILLUSTRATOR Fayez Jafri
PUBLISHER Disney
Publishing Worldwide
ISSUE July 26, 1999
CATEGORY Feature Story

■ 165

■ 168

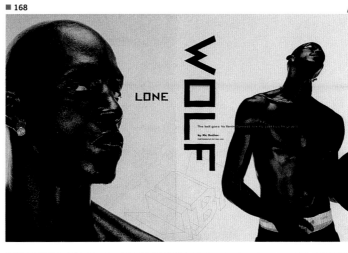

■ 167

■ 169

■ 165
PUBLICATION ESPN
DESIGN DIRECTOR F. Darrin Perry
ART DIRECTOR Peter Yates
DESIGNER Yvette L. Francis
PHOTO EDITOR Nik Kleinberg
PHOTOGRAPHER Drew Endicott
PUBLISHER Disney
Publishing Worldwide
ISSUE February 8, 1999
CATEGORY Feature Spread

■ 166
PUBLICATION ESPN
DESIGN DIRECTOR F. Darrin Perry
ART DIRECTOR Peter Yates
DESIGNER Peter Yates
PHOTO EDITOR Nik Kleinberg
PHOTOGRAPHER Andrew Brusso
PUBLISHER Disney
Publishing Worldwide
ISSUE March 8, 1999
CATEGORY Feature Spread

■ 167
PUBLICATION ESPN
DESIGN DIRECTOR Peter Yates
DESIGNER Jeanine Melnick
PHOTO EDITOR Nik Kleinberg
PHOTOGRAPHER John Huet
PUBLISHER Disney
Publishing Worldwide
ISSUE December 13, 1999
CATEGORY Feature Spread

■ 168
PUBLICATION ESPN
DESIGN DIRECTOR Peter Yates
DESIGNERS Peter Yates, Gabe Kuo
PHOTO EDITOR Nik Kleinberg
PHOTOGRAPHER Dah Len
PUBLISHER Disney
Publishing Worldwide
ISSUE November 15, 1999
CATEGORY Feature Story
 A **MERIT** Spread

■ 169
PUBLICATION ESPN
DESIGN DIRECTOR Peter Yates
DESIGNERS Peter Yates, Eric
Fehlberg, Gabe Kuo
ILLUSTRATOR Silverkid New York
PUBLISHER Disney
Publishing Worldwide
ISSUE November 15, 1999
CATEGORY Feature Spread

■ 170
PUBLICATION Details
DESIGN DIRECTOR Robert Newman
ILLUSTRATOR Mark Zingarelli
PHOTO EDITOR Greg Pond
TYPOGRAPHER David Coulson
PUBLISHER Condé Nast
Publications, Inc.
ISSUE February 1999
CATEGORY Feature Spread

■ 171
PUBLICATION Details
DESIGN DIRECTOR Robert Newman
DESIGNER John Giordani
PHOTO EDITOR Greg Pond
PHOTOGRAPHER Helmut Newton
PUBLISHER Condé Nast
Publications, Inc.
ISSUE March 1999
CATEGORY Feature Spread

■ 172
PUBLICATION Details
DESIGN DIRECTOR Robert Newman
DESIGNER Alden Wallace
PHOTO EDITOR Greg Pond
PHOTOGRAPHER Moshe Brakha
PUBLISHER Condé Nast
Publications, Inc.
ISSUE March 1999
CATEGORY Feature Spread

■ 173
PUBLICATION Details
DESIGN DIRECTOR Robert Newman
DESIGNER John Giordani
ILLUSTRATOR Marcus Burrowes
PHOTO EDITOR Greg Pond
PHOTOGRAPHER Moshe Brakha
PUBLISHER Condé Nast
Publications, Inc.
ISSUE April 1999
CATEGORY Feature Spread

■ 174
PUBLICATION Details
DESIGN DIRECTOR Robert Newman
DESIGNER John Giordani
PHOTO EDITOR Greg Pond
PHOTOGRAPHER Moshe Brakha
TYPOGRAPHER Dan Solo
PUBLISHER Condé Nast
Publications, Inc.
ISSUE May 1999
CATEGORY Feature Spread

■ 175
PUBLICATION Details
DESIGN DIRECTOR Robert Newman
DESIGNER John Giordani
PHOTO EDITOR Greg Pond
PHOTOGRAPHER Chris Buck
PUBLISHER Condé Nast
Publications, Inc.
ISSUE May 1999
CATEGORY Feature Spread

■ 176

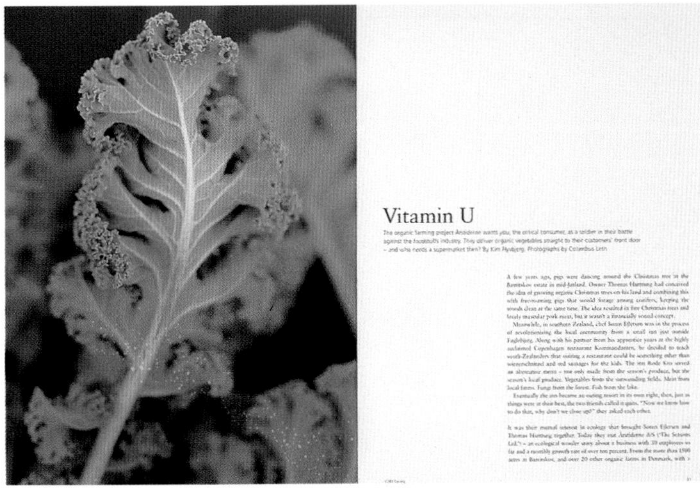

Moonlight Serenade

[body text illegible]

Vitamin U

[body text illegible]

■ 177

down-home garden gadgets

There are plenty of high-tech garden tools on the market, but it's fun to find vintage handmade ones or to invent your own out of whatever is at hand.

■ 178

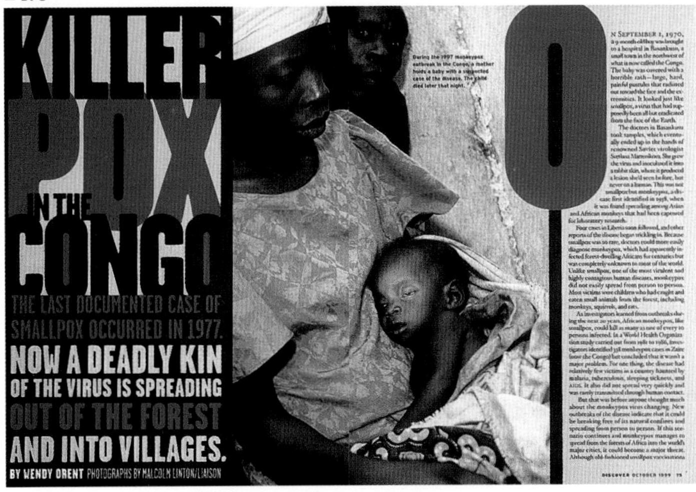

KILLER POX IN THE CONGO

THE LAST DOCUMENTED CASE OF SMALLPOX OCCURRED IN 1977. NOW A DEADLY KIN OF THE VIRUS IS SPREADING OUT OF THE FOREST AND INTO VILLAGES.

BY WENDY ORENT PHOTOGRAPHS BY MALCOLM LINTON/LIAISON

■ 179

DIGITAL DECISIONS

LANDMARK GRAPHICS CEO BOB PEEBLES AND HIS COLLEAGUES USE CUTTING-EDGE TECHNOLOGY TO HELP EXECUTIVES IN ONE OF THE WORLD'S MOST BASIC INDUSTRIES MAKE SMARTER DECISIONS. STEP INSIDE THE "DECISIONARIUM" — AND DECIDE WHETHER YOU'VE GOT WHAT IT TAKES TO MAKE THE RIGHT DECISIONS ABOUT YOUR BUSINESS.
BY CHUCK SALTER PORTRAITS BY NASH BAKER
PHOTO COLLAGES BY DOMINIQUE THIBODEAU

■ 176
PUBLICATION Copenhagen Living
CREATIVE DIRECTOR Anders Peter Mejer
DESIGNER Anders Peter Mejer
PHOTO EDITOR Anders Peter Mejer
PHOTOGRAPHERS Tor Jørgensen, Colombus Leth
STUDIO Embryo Design
PUBLISHER CPH Living Publishing
ISSUE November 12, 1999
CATEGORY Entire Issue

■ 177
PUBLICATION Country Home
ART DIRECTOR Paul Zimmerman
DESIGNER Susan L. Uedelhofen
PHOTOGRAPHER Tom McWilliam
PUBLISHER Meredith Corp.
ISSUE April 1999
CATEGORY Feature Spread

■ 178
PUBLICATION Discover
DESIGN DIRECTOR Michael J. Walsh
DESIGNER Michael J. Walsh
PHOTO EDITOR Jennifer Eckstein
PHOTOGRAPHER Malcolm Linton
PUBLISHER Disney
Publishing Worldwide
ISSUE October 1999
CATEGORY Feature Spread

■ 179
PUBLICATION Net Company
ART DIRECTOR Patrick Mitchell
DESIGNER Patrick Mitchell
PHOTOGRAPHERS Nash Baker,
Dominique Thibodeau
PUBLISHER Fast Company
ISSUE December 1999
CATEGORY Feature Spread

[the business
of the church]

InsanityInc

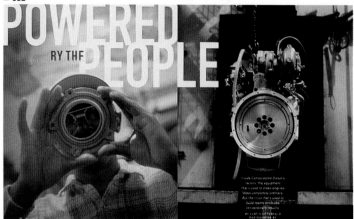

POWERED BY THE PEOPLE

"IN THE RIGHT ENVIRONMENT
PEOPLE AT ALL LEVELS
OF AN ORGANIZATION CAN
MAKE CONTRIBUTIONS."

"BEING PART OF A TEAM CREATES A DIFFERENT SENSE OF ACCOUNTABILITY.
EVERYBODY EXPECTS MORE FROM EVERYBODY ELSE."

■ 180
PUBLICATION Exchange
ART DIRECTOR Emily Weaver
DESIGNER Emily Weaver
PHOTOGRAPHER Pete Lacker
CLIENT Marriott School, BYU
PUBLISHER BYU
Publications & Graphics
ISSUE Spring 1999
CATEGORY Feature Story

■ 181
PUBLICATION Fast Company
ART DIRECTOR Patrick Mitchell
DESIGNER Patrick Mitchell
PHOTO EDITOR Alicia Jylkka
PHOTOGRAPHER Chris Buck
PUBLISHER Fast Company
ISSUE January 1999
CATEGORY Feature Spread

■ 182
PUBLICATION Fast Company
ART DIRECTOR Patrick Mitchell
DESIGNER Gretchen Smelter
PHOTO EDITOR Alicia Jylkka
PHOTOGRAPHER Chris Hartlove
PUBLISHER Fast Company
ISSUE July/August 1999
CATEGORY Feature Story

■ 183

A

■ 184

■ 185

■ 186

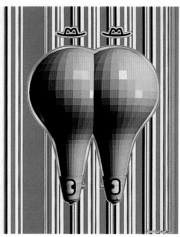

■ 187

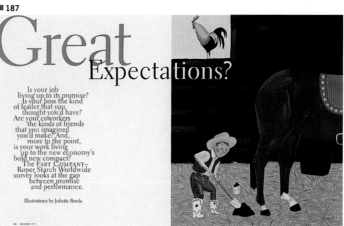

■ 183
PUBLICATION Fast Company
ART DIRECTOR Patrick Mitchell
DESIGNERS Patrick Mitchell,
Gretchen Smelter
PHOTO EDITOR Alicia Jylkka
PHOTOGRAPHERS Scogin Mayo,
Frank W. Ockenfels 3, Burk
Uzzle, Catherine Ledner
PUBLISHER Fast Company
ISSUE April 1999
CATEGORY Feature Story
    A **MERIT** Spread

■ 184
PUBLICATION Fast Company
ART DIRECTOR Patrick Mitchell
DESIGNERS Patrick Mitchell,
Emily Crawford
ILLUSTRATOR Istvan Banyai
PUBLISHER Fast Company
ISSUE May 1999
CATEGORY Feature Spread

■ 185
PUBLICATION Fast Company
ART DIRECTOR Patrick Mitchell
DESIGNER Gretchen Smelter
PHOTO EDITOR Alicia Jylkka
PHOTOGRAPHER Micheal McLaughlin
PUBLISHER Fast Company
ISSUE January 1999
CATEGORY Feature Spread

■ 186
PUBLICATION Fast Company
ART DIRECTOR Patrick Mitchell
DESIGNER Gretchen Smelter
ILLUSTRATOR John Hersey
PUBLISHER Fast Company
ISSUE September 1999
CATEGORY Feature Spread

■ 187
PUBLICATION Fast Company
ART DIRECTOR Patrick Mitchell
DESIGNER Patrick Mitchell
ILLUSTRATOR Juliette Borda
PUBLISHER Fast Company
ISSUE November 1999
CATEGORY Feature Spread

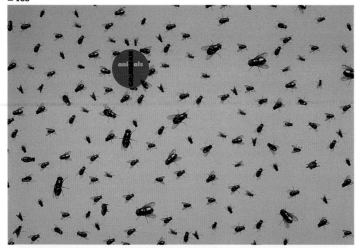

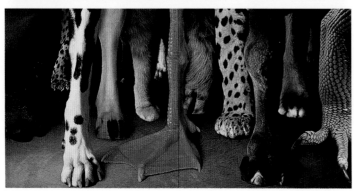

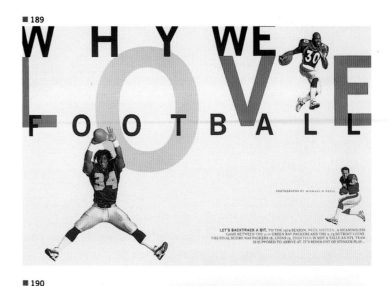

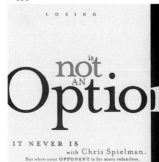

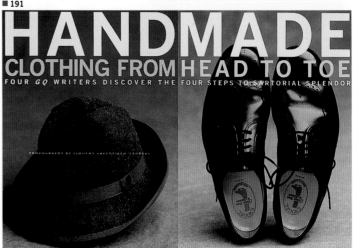

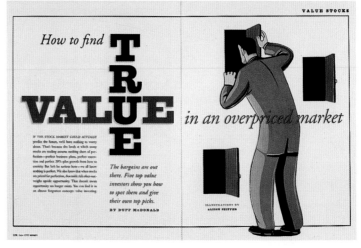

The Feeling Is

Dᴱ

MU
TUAL

If you own a
mutual life insurance policy,
hang on to it.
It may soon be as rare as
a Fabergé egg.

BY ANDREW FEINBERG

Photographs by Holly Lindem

BY MATTHEW JAMES RYAN

ILLUSTRATIONS BY BRIAN CAIRNS

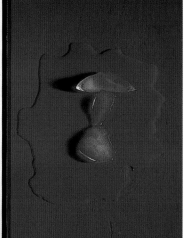

PHOTOGRAPHS BY Fredrik Brodén

THE Amazoning OF
FINANCIAL Services

By Laurie Jean Aron

gray matter

INTERVIEW BY BRUCE FELTON

Photographs by Chris Chapman

Global capitalism isn't the remedy for the world's
economic ills, argues noted British political
theorist JOHN GRAY.
It's the curse.

GLOBAL

OCTOBER/NOVEMBER 1999 | VOL. 2, NO. 3

FEATURES

DEPARTMENTS

■ 193
PUBLICATION Global
ART DIRECTOR Tom Brown
DESIGNER Tom Brown
PHOTOGRAPHER Holly Lindem
STUDIO Tom Brown Art & Design
PUBLISHER Deloitte & Touche, LLP
ISSUE March/April 1999
CATEGORY Feature Story

■ 194
PUBLICATION Global
ART DIRECTOR Tom Brown
DESIGNERS Tom Brown, Rob Hewitt
STUDIO Tom Brown Art & Design
PUBLISHER Deloitte & Touche, LLP
ISSUE November/December 1999
CATEGORY Contents & Departments

■ 195
PUBLICATION Global
ART DIRECTOR Tom Brown
DESIGNERS Tom Brown, Rob Hewitt
ILLUSTRATORS Brian Cairns, Tavis Coburn,
Jason Holley, John Hersey
PHOTOGRAPHERS Fredrik Brodén, Chris Chapman
STUDIO Tom Brown Art & Design
PUBLISHER Deloitte & Touche, LLP
ISSUE October/November 1999
CATEGORY Entire Issue

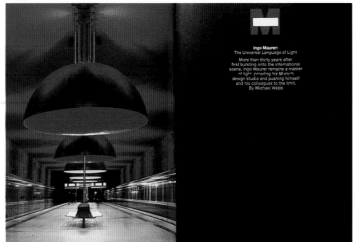

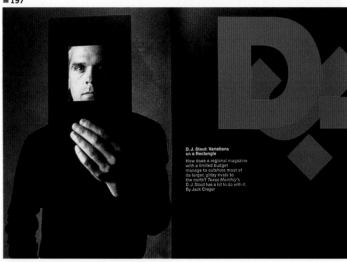

■ 196
PUBLICATION Graphis
CREATIVE DIRECTOR B. Martin Pedersen
ART DIRECTOR Massimo Acanfora
DESIGNERS B. Martin Pedersen,
Massimo Acanfora
PUBLISHER Graphis
ISSUE November/December 1999
CATEGORY Feature Spread

■ 197
PUBLICATION Graphis
CREATIVE DIRECTOR B. Martin Pedersen
ART DIRECTOR Massimo Acanfora
DESIGNERS B. Martin Pedersen,
Massimo Acanfora
PHOTOGRAPHER Michael O'Brien
PUBLISHER Graphis
ISSUE November/December 1999
CATEGORY Feature Spread

■ 198
PUBLICATION Graphis
CREATIVE DIRECTOR B. Martin Pedersen
ART DIRECTOR Massimo Acanfora
DESIGNERS B. Martin Pedersen,
Massimo Acanfora
ILLUSTRATOR Milton Glaser
PUBLISHER Graphis
ISSUE November/December 1999
CATEGORY Feature Spread

■ 199
PUBLICATION Guggenheim
ART DIRECTOR J. Abbott Miller
DESIGNERS J. Abbott Miller, Scott
Devendorf, Roy Brooks
STUDIO Pentagram Design, Inc.
PUBLISHER Guggenheim
Museum Publications
ISSUE Fall 1999
CATEGORY Entire Issue

■ 200

PUBLICATION Intelligence Report
DESIGN DIRECTOR Rodney Diaz
ART DIRECTOR Russell Estes
DESIGNER Russell Estes
PHOTO EDITORS Mark Potok, Richard Baudouin
PHOTOGRAPHER Scott Houston
PUBLISHER Southern Poverty Law Center
ISSUE Fall 1999
CATEGORY Redesign

■ 201

PUBLICATION Guardian Weekend
ART DIRECTOR Mark Porter
DESIGNERS Balwant Ahira, Maggie Murphy
PHOTO EDITOR Jane Greening
PHOTOGRAPHER Marc Burden, Paul Fusco
PUBLISHER Guardian Media Group
ISSUE October 9, 1999
CATEGORY Entire Issue

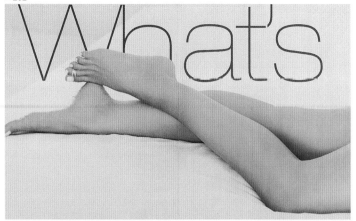

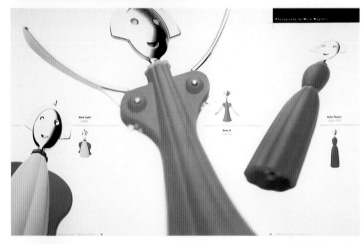

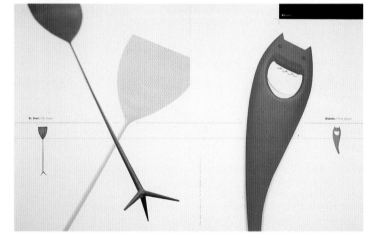

MARKET To Le Bazaar

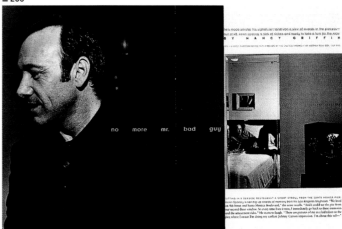

no more mr. bad guy

■ 205

PUBLICATION enRoute
CREATIVE DIRECTOR Danielle Le Bel
DESIGNER Denis Paquet
PHOTO EDITOR Julie Saindon
PHOTOGRAPHER Kurt-Michael Westermann
PUBLISHER Spafax Canada
CLIENT Air Canada
ISSUE May 1999
CATEGORY Feature Story

■ 206

PUBLICATION Los Angeles
CREATIVE DIRECTOR David Armario
DESIGNERS David Armario, Myla Sorensen
PHOTO EDITORS Lisa Thackaberry, Michelle Hauf
PHOTOGRAPHER Norman Jean Roy
PUBLISHER Fairchild Publications
ISSUE October 1999
CATEGORY Feature Story

TWENTY-SIX YEARS AGO, DESIGNER MARGO GRANT WALSH LEFT SKIDMORE FOR A SMALL FIRM CALLED GENSLER.

CHATEAU MARGO

BY ANDREA TRUPPIN

URBAN LEGEND

ARCHITECT
LAURINDA SPEAR
HELPED TO
TRANSFORM MIAMI'S
LOOK IN THE 80S.
LATELY SHE'S
BEEN SPREADING
HER PALETTE AND
PLAYFULNESS
TO OTHER CITIES.

BY KIRA L. GOULD

STEPHANIE ODEGARD
FITS THE LUXURIOUS
CARPETS SHE DESIGNS
INTO A VISION OF
SOCIAL PROGRESS

A LOOM OF ONE'S OWN

BY ANDREA MOED

snap to it!

LEGOLAND OFFERS A TINY, SHINY WORLD IN THE ERSATZ DREAM FACTORY OF SOUTHERN CALIFORNIA

BY MICHAEL DOOLEY
PHOTOGRAPHY BY JIMMY COHRSSEN

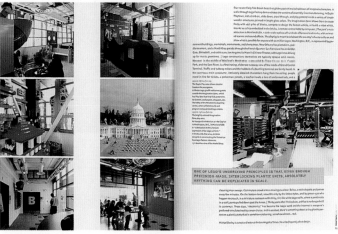

ONE OF LEGO'S UNDERLYING PRINCIPLES IS THAT, GIVEN ENOUGH PRECISION-MADE, INTERLOCKING PLASTIC UNITS, ABSOLUTELY ANYTHING CAN BE REPLICATED IN SCALE.

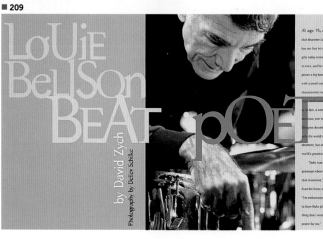

LoUie BeLLSon BEAT pOET

by David Zych
Photography by Detlev Schilke

METALSMITH

CONTENTS

FIRST AID
for
FICTION WRITERS

■ 212

■ 213

■ 211
PUBLICATION Poets & Writers
ART DIRECTORS Alissa Levin, Donald Partyka
DESIGNER Donald Partyka
STUDIO Point Five Design
PUBLISHER Poets & Writers Inc.
ISSUE November 12, 1999
CATEGORY Feature Spread

■ 212
PUBLICATION Pacifica
DESIGN DIRECTOR Kunio Hayashi
DESIGNER Kunio Hayashi
ILLUSTRATOR Kunio Hayashi
PHOTOGRAPHER David Fleetham
STUDIO Communication
Design Corporation
PUBLISHER Pacific Travelogue, Inc.
ISSUE April 1999
CATEGORY Feature Spread

■ 213
PUBLICATION Pacifica
DESIGN DIRECTOR Kunio Hayashi
DESIGNER Yoko Inui-Hamane
PHOTOGRAPHER Daniella Stallinger
STUDIO Communication
Design Corporation
PUBLISHER Pacific Travelogue, Inc.
ISSUE January 1999
CATEGORY Feature Spread

■ 214

PUBLICATION Martha Stewart Living
DESIGN DIRECTOR Eric A. Pike
ART DIRECTORS James Dunlinson, Scot Schy, Susan Corral, Stacey Dietz,
Linda Kocur, Helen Sanematsu, Brooke Hellewell
PHOTO EDITOR Heidi J. Posner
PHOTOGRAPHERS Gentl & Hyers, Minh & Wass, Christopher Baker, Beatriz
Da Costa, Lisa Hubbard, David Sawyer, John Dugdale, Victor Schrager,
Dana Gallagher, Charles Maraia, Anna Williams
PUBLISHER Martha Stewart Living Omnimedia
ISSUE December 1999/January 2000
CATEGORY Entire Issue

■ 215

PUBLICATION Martha Stewart Living
DESIGN DIRECTOR Eric A. Pike
ART DIRECTOR Claudia Bruno
DESIGNER Claudia Bruno
PHOTO EDITOR Heidi J. Posner
PHOTOGRAPHER Victor Schrager
PUBLISHER Martha Stewart Living
Omnimedia
ISSUE March 1999
CATEGORY Feature Spread

■ 216

PUBLICATION Martha Stewart Living
DESIGN DIRECTOR Eric A. Pike
DESIGNERS Eric A. Pike, Anthony
Cochran, Kerin Brooks
PHOTO EDITOR Heidi J. Posner
PHOTOGRAPHER William Abranowicz
PUBLISHER Martha Stewart Living
Omnimedia
ISSUE April 1999
CATEGORY Feature Story

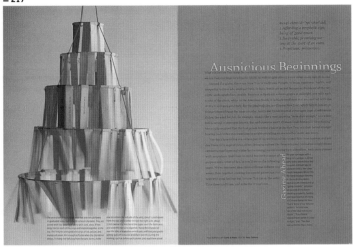

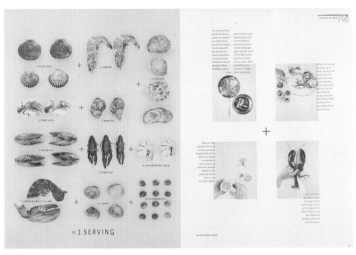

■ 217
PUBLICATION Martha Stewart Entertaining
CREATIVE DIRECTOR Gael Towey
ART DIRECTOR Claudia Bruno
DESIGNERS Claudia Bruno, Michele Outland
PHOTO EDITOR Heidi J. Posner
PHOTOGRAPHERS Frank Heckers, Coppi Barbieri, Gentl & Hyers,
Geoff Lung, Charles Maraia, Todd Eberle, Ken Kochey,
Chris Bakes, Maria Robledo, Wolfgang Woles
ISSUE November 1999
CATEGORY Entire Issue

■ 218
PUBLICATION Mirabella
CREATIVE DIRECTOR Shawn Young
ART DIRECTOR Shawn Young
DESIGNER Emiliano Neri
PHOTO EDITOR Loraine Pavich
PHOTOGRAPHERS Peggy Sirota, Larry Fink
PUBLISHER Hachette Filipacchi Magazines, Inc.
ISSUE October 1999
CATEGORY Redesign

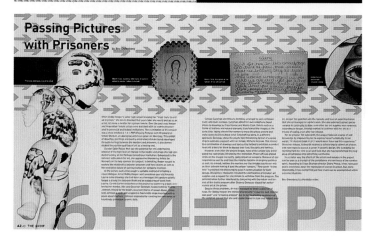

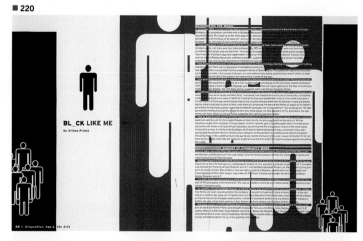

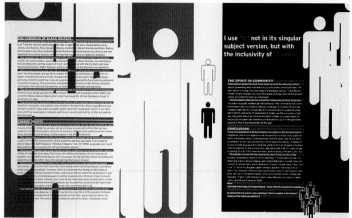

■ 219
PUBLICATION Mix
ART DIRECTORS Matthew P. Beckerle, Terry Lau
DESIGNERS Matthew P. Beckerle, Terry Lau
STUDIO creative activity /Beehive
PUBLISHER Parallélogramme Artist-Run Culture and Publishing Inc.
ISSUE March 5, 1999
CATEGORY Feature Story

■ 220
PUBLICATION Mix
ART DIRECTORS Matthew P. Beckerle, Terry Lau
DESIGNERS Matthew P. Beckerle, Terry Lau
ILLUSTRATOR Matthew P. Beckerle
STUDIO creative activity design company
PUBLISHER Parallélogramme Artist-Run Culture and Publishing Inc.
ISSUE September 5, 1999
CATEGORY Feature Story

■ 221
PUBLICATION Mix
ART DIRECTORS Matthew P. Beckerle, Terry Lau
DESIGNERS Matthew P. Beckerle, Terry Lau
STUDIO creative activity design company
PUBLISHER Parallélogramme Artist-Run Culture and Publishing Inc.
ISSUE September 5, 1999
CATEGORY Entire Issue

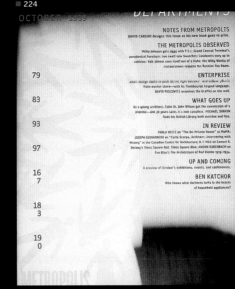

■ 222
PUBLICATION Metropolis
CREATIVE DIRECTOR Paula Scher
ART DIRECTOR Esther Bridavsky
DESIGNERS Anke Stohlmann,
Keith Daigle
STUDIO Pentagram Design, Inc.
PUBLISHER Bellerophon Publications
ISSUE December 1999
CATEGORY Entire Issue

■ 223
PUBLICATION Metropolis
CREATIVE DIRECTOR David Carson
DESIGNER David Carson
STUDIO David Carson Design
PUBLISHER Bellerophon Publications
ISSUE October 1999
CATEGORY Contents & Departments

■ 224
PUBLICATION Metropolis
CREATIVE DIRECTOR David Carson
DESIGNER David Carson
STUDIO David Carson Design
PUBLISHER Bellerophon Publications
ISSUE October 1999
CATEGORY Contents & Departments

■ 225
PUBLICATION Metropolis
CREATIVE DIRECTOR David Carson
DESIGNER David Carson
PHOTOGRAPHER Trevor Ray Hart
STUDIO David Carson Design
PUBLISHER Bellerophon Publications
ISSUE October 1999
CATEGORY Feature Spread

■ 226
PUBLICATION Network World
DESIGN DIRECTOR Rob Stave
ART DIRECTORS Tom Norton,
Paul M. Lee
DESIGNER Paul M. Lee
ILLUSTRATOR Val Mina
PUBLISHER International Data Group
ISSUE December 27, 1999
CATEGORY Single Page

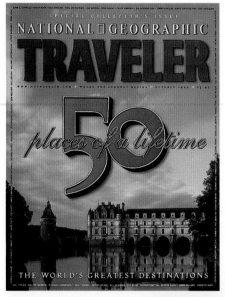

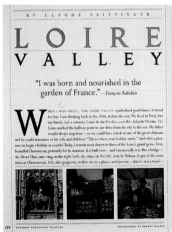

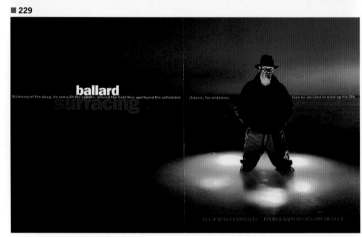

■ 227
PUBLICATION National Geographic Traveler
ART DIRECTOR Gerard Sealy
DESIGNERS Leigh Borghesani, Jonathan Halling, Gerard Sealy
PHOTO EDITORS Daniel R. Westergren, Carol Enquist, Linda B. Meyerriecks
PHOTOGRAPHERS Brooks Walker, Jeremy Walker
PUBLISHER National Geographic Society
ISSUE October 1999
CATEGORY Entire Issue

■ 228
PUBLICATION National Geographic Adventure
DESIGN DIRECTOR Tom Bentkowski
ART DIRECTOR Sam Serebin
DESIGNER Sam Serebin
PHOTO EDITOR Hadas Dembo
PHOTOGRAPHER Russell Kaye
PUBLISHER National Geographic Society
ISSUE Spring 1999
CATEGORY Feature Spread

■ 229
PUBLICATION National Geographic Adventure
DESIGN DIRECTOR Tom Bentkowski
ART DIRECTOR Sam Serebin
DESIGNER Tom Bentkowski
PHOTO EDITOR Hadas Dembo
PHOTOGRAPHER Gregory Heisler
PUBLISHER National Geographic Society
ISSUE Spring 1999
CATEGORY Feature Spread

■ 230

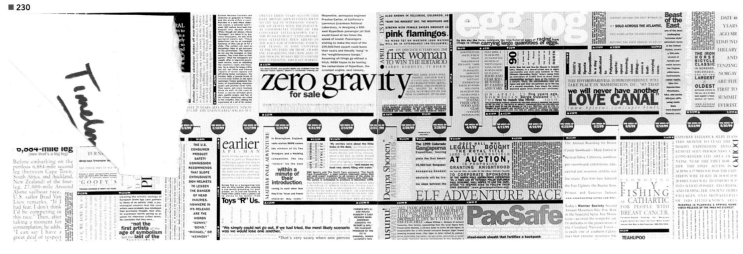

■ 231

■ 232

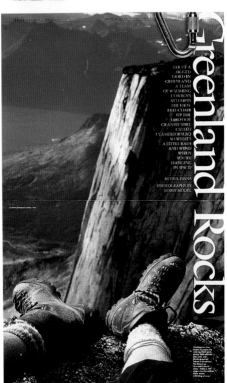

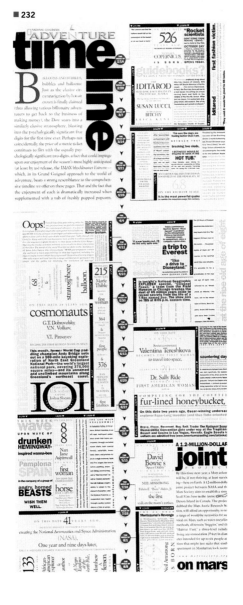

■ 230

PUBLICATION National Geographic Adventure
DESIGN DIRECTOR Tom Bentkowski
ART DIRECTOR Sam Serebin
DESIGNER Sam Serebin
PUBLISHER National Geographic Society
ISSUE Spring 1999
CATEGORY Contents & Departments

■ 231

PUBLICATION National Geographic Adventure
DESIGN DIRECTOR Tom Bentkowski
ART DIRECTOR Sam Serebin
DESIGNERS Tom Bentkowski,
Sam Serebin, Steve Walkowiak
PHOTO EDITOR Hadas Dembo
PHOTOGRAPHERS David Samuel Robbins,
Bobby Model, Bruno Barbey, Philip Harvey
PUBLISHER National Geographic Society
ISSUE Spring 1999
CATEGORY Entire Issue

■ 232

PUBLICATION National Geographic Adventure
DESIGN DIRECTOR Tom Bentkowski
ART DIRECTOR Sam Serebin
DESIGNER Sam Serebin
PUBLISHER National Geographic Society
ISSUE Summer 1999
CATEGORY Contents & Departments

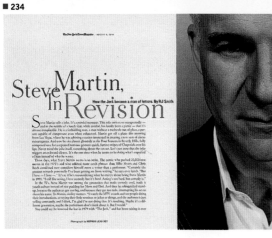

Baby in a Box
By Natalie Angier

A month sity of giving birth to her first child, Laura Pouzer, a college chemistry teacher, reclines on a padded table at Johns Hopkins University, the luxuriousness of her belly and her wit on equal display as she takes the infamous Stroop stress test...

Power Suffering
By Jennifer Egan

At sunset one evening in 1353, the 6-year-old Catherine Benincasa is said to have experienced the first of the mystical visions that would power her brief, extraordinary life...

A 'When I Was Little, In 1995'
By Kim Fiance

About 45 generations have passed during the last thousand years, generations in which a once profoundly unbalanced relationship between males and females has gradually shifted. But how far, exactly?...

Steve Martin, In Revision
How the Jerk became a man of letters. By RJ Smith

The Next Cardinal
With John J. O'Connor poised to retire, will the church choose a successor who can bring together the city's increasingly diverse Catholic population?
By Paul Elie

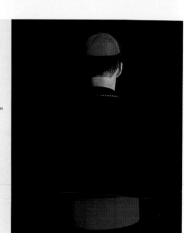

■ 233
PUBLICATION The New York Times Magazine
ART DIRECTOR Janet Froelich
DESIGNER Claude Martel
PHOTOGRAPHER Michelangelo Di Battista
STYLIST Stefan Campbell
PUBLISHER The New York Times
ISSUE January 31, 1999
CATEGORY Feature Spread

■ 234
PUBLICATION The New York Times Magazine
ART DIRECTOR Janet Froelich
DESIGNER Catherine Gilmore-Barnes
PHOTO EDITOR Kathy Ryan
PHOTOGRAPHER Norman Jean Roy
PUBLISHER The New York Times
ISSUE August 8, 1999
CATEGORY Feature Spread

■ 235
PUBLICATION The New York Times Magazine
ART DIRECTORS Janet Froelich, Joele Cuyler
DESIGNERS Joele Cuyler, Ignacio Rodriguez
PHOTO EDITORS Kathy Ryan, Sarah Harbutt
PHOTOGRAPHERS Tom Schierlitz, Andres Serrano,
Lisa Sarfati, Malerie Marder, Matthew Rolston,
Michael O'Neill, Justine Kurland, Catherine Opie
PUBLISHER The New York Times
ISSUE May 16, 1999
CATEGORY Feature Story

■ 236
PUBLICATION The New York Times Magazine
ART DIRECTOR Janet Froelich
DESIGNER Nancy Harris
PHOTO EDITOR Kathy Ryan
PHOTOGRAPHER Lyle Ashton Harris
PUBLISHER The New York Times
ISSUE October 10, 1999
CATEGORY Feature Spread

TRIUMPH OF THE IMAGE

For most of this millennium, art was reserved for the rich and the religious. Now, wherever we look, there's something to see. But is there no escape?

BY LUC SANTE

The Me Millennium

What Your Clothes Make of You

Dressing and identity.

By Amy M. Spindler

The Haunted Wardrobe

from a flea market, a life in 29 pieces.

By Lynn Hirschberg

Photographs by Tom Schierlitz

GEOFFREY JAMES

NEW FOUND LAND

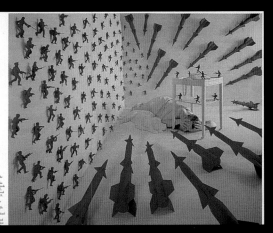

SANDY SKOGLUND

DUCK AND COVER

My Body

Models and ordinary women discuss what they were thinking as they posed nearly nude.

Concept by Vanessa Beecroft
Photographs by Mikael O'Neill

237
PUBLICATION The New York Times Magazine
ART DIRECTORS Janet Froelich, Joele Cuyler
DESIGNERS Joele Cuyler, Ignacio Rodriguez
ILLUSTRATOR Carroll Dunham
PHOTO EDITORS Kathy Ryan, Sarah Harbutt
PHOTOGRAPHERS Geoffrey James, Sandy Skoglund

238
PUBLICATION The New York Times Magazine
ART DIRECTORS Janet Froelich, Joele Cuyler
DESIGNERS Joele Cuyler, Ignacio Rodriguez
PHOTO EDITORS Kathy Ryan, Sarah Harbutt
PUBLISHER The New York Times
ISSUE October 17, 1999

239
PUBLICATION The New York Times Magazine
ART DIRECTOR Janet Froelich
DESIGNER Claude Martel
PHOTO EDITOR Kathy Ryan
PHOTOGRAPHERS Micahel O'Neill, Tom Schierlitz
PUBLISHER The New York Times

Who Am I?

Here and on pages to follow, six experts guess the identities of randomly selected New York pedestrians, trying to discern who they are by what they wear.

Photographs by Jake Chessum
Reporting by Abby Ellin and Degen Pener

The Experts' Guesses

The Answers

Who Am I?

The Experts' Guesses

The Answers

Who Am I?

The Experts' Guesses

The Answers

NASTY WORDS

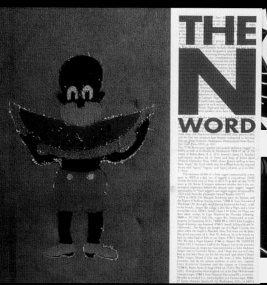

THE N WORD

■ 240
PUBLICATION The New York Times Magazine
ART DIRECTOR Janet Froelich
DESIGNERS Claude Martel, Andrea Fella
PHOTO EDITOR Kathy Ryan
PHOTOGRAPHER Jake Chessum
PUBLISHER The New York Times
ISSUE November 14, 1999
CATEGORY Feature Story

■ 241
PUBLICATION The Nose
CREATIVE DIRECTORS DK Holland, Seymour Chwast
ART DIRECTOR Seymour Chwast
DESIGNERS Seymour Chwast, Jim Hiesener, Barbara DiPaolo
ILLUSTRATOR Seymour Chwast
STUDIO The Pushpin Group Inc.
PUBLISHER The Pushpin Group Inc.
ISSUE May 1999
CATEGORY Entire Issue

■ 242

■ 243

■ 244

■ 245

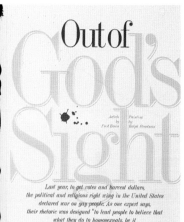

■ 246

■ 242
PUBLICATION Philadelphia
ART DIRECTOR Tim Baldwin
DESIGNER Tim Baldwin
ILLUSTRATOR Anita E. Kunz
PUBLISHER Metrocorp Publishing
ISSUE June 1999
CATEGORY Feature Spread

■ 243
PUBLICATION Philadelphia
ART DIRECTOR Tim Baldwin
DESIGNER Tim Baldwin
ILLUSTRATOR David Hughes
PUBLISHER Metrocorp Publishing
ISSUE March 1999
CATEGORY Feature Spread

■ 244
PUBLICATION Men's Journal
ART DIRECTOR Michael Lawton
DESIGNER Michael Lawton
ILLUSTRATOR Barry Blitt
PUBLISHER Wenner Media
ISSUE November 1999
CATEGORY Feature Spread

■ 245
PUBLICATION NewWest
ART DIRECTOR Steven Ralph Jerman
DESIGNERS Steven Ralph Jerman, Melinda Beck
ILLUSTRATOR Melinda Beck
PHOTO EDITOR Steven Ralph Jerman
STUDIO Jerman Design Incorporated
PUBLISHER Sandmark Publishing Co.
ISSUE September 1999
CATEGORY Feature Spread

■ 246
PUBLICATION Penthouse
CREATIVE DIRECTOR Frank DeVino
ART DIRECTOR Nicholas E. Torello
DESIGNER Nicholas E. Torello
ILLUSTRATOR Ralph Steadman
PUBLISHER General Media Communications, Inc.
ISSUE September 1999
CATEGORY Feature Spread

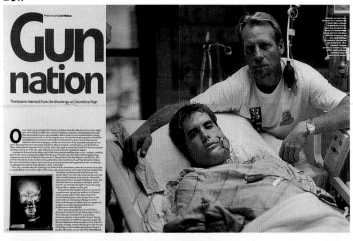

Gun nation

The lessons learned from the shootings at Columbine High

the rainbow coalition

The spring/summer season will see rich fabrics and even richer colours. The future is bright

GOLDEN GATE

Photographs by Richard Misrach

the force of Spirit

by Scott Russell Sanders

MAN KILLED BY PHEASANT

by John Price

■ 247
PUBLICATION The Observer Life
ART DIRECTOR Wayne Ford
DESIGNER Wayne Ford
PHOTO EDITOR Jennie Ricketts
PHOTOGRAPHER Zed Nelson
PUBLISHER
Guardian Newspapers Limited
ISSUE June 6, 1999
CATEGORY Feature Story

■ 248
PUBLICATION The Observer Life
ART DIRECTOR Wayne Ford
DESIGNER Wayne Ford
PHOTO EDITOR Jo Adams
PHOTOGRAPHER Francesca Sorrenti
PUBLISHER
Guardian Newspapers Limited
ISSUE March 21, 1999
CATEGORY Feature Story

■ 249
PUBLICATION Orion
CREATIVE DIRECTOR Hans Teensma
DESIGN DIRECTOR Katie Craig
PHOTO EDITOR Hadas Dembo
PHOTOGRAPHERS Richard Misrach,
Mary Schjeldahl
STUDIO Impress, Inc.
PUBLISHER Orion Society
ISSUE Autumn 1999
CATEGORY Entire Issue

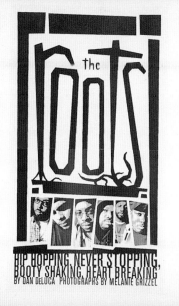

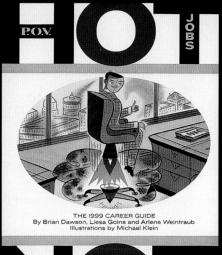

253

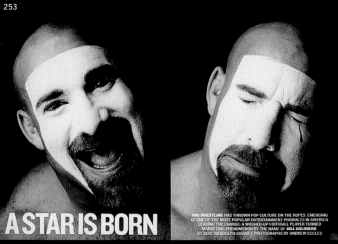

A STAR IS BORN

250

PUBLICATION Request
ART DIRECTOR David Yamada
DESIGNER David Yamada
PHOTOGRAPHER Melanie Grizzel
PUBLISHER Request Media
ISSUE April 1999
CATEGORY Single Page

251

PUBLICATION P.O.V.
DESIGN DIRECTOR Florian Bachleda
DESIGNERS Florian Bachleda, Pino Impastato
ILLUSTRATOR Michael Klein
PUBLISHER B.Y.O.B./Freedom Ventures, Inc.
ISSUE May 1999
CATEGORY Single Page

252

PUBLICATION P.O.V.
DESIGN DIRECTOR Florian Bachleda
DESIGNERS Pino Impastato, Edward Levine
ILLUSTRATOR Bill Russell
PHOTO EDITOR Evelyn Evans
PHOTOGRAPHERS Andrew Eccles, Jim Purdum, Barbara Ries, Max Hirshfeld
PUBLISHER B.Y.O.B./Freedom Ventures, Inc.
ISSUE April 1999
CATEGORY Feature Story

253

PUBLICATION P.O.V.
DESIGN DIRECTOR Florian Bachleda
DESIGNERS Florian Bachleda, Pino Impastato
PHOTOGRAPHER Andrew Eccles
PUBLISHER B.Y.O.B./Freedom Ventures, Inc.
ISSUE May 1999
CATEGORY Feature Spread

■ 254
PUBLICATION Philadelphia Inquirer Magazine
ART DIRECTORS Chrissy Dunleavy, Susan Syrnick
DESIGNER Chrissy Dunleavy
ILLUSTRATOR Harry Bliss
PUBLIHSER Philadelphia Inquirer
ISSUE July 25, 1999
CATEGORY Feature Story

■ 255
PUBLICATION Philadelphia Inquirer Magazine
ART DIRECTORS Chrissy Dunleavy, Susan Syrnick
DESIGNER Susan Syrnick
PHOTOGRAPHER James Muñoz
PUBLIHSER Philadelphia Inquirer
ISSUE September 12, 1999
CATEGORY Feature Story

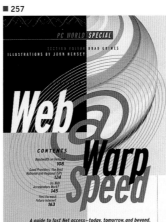

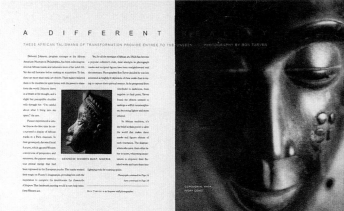

■ 256
PUBLICATION Philadelphia Inquirer Magazine
ART DIRECTORS Chrissy Dunleavy, Susan Syrnick
DESIGNER Chrissy Dunleavy
PHOTOGRAPHER Ron Tarver
PUBLIHSER Philadelphia Inquirer
ISSUE February 7, 1999
CATEGORY Feature Story

■ 257
PUBLICATION PC World
CREATIVE DIRECTOR Robert Kanes
ART DIRECTORS Carolyn Perot, Tim J. Luddy, Kate Godfrey
ILLUSTRATOR John Hersey
PHOTOGRAPHERS Paula Friedland, Danny Turner, Robert Holmgren, Amy Etra, Richard Howard
PUBLISHER International Data Group (IDG)
ISSUE March 1999
CATEGORY Feature Story

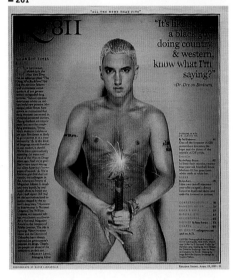

the wainwrights

THE BATTLES OF RAGE AGAINST THE MACHINE

BY DAVID FRICKE

THE MIGHTIEST BAND
IN ROCK & ROLL IS READY
TO TAKE ON RACISM, ECONOMIC
INJUSTICE AND POLITICAL
OPPRESSION — BUT FIRST
THEY HAD TO LEARN HOW
TO GET ALONG WITH ONE ANOTHER
PHOTOGRAPHED BY MARTIN SCHOELLER

coltrane davis monk & mingus

Nice & Naughty
By David Lipsky

Christina Ricci takes on her image as an angry, fun, kids-can't-stay tuned teen who will say anything

LIVE IN THE '90s
★★★★★ ★ ★★★★★★★★
BY DAVID FRICKE
★★★ STARRING ★★★
MADONNA, LOLLAPALOOZA, NIRVANA, METALLICA,
RED HOT CHILI PEPPERS/SMASHING PUMPKINS/PEARL JAM,
U2, SONIC YOUTH/SUN RA, PHISH, BECK,
THE CHEMICAL BROTHERS, CSN, ROLLING STONES,
PUFF DADDY AND THE FAMILY, BOB DYLAN, BEASTIE BOYS

the cooders

"WHEN JOACHIM WAS TWELVE YEARS
OLD, HE PLAYED ONSTAGE AT MADISON
SQUARE GARDEN WITH JOHN LEE
HOOKER. HE TOOK HIS PLACE
WITHOUT FEAR." —RY COODER

BY RY AND JOACHIM
COODER AT RY'S HOME
IN LOS ANGELES

264
PUBLICATION Rolling Stone
ART DIRECTOR Fred Woodward
DESIGNERS Fred Woodward, Ken DeLago
PHOTO EDITOR Rachel Knepfer
PHOTOGRAPHER Kurt Markus
PUBLISHER Straight Arrow Publishers
ISSUE November 11, 1999
CATEGORY Feature Story

265
PUBLICATION Rolling Stone
ART DIRECTOR Fred Woodward
DESIGNER Andy Omel
PHOTO EDITOR Rachel Knepfer
PHOTOGRAPHER Martin Schoeller
PUBLISHER Straight Arrow Publishers
ISSUE November 25, 1999
CATEGORY Feature Spread

266
PUBLICATION Rolling Stone
ART DIRECTOR Fred Woodward
DESIGNERS Fred Woodward, Gail Anderson
PHOTO EDITOR Rachel Knepfer
PHOTOGRAPHER Peggy Sirota
PUBLISHER Straight Arrow Publishers
ISSUE December 9, 1999
CATEGORY Feature Spread

267
PUBLICATION Rolling Stone
ART DIRECTOR Fred Woodward
DESIGNER Andy Omel
PHOTO EDITOR Rachel Knepfer
PHOTOGRAPHER Neil Preston
PUBLISHER Straight Arrow Publishers
ISSUE September 7, 1999
CATEGORY Feature Spread

 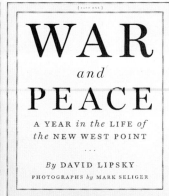

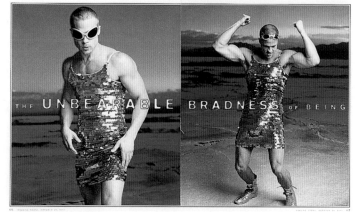

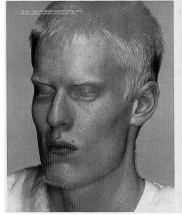 

■ 268
PUBLICATION Rolling Stone
ART DIRECTOR Fred Woodward
DESIGNERS Fred Woodward, Siung Tjia
PHOTO EDITOR Rachel Knepfer
PHOTOGRAPHER Mark Seliger
PUBLISHER Straight Arrow Publishers
ISSUE February 18, 1999
CATEGORY Feature Spread

■ 269
PUBLICATION Rolling Stone
ART DIRECTOR Fred Woodward
DESIGNERS Fred Woodward, Gail Anderson
PHOTO EDITOR Rachel Knepfer
PHOTOGRAPHER Mark Seliger
PUBLISHER Straight Arrow Publishers
ISSUE March 4 1999
CATEGORY Feature Spread

■ 270
PUBLICATION Rolling Stone
ART DIRECTOR Fred Woodward
DESIGNERS Fred Woodward, Siung Tjia
PHOTO EDITOR Rachel Knepfer
PHOTOGRAPHER Mark Seliger
PUBLISHER Straight Arrow Publishers
ISSUE October 28, 1999
CATEGORY Feature Spread

■ 271
PUBLICATION Rolling Stone
ART DIRECTOR Fred Woodward
DESIGNER Ken DeLago
PHOTO EDITORS Rachel Knepfer, Fiona McDonagh
PHOTOGRAPHER Mark Seliger
PUBLISHER Straight Arrow Publishers
ISSUE November 25, 1999
CATEGORY Feature Spread

■ 272
PUBLICATION Rolling Stone
ART DIRECTOR Fred Woodward
DESIGNERS Fred Woodward, Gail Anderson
PHOTO EDITORS Rachel Knepfer, Fiona McDonagh
PHOTOGRAPHER Mark Seliger
PUBLISHER Straight Arrow Publishers
ISSUE October 14, 1999
CATEGORY Feature Spread

■ 273
PUBLICATION Spin
ART DIRECTOR Lisa Steinmeyer
DESIGNER Garland Lyn
PHOTO EDITOR Cory Jacobs
PHOTOGRAPHER Alexei Hay
PUBLISHER Miller Publishing Group
ISSUE October 1999
CATEGORY Feature Spread

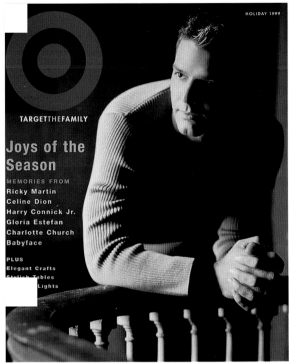

HOLIDAY 1999

TARGETTHEFAMILY

Joys of the Season

MEMORIES FROM

Ricky Martin
Celine Dion
Harry Connick Jr.
Gloria Estefan
Charlotte Church
Babyface

PLUS

Elegant Crafts
Stylish Tables
Lights

HOLIDAY ENTERTAINING

Punch It Up!

New flavors dress up a holiday favorite.

let it **snow**

HOME-GROWN

Holidays*

RICKY **martin**

CELINE
dion

HARRY **connick** Jr.

■ 274

PUBLICATION Target the Family
CREATIVE DIRECTOR Terry Ross Koppel
ART DIRECTOR Hitomi Sato
DESIGNERS Karen Yi, Jennifer Muller, Jason Lancaster
PHOTO EDITOR Maya Kaimal
PHOTOGRAPHER Evan Sklar
PUBLISHER Time Inc. Custom Publishing
ISSUE Holiday 1999
CATEGORY Redesign

■ 275

PUBLICATION Target the Family
CREATIVE DIRECTOR Terry Ross Koppel
ART DIRECTOR Hitomi Sato
DESIGNER Karen Yi
PHOTO EDITOR Maya Kaimal
PUBLISHER Time Inc. Custom Publishing
ISSUE Holiday 1999
CATEGORY Feature Story

design ■ MERIT

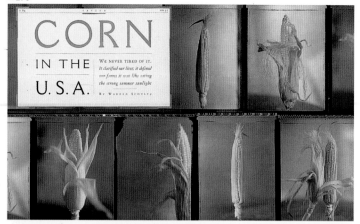

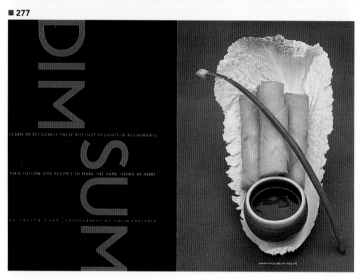

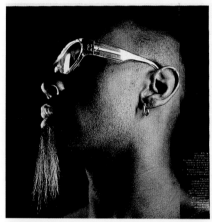

■ 276
PUBLICATION Saveur
CREATIVE DIRECTOR Michael Grossman
ART DIRECTOR Jill Armus
DESIGNER Julie Pryma
PHOTO EDITOR María Millán
PHOTOGRAPHER Lizzie Himmel
PUBLISHER Meigher Communications
ISSUE September/October 1999
CATEGORY Feature Spread

■ 277
PUBLICATION President's Choice Magazine
ART DIRECTOR Carol Moskot
DESIGNER Erika Oliveira
PHOTOGRAPHER Colin Faulkner
ISSUE July/August 1999
CATEGORY Feature Spread

■ 278
PUBLICATION Shift
CREATIVE DIRECTOR Carmen Dunjko
ART DIRECTOR Malcolm Brown
DESIGNERS Carmen Dunjko, Christine Stephens, Malcolm Brown
PHOTO EDITOR Bree Seeley
PHOTOGRAPHER Bryce Duffy
PUBLISHER Normal Net Inc.
ISSUE April 1999
CATEGORY Feature Story

■ 279
PUBLICATION Shift
CREATIVE DIRECTOR Carmen Dunjko
ART DIRECTOR Malcolm Brown
DESIGNERS Carmen Dunjko, Malcolm Brown
PHOTO EDITOR Bree Seeley
PHOTOGRAPHER Suzanne Langeuin
PUBLISHER Normal Net Inc.
ISSUE April 1999
CATEGORY Feature Spread

■ 280

 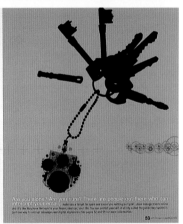

■ 281

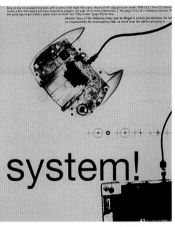 

■ 282

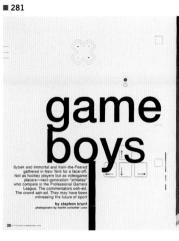 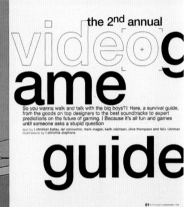

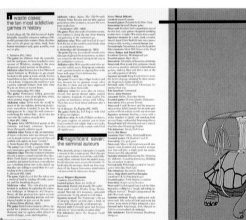

■ 280

PUBLICATION Shift
CREATIVE DIRECTOR Carmen Dunjko
ART DIRECTOR Malcolm Brown
DESIGNERS Carmen Dunjko,
Malcolm Brown
PHOTO EDITOR Bree Seeley
PHOTOGRAPHERS Jerome Albertini,
Sandy Nicholson
PUBLISHER Normal Net Inc.
ISSUE Summer 1999
CATEGORY Feature Story

■ 281

PUBLICATION Shift
CREATIVE DIRECTOR Carmen Dunjko
ART DIRECTOR Malcolm Brown
DESIGNERS Malcolm Brown,
Carmen Dunjko
PHOTO EDITOR Bree Seeley
PHOTOGRAPHER Martin Schoeller
PUBLISHER Normal Net Inc.
ISSUE July 1999
CATEGORY Feature Spread

■ 282

PUBLICATION Shift
CREATIVE DIRECTOR Carmen Dunjko
ART DIRECTOR Malcolm Brown
DESIGNERS Christine Stephens,
Carmen Dunjko, Malcolm Brown
ILLUSTRATOR Christine Stephens
PUBLISHER Normal Net Inc.
ISSUE September 1999
CATEGORY Feature Story

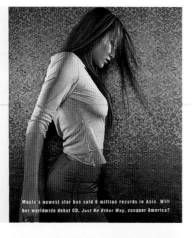

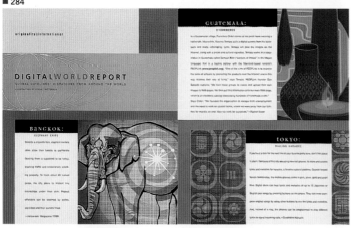

■ 283
PUBLICATION Sony Style
CREATIVE DIRECTOR Terry Ross Koppel
ART DIRECTOR Darcy Doyle
DESIGNER Terry Ross Koppel
PHOTO EDITOR Julie Claire
PHOTOGRAPHER Torkil Gudnason
PUBLISHER Time Inc. Custom Publishing
ISSUE Spring 1999
CATEGORY Feature Spread

■ 284
PUBLICATION Sony Style
CREATIVE DIRECTOR Terry Ross Koppel
ART DIRECTOR Darcy Doyle
DESIGNER Darcy Doyle
ILLUSTRATOR Stuart Patterson
PHOTO EDITOR Julie Claire
PUBLISHER Time Inc. Custom Publishing
ISSUE Spring 1999
CATEGORY Contents & Departments

■ 285
PUBLICATION Sony Style
CREATIVE DIRECTOR Terry Ross Koppel
ART DIRECTOR Darcy Doyle
DESIGNER Darcy Doyle
PHOTO EDITOR Julie Claire
PHOTOGRAPHER Chris Buck
PUBLISHER Time Inc. Custom Publishing
ISSUE Spring 1999
CATEGORY Contents & Departments

■ 286
PUBLICATION Sony Style
CREATIVE DIRECTOR Terry Ross Koppel
ART DIRECTOR Darcy Doyle
DESIGNER Kristina DiMatteo
ILLUSTRATOR Sally Bennett
PHOTO EDITOR Julie Claire
PHOTOGRAPHER Simon Watson
PUBLISHER Time Inc. Custom Publishing
ISSUE October 1999
CATEGORY Feature Story

milla
JOVOVICH

TIME
picks a person
of each century,
from
1000 to 1900

the most important ■ people of the
millennium

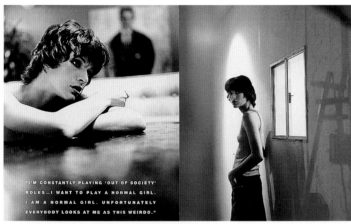

"I'M CONSTANTLY PLAYING 'OUT OF SOCIETY'
ROLES...I WANT TO PLAY A NORMAL GIRL.
I AM A NORMAL GIRL. UNFORTUNATELY
EVERYBODY LOOKS AT ME AS THIS WEIRDO."

I AM A HARD WORKER.
THAT'S THE RUSSIAN
IN ME COMING OUT.

TAKING RISKS

johann
gutenberg
(c. 1395-1468)
The obscure printer's innovation kindled reformations
and a yet unfinished information revolution

mohandas gandhi

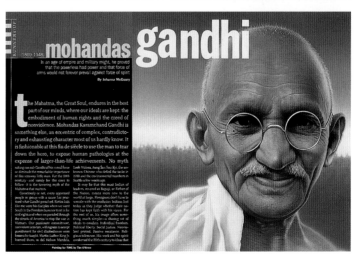

In an age of empire and military might, he proved
that the powerless had power and that force of
arms would not forever prevail against force of spirit
By Johanna McGeary

■ 287
PUBLICATION Sony Style
CREATIVE DIRECTOR Terry Ross Koppel
ART DIRECTOR Darcy Doyle
DESIGNER Terry Ross Koppel
PHOTO EDITOR Julie Claire
PHOTOGRAPHER Kate Garner
PUBLISHER Time Inc. Custom Publishing
ISSUE November 1999
CATEGORY Feature Story

■ 288
PUBLICATION Time
DESIGN DIRECTOR Arthur Hochstein
ART DIRECTOR Sharon Okamoto
DESIGNER Sharon Okamoto
ILLUSTRATORS Tim O'Brien, Laura Uram
PUBLISHER Time Inc.
ISSUE December 31, 1999
CATEGORY Entire Issue

The Tide of Prints

HAS DOMINIQUE MOCEANO FLIPPED?

LADIES and GENTLEMEN, the NEXT CORMAC McCARTHY

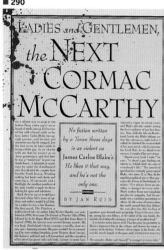

Has Madalyn Murray O'Hair Met Her Maker?

■ 289
PUBLICATION Technology Review
ART DIRECTOR Kelly McMurray
DESIGNER Kelly McMurray
PHOTOGRAPHER Fredrik Brodén
STUDIO kelly design, inc
PUBLISHER Massachusetts Institute of Technology
ISSUE January/February 1999
CATEGORY Feature Spread

■ 290
PUBLICATION Texas Monthly
CREATIVE DIRECTOR D. J. Stout
DESIGNERS D. J. Stout, Nancy McMillen
PHOTO EDITOR D. J. Stout
PHOTOGRAPHER James H. Evans
PUBLISHER Emmis Communications Corp.
CATEGORY Feature Spread

■ 291
PUBLICATION Texas Monthly
CREATIVE DIRECTOR D. J. Stout
DESIGNERS D. J. Stout, Nancy McMillen
PHOTO EDITOR D. J. Stout
PHOTOGRAPHER Don Glentzer
PUBLISHER Emmis Communications Corp.
ISSUE February 1999
CATEGORY Feature Spread

■ 292
PUBLICATION Texas Monthly
CREATIVE DIRECTOR D. J. Stout
DESIGNERS D. J. Stout, Nancy McMillen
PHOTO EDITOR D. J. Stout
PHOTOGRAPHER Wyatt McSpadden
PUBLISHER Emmis Communications Corp.
ISSUE May 1999
CATEGORY Feature Story

■ 293
PUBLICATION Travel & Leisure Golf
DESIGN DIRECTOR Tom Brown
ART DIRECTORS Dirk Barnett, Todd Albertson
DESIGNERS Tom Brown, Dirk Barnett, Todd Albertson
PHOTO EDITOR Maisie Todd
PHOTOGRAPHER Fredrik Brodén
PUBLISHER American Express Publishing Co.
ISSUE July/August 1999
CATEGORY Contents & Departments

THE RIGHT STUFF

HIGH-TECH AMMO

design ■ MERIT

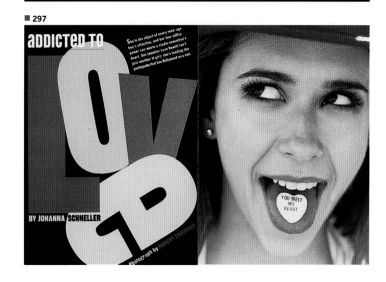

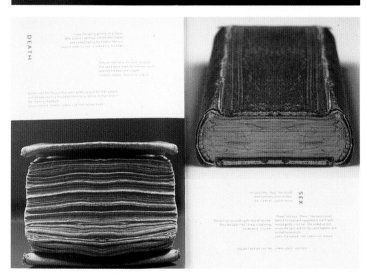

■ 294
PUBLICATION 2wice
ART DIRECTOR J. Abbott Miller
DESIGNERS J. Abbott Miller, Scott
Devendorf, Roy Brooks
PHOTOGRAPHER Marcus Tomlinson
STUDIO Pentagram Design, Inc.
PUBLISHER 2wice Arts Foundation
ISSUE Vol. 3, No. 2 1999
CATEGORY Entire Issue

■ 295
PUBLICATION TV Guide Ultimate Cable
DESIGN DIRECTOR Maxine Davidowitz
ART DIRECTOR Gloria Pantell
DESIGNER Gloria Pantell
PHOTO EDITOR Hazel Hammond,
Janet Csadenyi
PHOTOGRAPHER Danny Clinch
PUBLISHER TV Guide Inc.
ISSUE December 11, 1999
CATEGORY Feature Spread

■ 296
PUBLICATION UCLA Magazine
DESIGN DIRECTOR Charles Hess
DESIGNERS Dana Barton,
Jackie Morrow
PHOTO EDITOR Charles Hess
PHOTOGRAPHER Jason Beck
STUDIO C. Hess Design
PUBLISHER UCLA
ISSUE Winter 1999
CATEGORY Feature Spread

■ 297
PUBLICATION Us
ART DIRECTOR Richard Baker
DESIGNER Richard Baker
PHOTO EDITOR Jennifer Crandall
PHOTOGRAPHER Robert Erdmann
PUBLISHER US Magazine Co., L.P.
ISSUE February 1999
CATEGORY Feature Spread

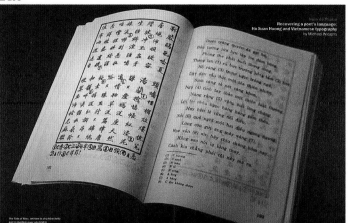

The fate of Nôm, written in chu Nôm (left) and in modern quoc ngu (right). Photograph by Jonce Vincot.

Gate of Vinh Tru Pagoda in Hanoi's old quarter, with inscriptions in chu Han and chu Nôm, and modern signs in the Latin-alphabet quoc ngu.

The short history

of Vietnamese typography is rooted in the country's ancient writing systems and its tumultuous history of foreign invasion—first and repeatedly by northern neighbor China, and later by the West. Each foreign invasion was followed by rebellion, internal turmoil, and further invasion. This periodic turmoil—and subsequent efforts to establish autonomy—is mirrored in the very writing systems the Vietnamese culture used to identify itself in its stories, histories, and documentation.

For 2000 years before this century two calligraphic writing systems were used: chu Han and chu Nôm. Chu Han, the Chinese writing system that was adopted in the first centuries, was used for poetry, and became the system through which the learned elite scholars, civil service profession, and Confucian teachings of mandarin rule were delivered. While it was a favorite of ruling-class scholars, chu Han, as did not represent spoken Vietnamese, so in the tenth century, chu Nôm, or the vernacular, was created. The calligraphic Nôm, which at times looks similar to chu Han, represents spoken Vietnamese. The two systems share some similarities, but there are more than 8000 Nôm characters which are completely unique, and the rest are Han Viet (Vietnamized chu Han—Chinese characters with Vietnamese pronunciation). At first Nôm was used to record names (family names, first names, place names, plant and animal names, etc.), folk poetry, sayings, customs, ceremonies, and events for the emperors. Quickly it was adopted for religious purposes. Finally it was used for recording histories and became the script of choice for poets, who used it particularly for its subversive possibilities. Stories and poetry, including great

Vietnamese classics, were written in Nôm. By 1800, Nôm had become the center of Vietnamese culture.

One writer whose work is still widely read throughout Vietnam is the famous nineteenth-century poet Ho Xuan Huong. Her poetry ranks with other Asian classics, yet outside of Vietnam few know of her, partly because of the years of war and colonization but more significantly because she wrote in Nôm. And she was a woman writing feminist poetry in a period of patriarchy. Her poems, filled with double entendre are cloaked in sexual innuendo, symbolically emasculated local leaders and community figureheads while at the same time addressing social and philosophical concerns. That she wrote in Nôm was one more subversive act.

I had read two of John Balaban's translations of Ho Xuan Huong's poetry in Locusts at the Edge of Summer, a book we published at Copper Canyon Press, which was nominated for the 1998 National

Above: Page from a phrasebook for reading Buddhist inscriptions in Han and Nôm characters. Opposite: Chu Han inscription.

LETTERING & TYPOGRAPHY IN THE WORLD AROUND US

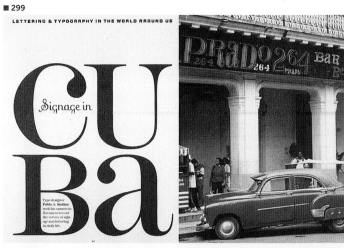

Signage in CUBA

Type designer Pablo A. Medina took his camera to Havana to record the variety of signage and lettering in daily life.

■ 298
PUBLICATION U&lc
CREATIVE DIRECTOR Clive Chiu
ART DIRECTOR Deanna Lowe
DESIGNER Deanna Lowe
PHOTOGRAPHERS James Worrell, Michael Wiegers
PUBLISHER International Typeface Corp.
ISSUE Fall 1999
CATEGORY Feature Story

■ 299
PUBLICATION U&lc
CREATIVE DIRECTOR Clive Chiu
ART DIRECTOR Deanna Lowe
DESIGNER Deanna Lowe
PHOTOGRAPHER Pablo A. Medina
PUBLISHER International Typeface Corp.
ISSUE Fall 1999
CATEGORY Feature Story

■ 300
PUBLICATION U&lc
CREATIVE DIRECTOR Clive Chiu
ART DIRECTOR Deanna Lowe
DESIGNER Deanna Lowe
PUBLISHER International Typeface Corp.
ISSUE Fall 1999
CATEGORY Contents & Departments

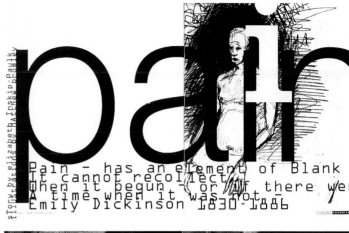

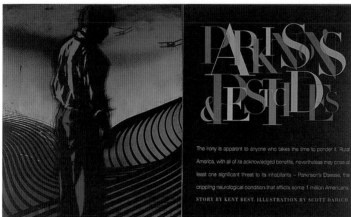

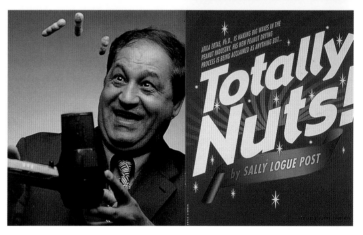

■ 301
PUBLICATION Vistas: Texas Tech Research
CREATIVE DIRECTORS Scott C. Dadich, Artie D. Limmer
ART DIRECTOR Scott C. Dadich
DESIGNERS Scott C. Dadich, Alyson Keeling
ILLUSTRATORS Matthew Bromley, Scott C. Dadich
PHOTO EDITOR Artie D. Limmer
PHOTOGRAPHERS Artie D. Limmer, Joey Hernandez, Melissa Goodlett
PUBLISHER Texas Tech University
ISSUE Fall 1999
CATEGORY Entire Issue

■ 302
PUBLICATION Vistas: Texas Tech Research
CREATIVE DIRECTORS Scott C. Dadich, Artie D. Limmer
ART DIRECTOR Scott C. Dadich
DESIGNERS Scott C. Dadich, Alyson Keeling
ILLUSTRATORS Matthew Bromley, Scott C. Dadich
PHOTO EDITOR Artie D. Limmer
PHOTOGRAPHERS Artie D. Limmer, Joey Hernandez, Melissa Goodlett
PUBLISHER Texas Tech University
ISSUE Fall 1999
CATEGORY Redesign

DECEMBER 1999

DEFINING THE YEAR,
WRAPPING UP
THE CENTURY,
AND POLISHING OFF
THE MILLENNIUM,
VANITY FAIR
PRESENTS

THE HALL 1999 OF FAME

PORTFOLIO BY ANNIE LEIBOVITZ
PHOTOGRAPHS BY JONATHAN BECKER, HARRY BENSON,
TODD EBERLE, SAM JONES, DAV D LACHAPELLE,
MICHAEL O'NEILL, HERB RITTS, AND NORMAN JEAN ROY
WITH TEXT BY JAMES WOLCOTT

FORTY MEN AND WOMEN WHO ROCKED THE STADIUMS, THE
CENSORS, AND THE SENSIBILITY; WHO FACED DOWN MICROSOFT,
MILOŠEVIĆ, AND THE CHINESE SOCCER TEAM; WHO TURNED
THE TOUR DE FRANCE INTO A TOUR DE FORCE, A CABLE SHOW
INTO MUST-SEE TV, AND A 45-YEAR-OLD MEN'S MAGAZINE
INTO A CAMP-HIPSTER ICON OF SEX AND THE SWINGIN' MAN

■ 303
PUBLICATION Vanity Fair
DESIGN DIRECTOR David Harris
ART DIRECTOR Gregory Mastrianni
PHOTO EDITORS Susan White,
Lisa Berman, Jeannie Rhodes
PHOTOGRAPHERS Annie Leibovitz, Herb Ritts,
Norman Jean Roy, Todd Eberlie, David Lachappelle,
Michael O'Neill, Jonathan Becker, Harry Benson
PUBLISHER Condé Nast Publications, Inc.
ISSUE December 1999
CATEGORY Feature Story

■ 304
PUBLICATION Vanity Fair
DESIGN DIRECTOR David Harris
ART DIRECTOR Gregory Mastrianni
PHOTO EDITORS Susan White, Lisa Berman
PHOTOGRAPHERS Annie Leibovitz, Herb Ritts, Bruce Weber,
Firooz Zahedi, Sam Jones, David LaChapelle, Helmut Newton,
Thierry Bouet, Peter Lindbergh, Michael O'Neill, Lorenzo Agius,
Art Streiber, David Hockney, Ellen von Unwerth
PUBLISHER Condé Nast Publications, Inc.
ISSUE April 1999
CATEGORY Feature Story

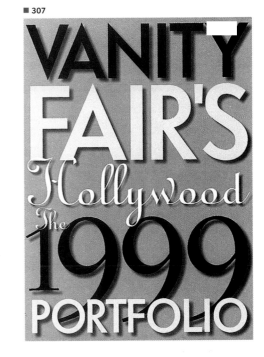

VANITY FAIR

THE EARLY YEARS:
1914~1936

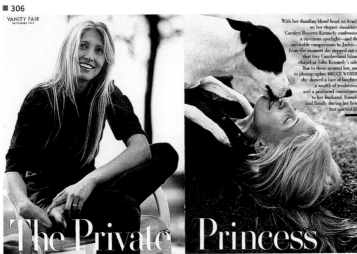

The Private Princess

In Cold, Blue Blood

■ 305

PUBLICATION Vanity Fair
DESIGN DIRECTOR David Harris
ART DIRECTOR Gregory Mastrianni
PHOTO EDITORS Susan White,
Lisa Berman, Jeannie Rhodes
PHOTOGRAPHERS Edward Steichen,
Nickolas Muray, George Hoyningen-Huene
PUBLISHER Condé Nast Publications, Inc.
ISSUE March 1999
CATEGORY Feature Story

■ 306

PUBLICATION Vanity Fair
DESIGN DIRECTOR David Harris
ART DIRECTOR Gregory Mastrianni
PUBLISHER Condé Nast Publications, Inc.
ISSUE April 1999
CATEGORY Single Page

■ 307

PUBLICATION Vanity Fair
DESIGN DIRECTOR David Harris
ART DIRECTORS Gregory Mastrianni,
Mimi Dutta, Julie Weiss
DESIGNERS Lisa Kennedy, Lee Ruelle
PHOTO EDITORS Susan White,
Lisa Berman, Jeannie Rhodes
PHOTOGRAPHER Bruce Weber
PUBLISHER Condé Nast Publications, Inc.
ISSUE September 1999
CATEGORY Entire Issue

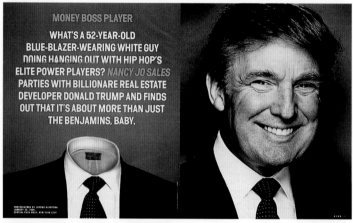

■ 308
PUBLICATION Vibe
DESIGN DIRECTOR Dwayne Shaw
DESIGNERS Dwayne Shaw,
Brandon Kavulla
PHOTO EDITOR George Pitts
PHOTOGRAPHER Piotr Sikora
PUBLISHER Miller Publishing Group
ISSUE February 1999
CATEGORY Feature Spread

■ 309
PUBLICATION Vibe
DESIGN DIRECTOR Dwayne Shaw
PHOTO EDITOR George Pitts
PHOTOGRAPHERS Piotr Sikora,
Andrew Williams
PUBLISHER Miller Publishing Group
ISSUE February 1999
CATEGORY Feature Story

■ 310
PUBLICATION Vibe
DESIGN DIRECTOR Dwayne Shaw
PHOTO EDITOR George Pitts
PHOTOGRAPHER Eve M. Fowler
PUBLISHER Miller Publishing Group
ISSUE March 1999
CATEGORY Feature Spread

■ 311
PUBLICATION Vibe
DESIGN DIRECTOR Dwayne Shaw
PHOTO EDITOR George Pitts
PHOTOGRAPHER Jerome Albertini
PUBLISHER Miller Publishing Group
ISSUE March 1999
CATEGORY Feature Spread

■ 312
PUBLICATION Vibe
ART DIRECTOR Brandon Kavulla
DESIGNER Brandon Kavulla
PHOTO EDITOR George Pitts
PHOTOGRAPHER Firooz Zahedi
PUBLISHER Miller Publishing Group
ISSUE August 1999
CATEGORY Feature Spread

■ 313

GROWN ASS WOMAN POWER

Missy Elliott knows exactly what she wants. And if she wants it, nucka, she'll take it. You got a problem with that, sucka? by Marc Weingarten

■ 314

For FREAKY TAH of the LOST BOYZ, hanging in the streets of Jamaica, Queens was the most natural thing in the world. But when a local beef escalated out of control, Tah paid the ultimate price. When a rapper lives the lifestyle of the rich and shameless, can he really go home again? By Greg Donaldson

QUEENS LOGIC

■ 315

Is the government out to get the OL' DIRTY BASTARD? Is the Ol' Dirty Bastard the second coming of Christ? Is the Ol' Dirty Bastard cracked out or cracking up? Sacha Jenkins looks high and low for the man behind the masks and wonders, Can he be saved?

LOOKING FOR JESUS

■ 316

the school of visual arts alumni magazine / fall 1999

VISUAL ARTS JOURNAL

PHOTOGRAPHY ISSUE

TOM BARIL
VERA LUTTER
FIVE TO WATCH
MFA PHOTOGRAPHY ALUMNI SURVEY

{ Five to Watch

5

{ Roderick Angle
MFA 1994 Photography

Tom Baril
close up

FOOD FOR THOUGHT

■ 313

PUBLICATION Vibe
ART DIRECTOR Brandon Kavulla
DESIGNER Brandon Kavulla
ILLUSTRATOR The Dynamic Duo Studio
PUBLISHER Miller Publishing Group
ISSUE August 1999
CATEGORY Feature Spread

■ 314

PUBLICATION Vibe
DESIGN DIRECTOR Robert Newman
DESIGNER Brandon Kavulla
ILLUSTRATOR Edmund Guy
PUBLISHER Miller Publishing Group
ISSUE December 1999
CATEGORY Feature Spread

■ 315

PUBLICATION Vibe
DESIGN DIRECTOR Robert Newman
DESIGNER Brandon Kavulla
PHOTO EDITOR George Pitts
PUBLISHER Miller Publishing Group
ISSUE September 1999
CATEGORY Feature Spread

■ 316

PUBLICATION Visual Arts Journal
CREATIVE DIRECTOR Silas H. Rhodes
ART DIRECTOR James D. McKibben
DESIGNER Janet Yonju Park
PHOTOGRAPHERS Roderick Angle,
Guy Aroch, Tom Baril
PUBLISHER Visual Arts Press, Ltd.
CLIENT School of Visual Arts
ISSUE Fall 1999
CATEGORY Entire Issue

The Washington Post Magazine

PORTRAIT
of the
CITY

IMAGES OF
WASHINGTON IN
THE AMERICAN
CENTURY

A SPECIAL MILLENNIUM ISSUE | NOVEMBER 21, 1999

McCarthy...was in many ways the most gifted demagogue ever bred on these shores. No bolder seditionist ever moved among us— nor any politician with a surer, swifter access to the dark places of the American mind.
—RICHARD H. ROVERE, SENATOR JOE McCARTHY (1959)

Bricks
and
Marble

As the afternoon goes on, Washington seems more and more a tender Southern city. The light psychic rust of its iron will, the sense of suffocation . . . the faded scent of its inhibition, its severity and its concealed corruption . . . all this seemed absent in the golden hovering on such leisurely twilight. —NORMAN MAILER, THE ARMIES OF THE NIGHT (1968)

HomeTown,
D.C.

'But I was born right here in D.C. Born, bred, and buttered, my mother used to say.' —EDWARD P. JONES, 'MARIE' (1992)

The
Seat of
Power

That's what we do in Washington, Harold said with sudden emotion. We fix things up. We compromise; that's the essence of our society. We give a little and get a little and out of the chaos comes an order that we can live with. It isn't perfect. But it's what we do. —WARD JUST, ECHO HOUSE (1997)

Audiences expand the mythologies of a director's world. We succeed when we give them something

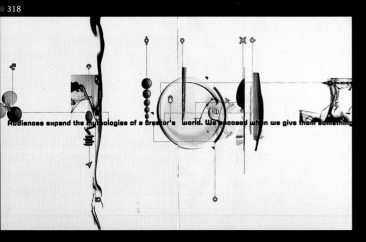

worthy of their

devotion

■ 317
PUBLICATION The Washington Post Magazine
ART DIRECTOR Kelly Doe
DESIGNER Kelly Doe
PHOTO EDITORS Molly Roberts, Gina Caruso, Keith Jenkins
PHOTOGRAPHERS Jacques Lowe, Arnold Newman, Alfred Eisenstaedt

■ 318
PUBLICATION Wired
DESIGN DIRECTOR Thomas Schneider
DESIGNER Giles Dunn
PUBLISHER Condé Nast Publications, Inc.
ISSUE February 1999

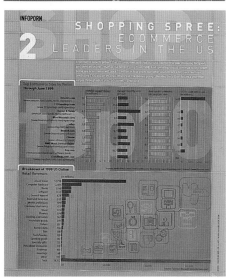

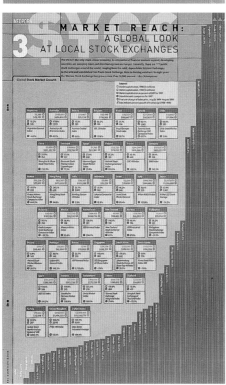

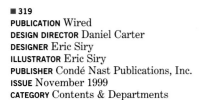

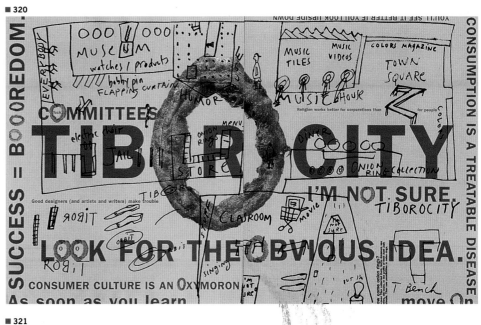

MUST READ July

MUST READ

Paranoia Technology

Tailor-Made Meds

Good Deal

MUST READ PEOPLE

I Surf My MTV

Redirector

Dell's Gatekeeper

Play Time

Scott's Landing

■ 319
PUBLICATION Wired
DESIGN DIRECTOR Daniel Carter
DESIGNER Eric Siry
ILLUSTRATOR Eric Siry
PUBLISHER Condé Nast Publications, Inc.
ISSUE November 1999
CATEGORY Contents & Departments

■ 320
PUBLICATION Wired
DESIGN DIRECTOR Daniel Carter
DESIGNER Richard Pandiscio
ILLUSTRATORS Richard Pandiscio, Maira Kalman
PHOTO EDITOR Christa Aboitiz
PHOTOGRAPHER Davies & Starr
PUBLISHER Condé Nast Publications, Inc.
ISSUE August 1999
CATEGORY Feature Story

■ 321
PUBLICATION Wired
DESIGN DIRECTOR Daniel Carter
DESIGNER Eric Siry
ILLUSTRATOR Peter Stemmler
PHOTO EDITOR Carolyn Rauch
PUBLISHER Condé Nast Publications, Inc.
ISSUE July 1999
CATEGORY Contents & Departments

the ninth

ze / ro

why
billionaires
should be
outlawed
by david sheff

23

Reasons Wall Street Hates Manuel Asencio

Just hope you don't own shares in reason number 24 By Jack Barth Photographs by John Goodman

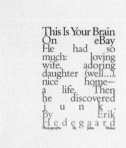

This Is Your Brain
On   eBay
He   had   so
much: loving
wife,   adoring
daughter (well...),
nice   home—
a   life.   Then
he   discovered
j u n k .
By   Erik
H e d e g a a r d
Photographs By John Weber

P6LYPSGDK2N
9OKG8P9FCUS
2HJ9**THIS**ZXO
UP3TI4S1PYU
YTG2SKCP**IS**K
A2FCANTLRBG
S9AR5OFCHE4
7TDVR WHICH E-BROKERS ARE BEST AT HANDLING
THEIR CUSTOMERS, AS WELL AS THEIR CUS-
TOMERS' TRADES? BY HARRIS COLLINGWOOD
DR7XE8RNPRB
X5**TEST**3XS4K
SLN6HBSGY7E

SEPTEMBER 1999 | WORTH 105

THIN WIRED DUKE

cyberspace oddity david bowie talks about fame,
fashion, and the net

It seems David Bowie wants to talk about his work. Not his music—although there's plenty of it, given that the chameleonic British rocker has spent the last 30 years creating such classic pop songs as "Fame," "Let's Dance," and "Ziggy Stardust." Not his movie roles—although there are plenty, ranging from his chilly star turn in Nicolas Roeg's *The Man Who Fell to Earth* to smaller parts in *The Last Temptation of Christ* and *Basquiat*. These days, when Bowie says "work," he means "network"—and specifically, he means BowieNet (www. davidbowie.com), his newborn boutique Internet service provider (ISP) and music

photographs by jill greenberg

■ 322
PUBLICATION Worth
ART DIRECTOR Philip Bratter
DESIGNER Anton Ioukhnovets
ILLUSTRATOR David Plunkert
PUBLISHER Worth Media
ISSUE June 1999
CATEGORY Feature Spread

■ 323
PUBLICATION Worth
ART DIRECTOR Philip Bratter
DESIGNER Deanna Lowe
PHOTO EDITOR Marianne Butler
PHOTOGRAPHER John Goodman
PUBLISHER Worth Media
ISSUE July/August 1999
CATEGORY Feature Spread

■ 324
PUBLICATION Worth
ART DIRECTOR Philip Bratter
DESIGNER Philip Bratter
PHOTO EDITOR Marianne Butler
PHOTOGRAPHER John Weber
PUBLISHER Worth Media
ISSUE September 1999
CATEGORY Feature Spread

■ 325
PUBLICATION Worth
ART DIRECTOR Philip Bratter
DESIGNERS George Karabotsos,
Philip Bratter
PUBLISHER Worth Media
ISSUE September 1999
CATEGORY Single Page

■ 326
PUBLICATION Yahoo! Internet Life
ART DIRECTOR Gail Ghezzi
PHOTO EDITOR Gail Henry
PHOTOGRAPHER Jill Greenberg
PUBLISHER Ziff-Davis, Inc.
ISSUE April 1999
CATEGORY Feature Spread

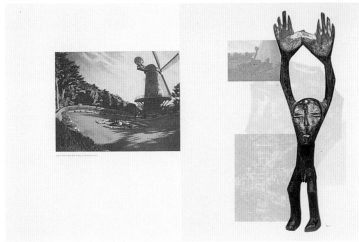

■ 327
PUBLICATION General Magic 1998 Annual Report
CREATIVE DIRECTOR Bill Cahan
DESIGNER Bob Dinetz
STUDIO Cahan & Associates
ISSUE May 1999
CATEGORY Entire Issue

■ 328
PUBLICATION de Young Private Case
CREATIVE DIRECTOR Bill Cahan
DESIGNER Michael Braley
ILLUSTRATOR Nanette Biers
PHOTOGRAPHER Christian Kerez
STUDIO Cahan & Associates
CLIENT Fine Arts Museum
ISSUE April 1999
CATEGORY Entire Issue

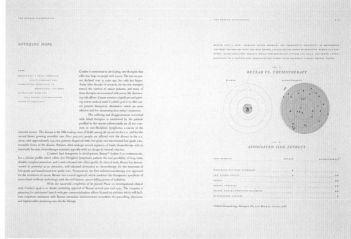

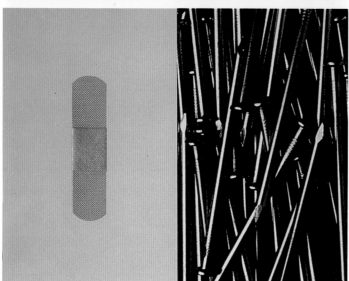

VALENTIS

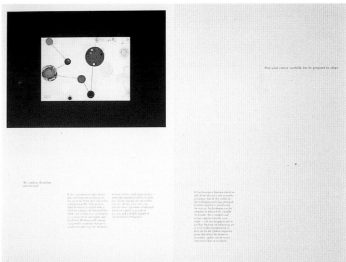

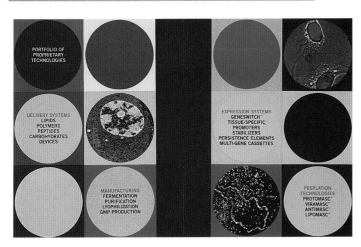

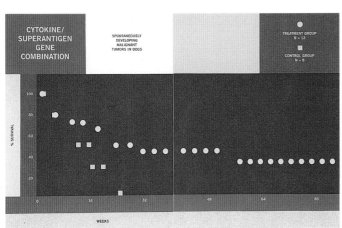

■ 331

PUBLICATION Valentis 1998 Annual Report
CREATIVE DIRECTOR Bill Cahan
DESIGNER Sharrie Brooks
STUDIO Cahan & Associates
ISSUE October 1999
CATEGORY Entire Issue

■ 332

PUBLICATION Silicon Valley Bank 1998 Annual Report
CREATIVE DIRECTOR Bill Cahan
DESIGNER Sharrie Brooks
ILLUSTRATOR Jason Holley
STUDIO Cahan & Associates
ISSUE August 1999
CATEGORY Entire Issue

all that glitters: how hiv caught fire in south africa by mark schoofs

INSIDE OUR HEADS

335

The Boston Globe
2000
MARCH 14, 1999

Visions

Reflections, forecasts,
and fantasies on the nation,
millennial angst, community,
consumerism, language, war,
preservation, race,
arts and culture, aging,
possessions, sports, family,
and utopia

Stop that millennial moping, America
A PROPOSAL FOR A FRESH START

Next...

Stumbling

The American struggle with race
is filled with rich paradoxes:
painful yet redemptive, ageless yet newly exotic,
hopeful yet filled with years
of hopelessness.

at the color line

■ 336
PUBLICATION La Luna
DESIGN DIRECTOR Carmelo Caderot
ART DIRECTOR Rodrigo Sanchez
DESIGNERS Rodrigo Sanchez,
Francisco Dorado, Chano Del Río
PHOTO EDITOR Rodrigo Sanchez
ISSUE June 11, 1999
CATEGORY Entire Issue

■ 337
PUBLICATION National Post
ART DIRECTOR Leanne M. Shapton
DESIGNER Leanne M. Shapton
PUBLISHER Southam Inc.
ISSUE December 2, 1999
CATEGORY Feature Spread

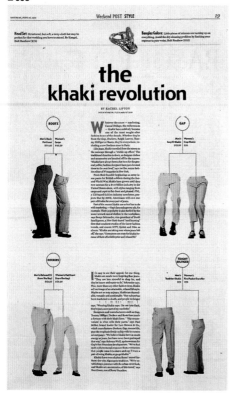

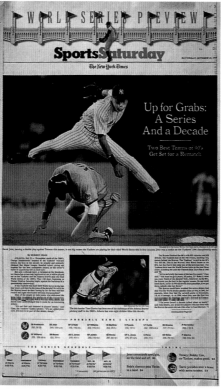

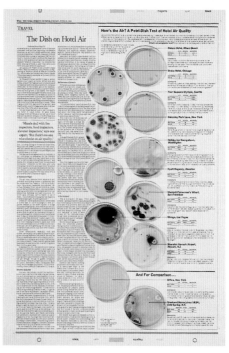

■ 338
PUBLICATION Weekend Post
ART DIRECTOR Friederike N. Gauss
DESIGNER Antonio Enrico De Luca
PHOTOGRAPHER Patty Watteyne
PUBLISHER National Post Southam Inc.
ISSUE June 26, 1999
CATEGORY Contents & Departments

■ 339
PUBLICATION The New York Times
ART DIRECTOR Nicholas Blechman
ILLUSTRATOR Tibor Kalman
PUBLISHER The New York Times
ISSUE January 1, 1999
CATEGORY Single Page

■ 340
PUBLICATION The New York Times
DESIGNERS Wayne Kamidoi,
Joe Ward, Bedel Saget
ILLUSTRATOR Joe Ziff
PHOTOGRAPHERS G. Paul Burnett,
Ozier Muhammed
PUBLISHER The New York Times
ISSUE October 23, 1999
CATEGORY Entire Issue

■ 341
PUBLICATION The Wall Street Journal
Weekend Journal
ART DIRECTOR Stephen Fay
ILLUSTRATOR Joe Fournier
PHOTO EDITOR Elizabeth Williams
PHOTOGRAPHER Peter Ardito
PUBLISHER Dow Jones & Co., Inc.
ISSUE June 18, 1999
CATEGORY Feature Story

online

PUBLICATION Nickelodeon Website
CREATIVE DIRECTOR David L. Vogler
DESIGN DIRECTOR David L. Vogler
ART DIRECTOR Michael Redding
DESIGNERS Michael Beeler, Colm Fox, Jason Arena,
Patrick Dorey, Chiaki Watanabe-Darcy, Jenny Nordeman,
Kevin Laughran, Michele Dauchtry, Dave Maro,
Melani Larson, Andrea Koronkiewicz, Beegee Tolpa
DESIGNER PUBLISHER Nickelodeon Online
ONLINE ADDRESS www.Nick.com
ISSUE December 1, 1999
CATEGORY Website

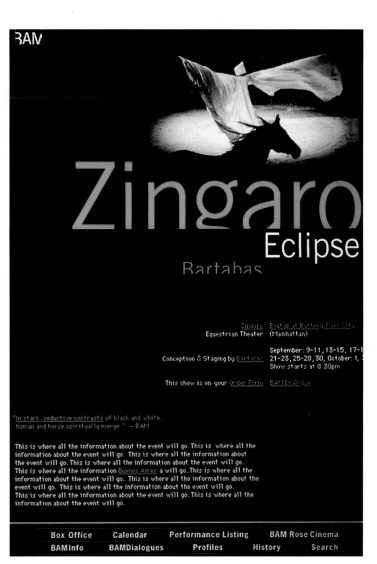

online ■ SILVER

■ 343
PUBLICATION BAM
CREATIVE DIRECTOR John DiRé
ART DIRECTOR Sasha Kurtz
DESIGNERS John Rabasa, Pat Stern,
Sasha Kurtz, Lesli Karavil
PUBLISHER Brooklyn Academy of Music
ONLINE ADDRESS www.bam.org
CATEGORY Website

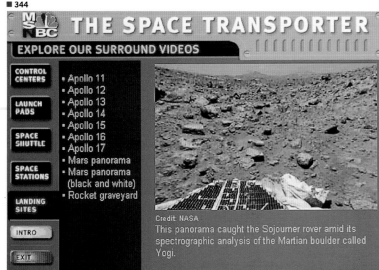

THE SPACE TRANSPORTER

EXPLORE OUR SURROUND VIDEOS

- CONTROL CENTERS
- LAUNCH PADS
- SPACE SHUTTLE
- SPACE STATIONS
- LANDING SITES
- INTRO
- EXIT

- Apollo 11
- Apollo 12
- Apollo 13
- Apollo 14
- Apollo 15
- Apollo 16
- Apollo 17
- Mars panorama
- Mars panorama (black and white)
- Rocket graveyard

Credit: NASA
This panorama caught the Sojourner rover amid its spectrographic analysis of the Martian boulder called Yogi.

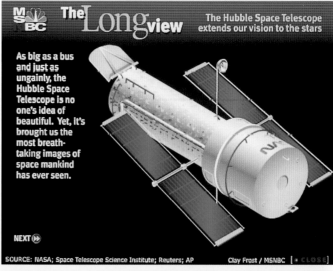

The Longview

The Hubble Space Telescope extends our vision to the stars

As big as a bus and just as ungainly, the Hubble Space Telescope is no one's idea of beautiful. Yet, it's brought us the most breathtaking images of space mankind has ever seen.

NEXT ▶▶

SOURCE: NASA; Space Telescope Science Institute; Reuters; AP   Clay Frost / MSNBC   [▪ CLOSE]

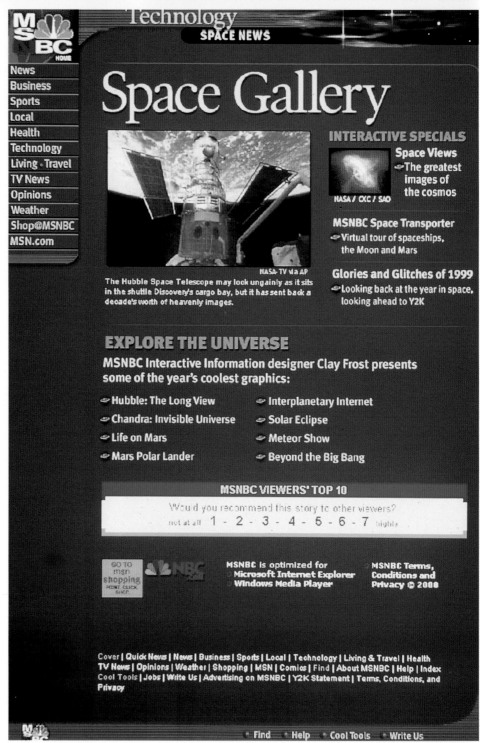

Technology
SPACE NEWS

MSNBC HOME

- News
- Business
- Sports
- Local
- Health
- Technology
- Living - Travel
- TV News
- Opinions
- Weather
- Shop@MSNBC
- MSN.com

Space Gallery

NASA-TV via AP
The Hubble Space Telescope may look ungainly as it sits in the shuttle Discovery's cargo bay, but it has sent back a decade's worth of heavenly images.

INTERACTIVE SPECIALS

NASA / CXC / SAO

Space Views
↪ The greatest images of the cosmos

MSNBC Space Transporter
↪ Virtual tour of spaceships, the Moon and Mars

Glories and Glitches of 1999
↪ Looking back at the year in space, looking ahead to Y2K

EXPLORE THE UNIVERSE

MSNBC Interactive Information designer Clay Frost presents some of the year's coolest graphics:

- ↪ Hubble: The Long View
- ↪ Chandra: Invisible Universe
- ↪ Life on Mars
- ↪ Mars Polar Lander
- ↪ Interplanetary Internet
- ↪ Solar Eclipse
- ↪ Meteor Show
- ↪ Beyond the Big Bang

MSNBC VIEWERS' TOP 10

Would you recommend this story to other viewers?
not at all 1 - 2 - 3 - 4 - 5 - 6 - 7 highly

GO TO msn shopping POINT. CLICK. SHOP.

NBC

MSNBC is optimized for Microsoft Internet Explorer Windows Media Player

MSNBC Terms, Conditions and Privacy © 2000

Cover | Quick News | News | Business | Sports | Local | Technology | Living & Travel | Health
TV News | Opinions | Weather | Shopping | MSN | Comics | Find | About MSNBC | Help | Index
Cool Tools | Jobs | Write Us | Advertising on MSNBC | Y2K Statement | Terms, Conditions, and Privacy

▪ Find   ▪ Help   ▪ Cool Tools   ▪ Write Us

■ 344
PUBLICATION MSNBC.com
DESIGN DIRECTORS Bo Hok Cline, Greg Harris
DESIGNERS Clay Frost, Brian Frick, Mike Grigg
PHOTO EDITOR Brian Storm
PUBLISHER MSNBC.com
ONLINE ADDRESS www.MSNBC.com
CATEGORY Feature

SILVER ■ online

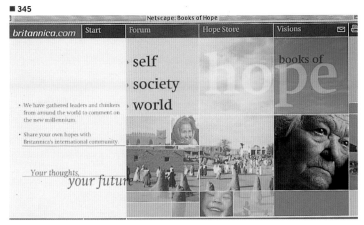

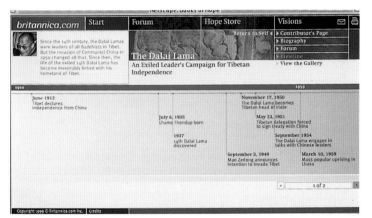

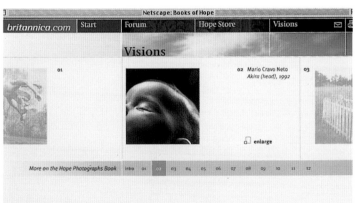

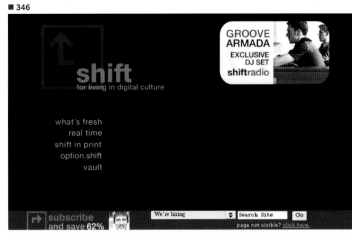

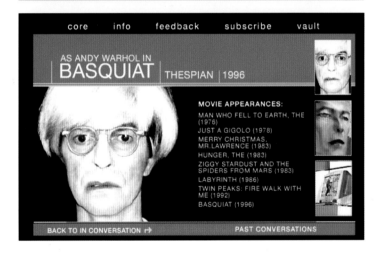

■ 345
PUBLICATION Britannica.com
CREATIVE DIRECTOR Terry Irwin
ART DIRECTORS Mark Davis, David Peters
DESIGNERS Carlo Bernoulli, Thomas Bircher,
Hyungjung Kim, Michelle Koza, Kris Krois
STUDIO MetaDesign SF
PUBLISHER Britannica
ONLINE ADDRESS www.britannica.com/hope/
CATEGORY Website

■ 346
PUBLICATION Shift Online
CREATIVE DIRECTOR Carmen Dunjko
DESIGN DIRECTOR Dave Sylvestre
DESIGNERS Dave Sylvestre, Steve Park
PUBLISHER Normal Net Inc.
ONLINE ADDRESS www.shift.com/shiftonline/html/core/core.html
ISSUE December 20, 1999
CATEGORY Website

AOL teens

 Chatting LIVE Tonight
Pop star Christina Aguilera is here for Q&A!

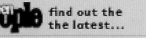 **What Career's For YOU?**
Check out the personal Career Finder in Real Life.

 The Sega Dreamcast
Is the latest game system the best game system?

- music
- movies & tv
- celeb fan club
- gametech
- **sports**
- girls
- real life
- chat & boards
- style special
- search

Walled In
Jakob Dylan talks to MTV about the Wallflowers' upcoming tour. Get the news.

Sarah Michelle Gellar
She's played everything from a vampire slayer to a twisted debutante. Who's the real Sarah?

⇨ **Meet Skater Tony Hawk**

▷ **POLL: The Best TV Shows?**

▷ **Health Resources for Teens**

MTV Online for the groovin people

EX animations for cool people

Teen People find out the the latest...

ChannelOne everything you need.

Keyword:Teens

AOL teens — Explore AOL Teens [Go]

÷ **gametech**   go chat   go post

Technology Feature
Now create your very own Slingo or X-Press rooms. Click here!

Believe in Magic?
Become a magic mand and cast a spell over the lands of Magestorm!

Magic & Monsters
Discover a realm where you are the bold adventurer, out on a maiden voyage of discovery.
-- King of Narmenia
-- Sherwood Forest

Resources: Cheat Codes | Resource Link
Complete Games List | Cheat Codes | Resource

Featuring...
MTV Online for the groovin people
EX animations for cool people
Teen People find out the the latest...
ChannelOne everything you need.

Kodak Max. Get great pictures. Anywhere. Anytime. CLICK HERE

Keyword: Teens

AOL teens — Explore AOL Teens [Go]

÷ **sports**   go chat   go post

▢ extreme | ▢ high school | ▢ college/pro

Superbowl fever!
Who do you think is going to be in the playoffs? Click here.

Grant Hill Speaks
Grant Hill talks about his game and about his future in basketball.

Serena Williams
Serena Williams has been winning tournaments left and right. Learn more about her winning streak.
-- U.S. Open pics
-- Wimbledon pics

Poll: Do you think that Women's Soccer should have a national league? Vote in our poll!

Featuring...
MTV Online for the groovin people
EX animations for cool people
Teen People find out the the latest...
ChannelOne everything you need.

Kodak Max. Get great pictures. Anywhere. Anytime. CLICK HERE

Keyword: Teens

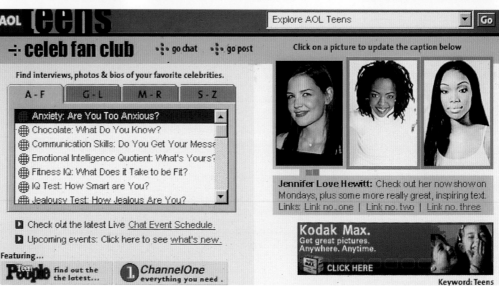

AOL teens — Explore AOL Teens [Go]

÷ **celeb fan club**   go chat   go post

Click on a picture to update the caption below

Find interviews, photos & bios of your favorite celebrities.

| A - F | G - L | M - R | S - Z |

- Anxiety: Are You Too Anxious?
- Chocolate: What Do You Know?
- Communication Skills: Do You Get Your Messa
- Emotional Intelligence Quotient: What's Yours?
- Fitness IQ: What Does it Take to be Fit?
- IQ Test: How Smart are You?
- Jealousy Test: How Jealous Are You?

Jennifer Love Hewitt: Check out her now show on Mondays, plus some more really great, inspiring text.
Links: Link no. one | Link no. two | Link no. three

▷ Check out the latest Live Chat Event Schedule.

▷ Upcoming events: Click here to see what's new.

Featuring...
Teen People find out the the latest...
ChannelOne everything you need.

Kodak Max. Get great pictures. Anywhere. Anytime. CLICK HERE

Keyword: Teens

■ 347
PUBLICATION Teens
CREATIVE DIRECTOR Robert Raines
DESIGN DIRECTOR Phoebe Espiritu
ART DIRECTORS Jennifer Meehan, Enrique Domenech
DESIGNERS Ehrique Domenech, Jennifer Hannon
PUBLISHER America Online
CATEGORY Home page

photography

ALTERNATIVE INVESTMENTS

hedgechic

At a time when even hedge funds need hedging, a fund of funds
can tailor your search for a way to reduce risk and to diversify

By Frances Denmark ❧ Photographs by Hugh Kretschmer

Hedge funds have always been an intriguing investment category

Hedge funds aren't easy to track down

Liquidity is sometimes a problem

■ 348

PUBLICATION Bloomberg Wealth Manager
ART DIRECTOR Laura Zavetz
DESIGNER Laura Zavetz
PHOTOGRAPHER Hugh Kretschmer
PUBLISHER Bloomberg L.P.
ISSUE September/October 1999
CATEGORY Photo Illustration

SHINORAMA 1
photographs by Kishin Shinoyama

Eight years back, when I saw Kishin Shinoyama shooting Tokyo, I lit upon the catchphrase "Tokyo is a photograph." Up until then, photography had depicted reality as reality. Only lately have I come to realize that photography is in fact a device for reassembling illusions. And at the same time, the city of Tokyo was becoming ever more rarefied, so that paradoxically it only attained existence as "Tokyo" in photographs of its illusions. By the latter half of the 80s, this permutation of mine was confirmed reality. Any and all varietals of "caritas" bloomed forth proudly in Tokyo. Shinoyama, commanding virtually every technique of 20th-century art, challenged the all-consuming power of this vainglorious city with his own "desiring eye." Whereupon Kishin Shinoyama became possessed by "Tokyo" and Kishin Shinoyama's photography itself became emblematic of "Tokyo." Herein it soon becomes apparent that "Tokyo is Kishin Shinoyama."
ARATA ISOZAKI (ARCHITECT), FROM TOKYO MIRAI SEIKI (TOKYO FUTURE CENTURY), PUBLISHED BY SHOGAKUKAN, 1992

■ 349
PUBLICATION Big
CREATIVE DIRECTOR Marcelo Jünemann
ART DIRECTOR Markus Kiersztan
DESIGNERS Garland Lyn, David Lee
PHOTOGRAPHER Kishin Shinoyama
PUBLISHER Big Magazine, Inc.
ISSUE #26, December 1999
CATEGORY Portrait Story

1999

Jude Walter, at right, will be one hundred the next time the calendar turns to zeros. He may be joined by several others from these pages, given the trend of human longevity, but if any of them face 2099 with the same bright, open eyes of Joseph Napolitano (page 103), who turned one hundred in August, they will be hugely blessed. Imagine what he has seen—and then what all these men and boys have seen. Some of it is in their faces. What follows are portraits we photographed of men born in every year of this century. You are in here. So is your father. So is Don Knotts. A long life to you all. Long life, Ice Cube. Long life, master Jude. And, especially, long life, Mr. Napolitano.

1999 Jude Walter Infant. Greatest achievement: Standing up in his crib.

1998 Jake Dillon Webber Baby. Greatest achievement: Saying "Mama" and "Dada."

1997 Dan Hosannah Toddler. Greatest achievement: Learning Japanese and English at the same time.

1996 Jack Freedman Preschooler. Best day: "I fed Bo the sea lion and his sea-lion friends at the Miami Seaquarium on January 28, 1999."

1995 Danny Jacobs Pre-kindergartner. Greatest achievement: Singing "Take Me Out to the Ball Game."

1994 Max Resetar Kindergartner. Best day: "I lost my first tooth on August 20, 1999."

1993 Joshua Rodriguez First grader. Best day: "I got a color Game Boy, April 16, 1999."

1992 T. J. Nieves Second grader. Greatest achievement: "Going to school."

1991 Alexis Antonio Salcedo Second grader. Greatest achievement: "Being an uncle."

1990 Eric Wong Fourth grader. Greatest achievement: "Beating my cousin in basketball."

1989 Andy Silveus Fourth grader. Greatest achievement: "Doing math. The advanced work is easier because there are less problems and they are more fun."

1988 Haley Joel Osment Actor / Fifth grade / sixth grader. Greatest achievement: "Receiving straight A's during the entire fifth-grade school year."

1987 Noah Kraft Seventh grader. Best day: "The day I won a sixty-four-draw tennis tournament."

1986 Douglas Kupferman Eighth grader / son of Conrad Kupferman (1952). Best day: "My bar mitzvah in Israel, July 3, 1997."

1985 Anthony C. Golden Eighth grader. Greatest achievement: "I'm interested in becoming a sky diver in the future."

1984 Ben Meeker Tenth grader. Greatest achievement: "Playing cello with the Westchester Youth Symphony at Carnegie Hall."

1983 Ross Kirsh Eleventh grader. Best day: "Meeting the New Jersey Devils hockey team, September 11, 1997."

1975↑

1982 Shawn Reynolds Maintenance man. Best day: "I met my wonderful girlfriend, Ginger, December 5, 1998."

1981 George DeLucia Waiter. Greatest achievement: "Living."

1980 Alejandro Gutierrez College student. Greatest achievement: "Placing first in the coed category of the '98 ocean-to-ocean Panama Canal Cayuco Race."

1979 Suresh Madhavan Premed student. Greatest achievement: "Because my mom is single, I basically raised myself alone."

1978 Aviance Urrutia Salesman. Best day: "I remember having a blast at Twilo nightclub on February 13, 1993. Extreme excitement."

1977 Wally Szczerbiak Professional basketball player. Greatest achievement: "Being drafted number six to play in the NBA for Minnesota."

1976 Heath Silvercloud College student. Greatest achievement: "With all the distractions and perils of life, remaining true to myself and staying as real as I can."

1975 Robert Viera Gay Graphic artist. Best day: "I met my soul mate. There was no physical attraction involved, just pure innocence and discovery."

1974↑

1950↑

1949↑

1925↑

1924↑

1899↑

■ 350
PUBLICATION Esquire
DESIGN DIRECTOR John Korpics
PHOTO EDITOR Simon Barnett
PHOTOGRAPHER Matthew Welch
PUBLISHER The Hearst Corporation-Magazines Division
ISSUE December 1999
CATEGORY Portrait Story

THE 1999 HALL OF FAME

THE SOPRANOS

Because, despite getting rooked at the Emmys by West Coast voters suffering from too much sunshine and chopped salad, the cast of this HBO series has the deepest bench strength and scariest footprints of any television ensemble, not to mention the coolest character names (Uncle Junior, Big Pussy Bompensiero). Because there hasn't been such a viper-mother as Nancy Marchand's Livia since I, Claudius, a more put-upon son than James Gandolfini's Tony Soprano, who shuffles into his middle crisis like a hibernating bear, his eyelids at half-mast from the weight of all the goombahs he has to whack, or a more miffed daughter-in-law than Edie Falco's Carmela, whose clipped delivery could slice foreskins (her recurring cry: "What am I an idiot?"). Because, brilliantly devised and co-written by David Chase, this maxi mini-series cruises the Jersey suburbs like a stolen hearse, eyeing the American Dream through dark tinted glass.

From left: David Chase (creator and co-writer of the series), Jamie-Lynn Sigler (Meadow Soprano), Robert Iler (Anthony Soprano Jr.), Dominic Chianese (Uncle Junior), Nancy Marchand (Livia Soprano), Edie Falco (Carmela Soprano), James Gandolfini (Tony Soprano), Lorraine Bracco (Dr. Jennifer Melfi), Michael Imperioli (Christopher Moltisanti), Steve Van Zandt (Silvio Dante), Tony Sirico (Paulie Walnuts), Jerry Adler (Hesh Rabkin), and Vincent Pastore (Big Pussy Bompensiero).

Photographed by ANNIE LEIBOVITZ in New York City on September 7, 1999

photography ■ GOLD

You Had to Be There

Fresh from the runway of history, the
actress Salma Hayek is the height of fashion.

Photographs by Matthew Rolston · Styled by Elizabeth Stewart

THE HIGHER THEY COME
Venetian courtesans
in the 15th
century dressed in
extremes — none more
evident than the new-fanci-
high chopines on their
little feet. But Venice has
never been easy to get
around in, whether you're
a mistress or not. Silver-
stitched taffeta ball gown
$5,600, by Oscar de la
Renta. At Bergdorf
Goodman. Saks Fifth
Avenue, Helmut Marcus.
Shoes, made to order,
by Christian Louboutin.
Rings by Cynthia
Bach at Neiman Marcus.
Flower hair
snaps by Cristy Larken
for Pink World.

**LET THEM EAT
TULLE PASTE**
Marie Antoinette,
married by proxy at age
15, grew up to be
the arbiter of late-18th-
century rococo
indulgence; hair was
stiffened to Your Eiffel
heights and whitened
with papier-mâché paste,
panniers stretched
skirts and breasts were
shoved up while
décolletages dipped way
down. This dress was
designed by the costume
designer Adrian
for the 1938 film "Marie
Antoinette," starring
Norma Shearer. From the
private collection
of Larry McEwen,
a costume collector.
Jewelry from Fred
Leighton.

**LIFT AND
SEPARATE**
For centuries women
wore no underwear,
not bothering anyone.
That changed
radically in the 20th
century, when the
brassiere made its debut
and the word "support"
acquired new meaning.
After that, synthetic
materials and
elastic spawned the
intimate-apparel
revolution. Original
1940's bra (34B) and
girdle (28) from
Maidenform. Stockings
from Fogal.

**GUINEVERE:
LET DOWN YOUR
HAIR**
Being fashionable
in the 1100's meant a
flowing gown with
train, flared sleeves,
rounded neckline
and superlong hair
unbound or plaited.
This gray silk-chiffon
gown with chain
mail is from Gianni
Versace's fall 1998
collection. Silver
headband and hair tips
by Robert Lee Morris,
by special order.
Hair: Robert Verica for
Nubest and Company.
Makeup: Francesca
Tolot at Cloutier.
Manicurist: Lisa
Jachno for Cloutier.
Fashion assistant:
George Kotsiopoulos.

■ 352
PUBLICATION The New York Times Magazine
ART DIRECTORS Janet Froelich, Joele Cuyler
DESIGNERS Joele Cuyler, Ignacio Rodriguez
PHOTOGRAPHER Matthew Rolston
PHOTO STYLIST Elizabeth Stewart
PUBLISHER The New York Times
ISSUE May 16, 1999
CATEGORY Fashion/Beauty Story

PEOPLE USED TO THINK THE BRAIN

WAS STATIC AND INEVITABLY

DECLINED WITH AGE. ACTUALLY,

THE BRAIN NEVER STOPS

CHANGING—AND WE NEVER STOP

LEARNING. BY DON COLBURN

ILLUSTRATION BY WILLIAM DUKE

The Infinite Brain

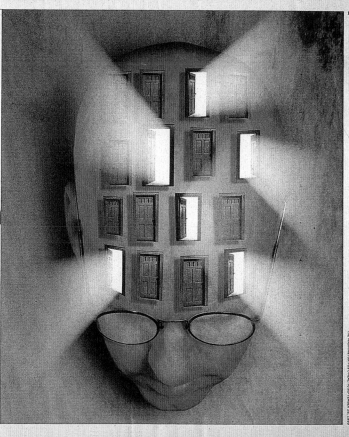

It's about three pounds

of wrinkled, pinkish-gray matter with the consistency of jelly—and yet, in Emily Dickinson's words, "wider than the sky."

The human brain's nearly infinite reach comes from the elaborate circuitry of its billions of neurons—a marvel that has led some to call it the world's most complex computer.

But scientists are zeroing in on another quality of the brain that distinguishes it from even the most powerful PC: its adaptability.

It turns out the brain is plastic.

Not that it's made of vinyl. Plastic in the sense of flexible and dynamic.

The brain is not a cerebral black box, wired forever by age 2 or 3, as once thought. It remodels itself *See* BRAIN, *Page 14*

THE WASHINGTON POST/HEALTH/SEPTEMBER 28, 1999

photography ■ GOLD

[The Washington Post]

HEALTH

TUESDAY, SEPTEMBER 28, 1999

The Infinite Brain

PLUS: New NIH Warning on Blood Pressure ■ Reagan's Daughter on Caring for Alzheimer's Patients

■ 353
PUBLICATION The Washington Post/ Health Section
ART DIRECTOR Stacie Harrison Reistetter
ILLUSTRATOR William Duke
ISSUE September 28, 1999
CATEGORY Photo Illustration

Your ad here

What's wrong with a little self-promotion?

PHOTOGRAPHY BY STEPHANE SEDNAOUI

So you've got the billboard, now it's time to work on your slogan: Ralph Lauren Swimwear crocheted bikini top, $224 (with bottoms); Ralph by Ralph Lauren corduroy short shorts, $45.

■ 354
PUBLICATION Jane
ART DIRECTOR Johan Svensson
DESIGNER Amy Demas
PHOTO EDITOR Cary Estes Leitzes
PHOTOGRAPHER Stephane Sednaoui
PUBLISHER Fairchild Publications
ISSUE December 1999
CATEGORY Fashion/Beauty Story

✠ THE ✠✠

THE OSCAR-WINNING ACTOR WHO

PASSION

SAYS HE BUILT A CAREER ON BEING

✠✠ OF ✠✠

"UNPREDICTABLE AND FRIGHTENING"

NICOLAS

REVEALS A SIDE NOBODY KNOWS

✠✠ CAGE

BY FRED SCHRUERS

photogra

The Commute

I BEGAN TO PHOTOGRAPH THE 350-MILE stretch of highway between Rochester, New York (where I teach photography), and New York City (where I reside) as a way to deal with the tedium of the commute. But as I began to look at the highway through my camera, to stop and to talk to the people along the way, I found that the drive was deepening my sense of America. We are a country of cars and commuters, forever in transit. The road, the rest stop, the diner, the gas station, and the loneliness of the long distance commuter define our culture. The special landscape of the highway, manmade and strange, is usually ignored by the motorist flying past at five miles above the legal speed limit. After photographing along Route 17 for three years, I have learned to slow down and enjoy the ride.

—MARK HAVEN

Above: Sunday night, heading back to Rochester, near Bear Mountain, September 1994

Opposite: Beaverkill River, Roscoe, September 1994

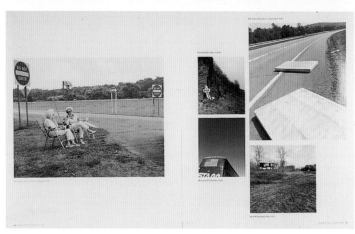

■ 356
PUBLICATION DoubleTake
DESIGNERS William Drenttel, Jessica Helfand, Jeff Tyson
PHOTO EDITOR Richard B. Woodward
PHOTOGRAPHER Mark Haven
PUBLISHER DoubleTake Community Service Corporation
ISSUE Summer 1999
CATEGORY Reportage Story

the lives of men   By Ron Carlson

Say Hello to My Little Friend

Just because it's the part of you that goes forth first into the world does not mean that you must always follow

IT WOULD BE EXCITING if, in writing about the most openly celebrated and reviled body part, I could shatter a few myths and create a few others, but we all know already that it is the center of so many of the world's mythologies, the source of all major and minor religions, the focus and motor of all marketing, in fact the basis of capitalism (to which it gave its name) and every nonsocial economy, the name and nickname of every rock group and many musical chorales, the true axis of planet Earth in this solar system, the hinge that opens the door to understanding, the axle in the big wheel of desire and regret, the bolt that keeps the door to understanding forever sealed, the first radical pillar of society, and the lone last digit of the secret combination on the lock to heaven, so I am going to have to settle for a few minor remarks about the penis, which, like nuclear power, has been

70 ESQUIRE JUNE 1999

DAN WINTERS

photography ■ SILVER

■ 357
PUBLICATION Esquire
DESIGN DIRECTOR Robert Priest
ART DIRECTOR Rockwell Harwood
DESIGNER Paul Scirecalabrissotto
PHOTO EDITOR Simon Barnett
PHOTOGRAPHER Dan Winters
PUBLISHER The Hearst Corporation-Magazines Division
ISSUE June 1999
CATEGORY Portrait Spread

PRO FOOTBALL >> BRETT FAVRE

BUSTIN' LOOSE

BY TIM KEOWN

BRETT FAVRE IS ALL GROWN UP—AND PLAYING THE BEST BALL OF HIS LIFE

PHOTOGRAPHS BY CHRISTOPHER KOLK

■ 358
PUBLICATION ESPN
DESIGN DIRECTOR Peter Yates
ART DIRECTOR Yvette L. Francis
DESIGNER Yvette L. Francis
PHOTO EDITOR Nik Kleinberg
PHOTOGRAPHER Christopher Kolk
PUBLISHER Disney Publishing Worldwide
ISSUE November 1, 1999
CATEGORY Portrait Spread

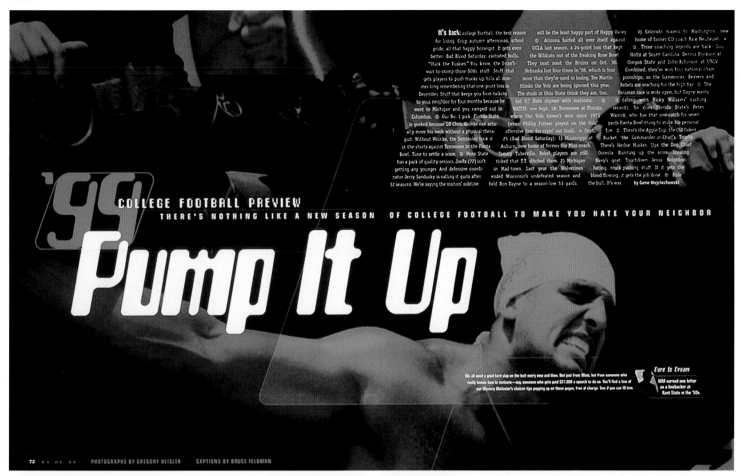

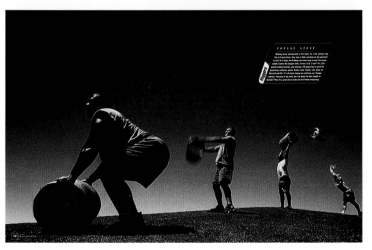

■ 359
PUBLICATION ESPN
DESIGN DIRECTOR Peter Yates
ART DIRECTOR Yvette L. Francis
DESIGNER Chris Rudzik
PHOTO EDITOR John Toolan
PHOTOGRAPHER Gregory Heisler
PUBLISHER Disney Publishing Worldwide
ISSUE September 6, 1999
CATEGORY Portrait Story

photography ■ SILVER

Sunday Best

Back in the 40's, country people would have
their pictures taken after church by a visiting
photographer. We decided to revive that tradition
in the mountains of eastern Kentucky, where
the churchgoers were dressed in clothes evocative
of that earlier time but every bit as stately
as their own Sunday best.

Photographs by Shelby Lee Adams[1]
Styled by Mimi Lombardo

Church Elders

Arnold Shepherd, the pastor of the Church of
the Lord Jesus Christ,[2] in Punchean Camp,[3] and his wife, Gladys, could not have
been more welcoming. "Come back and see us anytime," said Arnold.
"You know where we're at." Arnold's wool suit, $398, from Brooks Brothers.
Call 800-274-1815 for stores. Shirt, $79.50, from Banana Republic. Gladys's
rayon dress, $175, from Jill Anderson, 331 East Ninth Street.

■ 360
PUBLICATION The New York Times Magazine
ART DIRECTOR Janet Froelich
DESIGNER Claude Martel
PHOTOGRAPHER Shelby Lee Adams
PHOTO STYLIST Mimi Lombardo
PUBLISHER The New York Times
ISSUE April 1, 1999
CATEGORY Portrait Story

A Gothic Romance

Once again, fashion flirts with Camelot.

Photographs by Guzman Styled by Polly Hamilton Set design by Marla Weinhoff Credits on following page.

■ 361
PUBLICATION The New York Times Magazine
ART DIRECTOR Janet Froelich
DESIGNER Claude Martel
PHOTOGRAPHER Guzman
PHOTO STYLIST Polly Hamilton
PUBLISHER The New York Times
ISSUE June 20, 1999
CATEGORY Fashion/Beauty Story

The
PRESENCE

QUEEN LATIFAH, actress, rapper,
writer, self-anointed royal.

After growing up in Newark and working at
Burger King, she spoke for aviation when she said of acting:
"It's not as hard as being a cashier." Proved her point
by seamlessly moving from a thriving rap career—five albums
(one gold), four Grammy nominations—to a string of rollicking films
that began with her sassy-girl performance
in Spike Lee's Jungle Fever (1991)
and reached another level last year
when she played the smarty-pants jazz singer
in Living Out Loud.

In Arabic, latifah means "sensitive" (which she is) and
"delicate" (which she isn't). The Queen still shares a house
in Wayne, New Jersey, with her mother, Rita Bray Owens.

Upcoming: a nurse in The Bone Collector,
starring Denzel Washington.

Lyrics from Latifah's signature song, "U.N.I.T.Y." (1993):
"Instincts lead me to another flow
Every time I hear a brother call a girl a bitch or a ho,
Trying to make a sister feel low,
You know all of that's got to go."

Photographed (with the Boys Choir of Harlem)
by Bruce Weber in New York City on
December 16, 1998.

photography ■ SILVER

■ 362
PUBLICATION The New Yorker
PHOTO EDITOR Elisabeth Biondi
PHOTOGRAPHER Richard Avedon
PUBLISHER Condé Nast Publications, Inc.
ISSUE February/March 1999
CATEGORY Portrait Single Page

■ 363
PUBLICATION Vanity Fair
DESIGN DIRECTOR David Harris
ART DIRECTOR Gregory Mastrianni
PHOTO EDITORS Susan White, Lisa Berman, Sharon Suh
PHOTOGRAPHER Bruce Weber
PUBLISHER Condé Nast Publications, Inc.
ISSUE April 1999
CATEGORY Portrait Spread

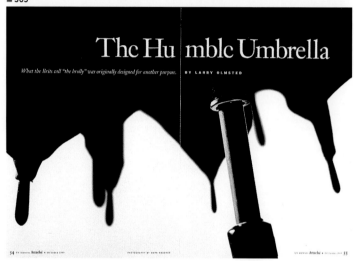

Thc Hu mblc Umbrella

What the Brits call "the brolly" was originally designed for another purpose. BY LARRY OLMSTED

THE INTERVIEW: Skier Jonny Moseley | FASHION: Girls' clothes

The Boston Globe Magazine
JANUARY 31, 1999

Selling the farm *It was just one more*
Vermont dairy farm that couldn't make a go of it. But it was theirs.

PHOTOGRAPHS AND TEXT BY BILL GREENE

Selling the farm

It was just one more
Vermont dairy farm that
couldn't make a go of it.
But it was theirs.

PHOTOGRAPHS AND TEXT
BY BILL GREENE

■ 364
PUBLICATION Atomic
CREATIVE DIRECTOR Jeffrey R. Griffith
DESIGNER Jeffrey R. Griffith
PHOTOGRAPHER Bill Phelps
ISSUE December 20, 1999
CATEGORY Fashion/Beauty Spread

■ 365
PUBLICATION Attaché
ART DIRECTOR Paul Carstensen
DESIGNER Paul Carstensen
PHOTOGRAPHER Mark Wagoner
PUBLISHER Pace Communications
CLIENT US Airways
ISSUE October 1999
CATEGORY Still Life/Interiors Spread

■ 366
PUBLICATION The Boston Globe Magazine
ART DIRECTOR Catherine Aldrich
PHOTO EDITOR Catherine Aldrich
PHOTOGRAPHER Bill Greene
PUBLISHER The Globe Newspaper Co.
ISSUE January 31, 1999
CATEGORY Reportage Story

Big

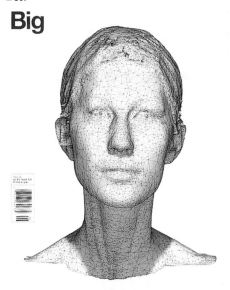

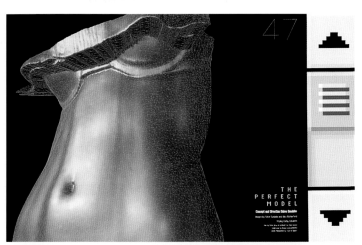

photography ■ MERIT

■ 367
PUBLICATION Big
CREATIVE DIRECTOR Marcelo Jünemann
ART DIRECTORS Stuart Spalding, Lee Swillingham
PHOTOGRAPHER Sølve Sündsbø
PUBLISHER Big Magazine, Inc.
ISSUE June 1999, #23
CATEGORY Photo Illustration

■ 368
PUBLICATION Condé Nast Traveler
DESIGN DIRECTOR Robert Best
ART DIRECTOR Carla Frank
DESIGNER Carla Frank
PHOTO EDITOR Kathleen Klech
PHOTOGRAPHER Hakan Ludwigson
PUBLISHER Condé Nast Publications, Inc.
ISSUE March 1999
CATEGORY Reportage Story

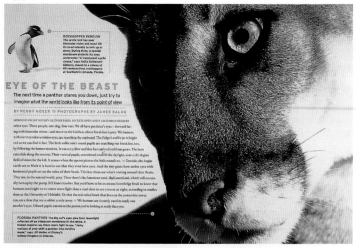

EYE OF THE BEAST

The next time a panther stares you down, just try to imagine what the world looks like from its point of view

BY PENNY MOSER ✦ PHOTOGRAPHS BY JAMES BALOG

NEANDERTHALS IN LOVE

He-man love guru **Justin Sterling** advises his rabid following that a little less sensitivity and a lot more **knuckle scraping** make for a real ladies' man.

BY STEPHEN PAPA PHOTOGRAPHS BY CARLOS SERRAO

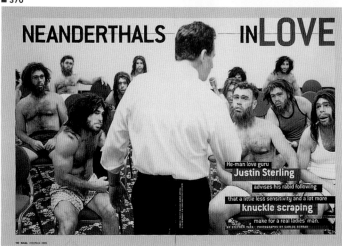

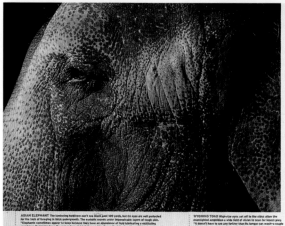

■ 369
PUBLICATION Details
DESIGN DIRECTOR Robert Newman
DESIGNER John Giordani
PHOTO EDITOR Greg Pond
PHOTOGRAPHER Dan Winters
PUBLISHER Condé Nast Publications, Inc.
ISSUE April 1999
CATEGORY Portrait Spread

■ 370
PUBLICATION Details
CREATIVE DIRECTOR Dale Hrabi
ART DIRECTOR Jamie Lipps
PHOTO EDITORS Doris Brautigan, Axel Kessler
PHOTOGRAPHER Carlos Serrao
PUBLISHER Condé Nast Publications, Inc.
ISSUE December 1999
CATEGORY Photo Illustration

■ 371
PUBLICATION Discover
DESIGN DIRECTOR Michael J. Walsh
DESIGNER Kory Kennedy
PHOTOGRAPHER James Balog
PUBLISHER Disney Publishing Worldwide
ISSUE December 1999
CATEGORY Reportage Story

photography ■ MERIT

■ 372
PUBLICATION enRoute
CREATIVE DIRECTOR Danielle Le Bel
DESIGNER Denis Paquet
PHOTO EDITOR Julie Saindon
PHOTOGRAPHER Kurt-Michael Westermann
PUBLISHER Spafax Canada
CLIENT Air Canada
ISSUE May 1999
CATEGORY Reportage Story

■ 373
PUBLICATION enRoute
CREATIVE DIRECTOR Danielle Le Bel
DESIGNER Denis Paquet
PHOTO EDITOR Julie Saindon
PHOTOGRAPHER Edward Gajdel
PUBLISHER Spafax Canada
CLIENT Air Canada
ISSUE April 1999
CATEGORY Portrait Spread

■ 374
PUBLICATION Food & Wine
CREATIVE DIRECTOR Stephen Scoble
ART DIRECTOR Lou DiLorenzo
DESIGNER Lou DiLorenzo
PHOTO EDITOR Kim Gougenheim
PHOTOGRAPHER Zubin Schroff
PUBLISHER American Express Publishing Co.
ISSUE February 1999
CATEGORY Reportage Spread

family pictures

smoke

■ 375
PUBLICATION DoubleTake
DESIGNERS William Drenttel, Jessica Helfand, Jeff Tyson
PHOTO EDITOR Richard B. Woodward
PHOTOGRAPHER Nicholas Nixon
PUBLISHER DoubleTake Community Service Corporation
ISSUE Spring 1999
CATEGORY Reportage Story

■ 376
PUBLICATION DoubleTake
DESIGNERS William Drenttel, Jessica Helfand, Jeff Tyson
PHOTO EDITOR Richard B. Woodward
PHOTOGRAPHER Michael Ackerman
PUBLISHER DoubleTake Community Service Corporation
ISSUE Summer 1999
CATEGORY Reportage Story

ON THE EVE: MOSCOW 1998

PHOTOGRAPHS BY MARY BERRIDGE

READY TO WARE

Decorating with fashion accessories is a natural. What with-it, well-dressed gal hasn't transformed a favorite pashmina shawl into a smart throw? Or decorated a country-house wall with scads of artfully hung straw hats? We've seen raffia totes transformed into firewood receptacles and Bakelite bracelets functioning as curtain rings, but—to reverse the scenario—can home furnishings be wearable?

You bet. For creative, adventurous, witty souls, there's a whole world of wardrobe possibilities in every room of the house. From the practical to the preposterous, these eight pages celebrate the concept of double duty. Don't forget that grain of salt!

MAKE HEADLINES IN A CHANDELIER CHAPEAU

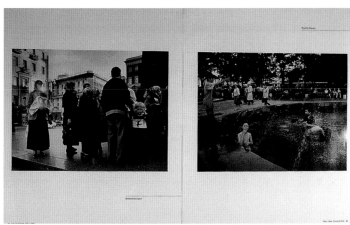

BAG A BIN FOR THROWAWAY CHIC

GET A HANDLE ON FACE-SETTING PLACE SETTINGS

LOCK ONTO AN ADORABLE CHOKER

BUCKLE UP WITH A KNOCK, KNOCK KNOCKOUT BELT

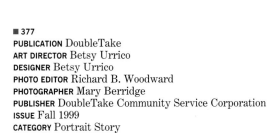

SWITCH ON TO AN ELECTRIFYING SHADE

STEP UP TO CRYSTAL-CLEAR STYLE

■ 377
PUBLICATION DoubleTake
ART DIRECTOR Betsy Urrico
DESIGNER Betsy Urrico
PHOTO EDITOR Richard B. Woodward
PHOTOGRAPHER Mary Berridge
PUBLISHER DoubleTake Community Service Corporation
ISSUE Fall 1999
CATEGORY Portrait Story

■ 378
PUBLICATION Elle Decor
CREATIVE DIRECTOR Nora Sheehan
DESIGNER Nora Sheehan
PHOTO EDITOR Quintana Dunne
PHOTOGRAPHER Torkil Gunardson
PUBLISHER Hachette Filipacchi Magazines, Inc.
ISSUE April 1999
CATEGORY Still Life/Interiors Story

photography ■ MERIT

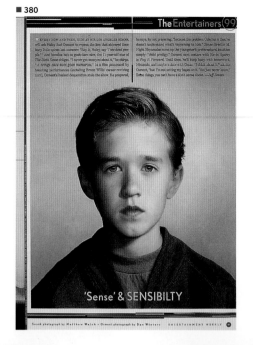

■ 379
PUBLICATION Entertainment Weekly
DESIGN DIRECTOR Geraldine Hessler
DESIGNER Erin Whelan
PHOTO EDITOR Freyda Tavin
PHOTOGRAPHER Amy Guip
PUBLISHER Time Inc.
ISSUE September 3, 1999
CATEGORY Portrait Single Page

■ 380
PUBLICATION Entertainment Weekly
DESIGN DIRECTOR Geraldine Hessler
DESIGNERS Geraldine Hessler,
John Walker
PHOTO EDITOR Denise Sfraga
PHOTOGRAPHER Dan Winters
PUBLISHER Time Inc.
ISSUE December 24–31, 1999
CATEGORY Portrait Single Page

■ 381
PUBLICATION Entertainment Weekly
DESIGN DIRECTOR Geraldine Hessler
DESIGNER Ellene Standke
PHOTOGRAPHER Matt Mahurin
PUBLISHER Time Inc.
ISSUE September 24, 1999
CATEGORY Photo Illustration

■ 382
PUBLICATION Entertainment Weekly
DESIGN DIRECTOR John Korpics
ART DIRECTOR Geraldine Hessler
DESIGNERS Geraldine Hessler,
Jennifer Procopio
PHOTO EDITOR Michele Romero
PHOTOGRAPHER Anton Corbijn
PUBLISHER Time Inc.
ISSUE May 28, 1999
CATEGORY Portrait Story

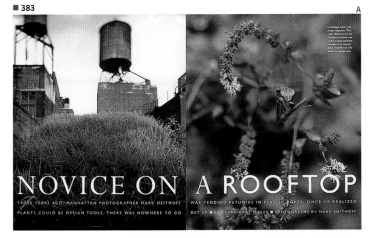

NOVICE ON A ROOFTOP

THREE YEARS AGO, MANHATTAN PHOTOGRAPHER MARK HEITHOFF WAS TENDING PETUNIAS IN PLASTIC BOXES. ONCE HE REALIZED PLANTS COULD BE DESIGN TOOLS, THERE WAS NOWHERE TO GO BUT UP ■ BY SARAH GRAY MILLER ■ PHOTOGRAPHS BY MARK HEITHOFF

SWAMP THINGS

FORGET SWEET ROSES AND LUSH PEONIES. SARRACENIA—THE BIZARRE-LOOKING BOG DWELLER—IS PRETTY AS A PITCHER

No one could find fault with the straightforward American beauty of Christie Brinkley, or with Cindy Crawford's more voluptuous look. But today, it's Cate Blanchett's wan fragility, Christina Ricci's plump gloom that land magazine covers. The age of ugly pretty has arrived. Hybrid tea roses had their day in the sun. Now it's garish gargantuan foliage, morbid black flowers that we crave. Bring on the prominently veined pitchers of sarracenia (right)—horticulture's current "it" girl. These odd-shaped leaves seem deceptively delicate, painfully thin, but their appetites are voracious. Peer inside, and you'll see science fiction

BY ADAM LEVINE ■ PHOTOGRAPHS BY MARYGRAY HUNTER

> IN THE PAST, WETLANDS WERE VIEWED AS DANGEROUS, SNAKE-RIDDEN, GOOD-FOR-NOTHING SWAMPS, FULL OF MOSQUITOES

THE LAST *Paradise*

photography ■ MERIT

■ 384
PUBLICATION Garden Design
CREATIVE DIRECTOR Michael Grossman
ART DIRECTOR Toby Fox
DESIGNER Chad Tomlinson
PHOTO EDITOR Stella Kramer
PHOTOGRAPHER Marygray Hunter
PUBLISHER Meigher Communications
ISSUE May 1999
CATEGORY Still Life/Interiors Story

■ 385
PUBLICATION Hemispheres
DESIGN DIRECTOR Jaimey Easler
ART DIRECTORS Jaimey Easler, Jody Mustain, Kevin de Miranda
PHOTOGRAPHER Gian Paolo Barbieri
PUBLISHER Pace Communications
CLIENT United Airlines
ISSUE May 1999
CATEGORY Reportage Spread

■ 383
PUBLICATION Garden Design
CREATIVE DIRECTOR Michael Grossman
ART DIRECTOR Toby Fox
DESIGNER Chad Tomlinson
PHOTO EDITOR Stella Kramer
PHOTOGRAPHER Mark Heithoff
PUBLISHER Meigher Communications
ISSUE May 1999
CATEGORY Still Life/Interiors Story
A MERIT Still Life/Interiors Spread

FAT GUY FROM CLEVELAND WALKS INTO A BAR

THE COMMON TOUCH of the Leading Man

As this story demonstrates, sometimes trying not to be a dick takes work

By JOHN H. RICHARDSON

Photographs by SAM JONES

Esquire THE FATHER'S KISS

THE BETTER MAN SERIES

Hey, Nature Boy!

STEVE IRWIN KEEPS PLENTY BUSY RASSLIN' RATTLERS AND CORRALLING CROCS ON ANIMAL PLANET, BUT HE CAN STILL FIND TIME TO OFFER A FEW POINTERS ON CRITTER PROBLEMS OF THE DOMESTIC VARIETY

PHOTOGRAPH BY DAN WINTERS

■ 386
PUBLICATION Esquire
DESIGN DIRECTOR Robert Priest
ART DIRECTOR Rockwell Harwood
DESIGNER Joshua Liberson
PHOTO EDITOR Patti Wilson
PHOTOGRAPHER Sam Jones
PUBLISHER The Hearst Corporation-Magazines Division
ISSUE April 1999
CATEGORY Portrait Story

■ 387
PUBLICATION Esquire
DESIGN DIRECTOR Robert Preiest
ART DIRECTOR Hannah McCaughey
PHOTO EDITOR Simon Barnett
PHOTOGRAPHER Sam Jones
PUBLISHER The Hearst Corporation-Magazines Division
ISSUE October 1999
CATEGORY Portrait Spread

■ 388
PUBLICATION Esquire
DESIGN DIRECTOR Robert Priest
ART DIRECTOR Rockwell Harwood
PHOTO EDITOR Simon Barnett
PHOTOGRAPHER Gregory Heisler
PUBLISHER The Hearst Corporation-Magazines Division
ISSUE June 1999
CATEGORY Portrait Spread

■ 389
PUBLICATION Esquire
DESIGN DIRECTOR Robert Priest
ART DIRECTOR Rockwell Harwood
DESIGNER Paul Scirecalabrissotto
PHOTO EDITOR Simon Barnett
PHOTOGRAPHER Dan Winters
PUBLISHER The Hearst Corporation-Magazines Division
ISSUE August 1999
CATEGORY Portrait Spread

BEING
Max
Cleland

HE HAS ONE ARM AND NO LEGS.
HE IS A UNITED STATES SENATOR.
THIS IS HOW HE LIVES.

BY CHARLES BOWDEN
PHOTOGRAPHS BY BRUCE DAVIDSON

SCENES
FROM
A
(GROUP)
MARRIAGE

BY JOHN H. RICHARDSON

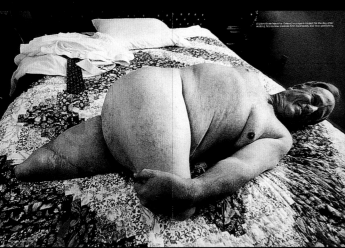

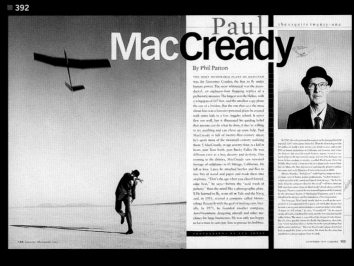

Paul
MacCready
the esquire twenty-one

By Phil Patton

photography ■ **MERIT**

■ 390
PUBLICATION Esquire
DESIGN DIRECTOR Robert Priest
ART DIRECTOR Rockwell Harwood
DESIGNER Robert Priest
PHOTO EDITOR Simon Barnett
PHOTOGRAPHER Bruce Davidson
PUBLISHER The Hearst Corporation-
Magazines Division
ISSUE August 1999
CATEGORY Portrait Story

■ 391
PUBLICATION Esquire
DESIGN DIRECTOR Robert Priest
ART DIRECTOR Rockwell Harwood
DESIGNER Joshua Liberson
PHOTO EDITOR Patti Wilson
PHOTOGRAPHER Mary Ellen Mark
PUBLISHER The Hearst Corporation-
Magazines Division
ISSUE May 1999
CATEGORY Portrait Spread

■ 392
PUBLICATION Esquire
DESIGN DIRECTOR John Korpics
ART DIRECTOR Rockwell Harwood
PHOTO EDITOR Simon Barnett
PHOTOGRAPHER Sam Jones
PUBLISHER The Hearst Corporation-
Magazines Division
ISSUE November 1999
CATEGORY Portrait Spread

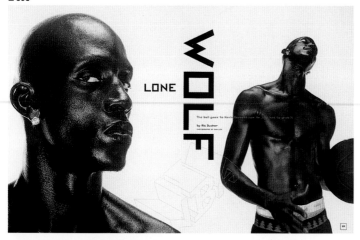

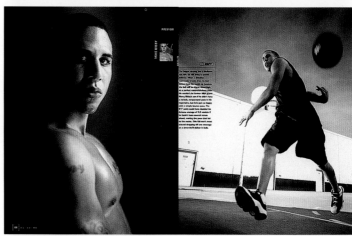

■ 393
PUBLICATION ESPN
DESIGN DIRECTOR Peter Yates
ART DIRECTOR Yvette L. Francis
DESIGNERS Peter Yates, Yvette L. Francis
PHOTO EDITOR Nik Kleinberg
PHOTOGRAPHER Dah Len
PUBLISHER Disney Publishing Worldwide
ISSUE November 15, 1999
CATEGORY Portrait Spread

■ 394
PUBLICATION ESPN
DESIGN DIRECTOR F. Darrin Perry
ART DIRECTOR Peter Yates
DESIGNER Bruce Glace
PHOTO EDITOR John Toolan
PHOTOGRAPHER Piotr Sikora
PUBLISHER Disney Publishing Worldwide
ISSUE March 22, 1999
CATEGORY Portrait Spread

■ 395
PUBLICATION ESPN
DESIGN DIRECTOR F. Darrin Perry
DESIGNERS F. Darrin Perry, Peter Yates
PHOTO EDITORS Nik Kleinberg, Gladees Prieur
PHOTOGRAPHER John Huet
PUBLISHER Disney Publishing Worldwide
ISSUE February 22, 1999
CATEGORY Portrait Story

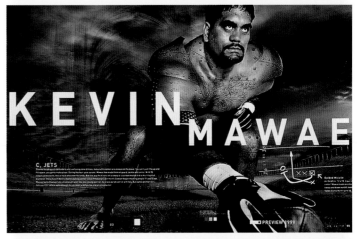

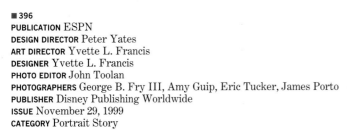

■ 396
PUBLICATION ESPN
DESIGN DIRECTOR Peter Yates
ART DIRECTOR Yvette L. Francis
DESIGNER Yvette L. Francis
PHOTO EDITOR John Toolan
PHOTOGRAPHERS George B. Fry III, Amy Guip, Eric Tucker, James Porto
PUBLISHER Disney Publishing Worldwide
ISSUE November 29, 1999
CATEGORY Portrait Story

■ 397
PUBLICATION ESPN
DESIGN DIRECTOR Peter Yates
ART DIRECTOR Yvette L. Francis
DESIGNER Peter Yates
PHOTO EDITORS John Toolen, Nik Kleinberg
PHOTOGRAPHERS John Huet, Claude Shade
PUBLISHER Disney Publishing Worldwide
ISSUE September 20, 1999
CATEGORY Photo Illustration

photography ■ MERIT

■ 398
PUBLICATION ESPN
DESIGN DIRECTOR F. Darrin Perry
ART DIRECTOR Peter Yates
DESIGNER Chris Rudzik
PHOTO EDITOR Gladees Prieur
PHOTOGRAPHER Peter Gregoire
PUBLISHER Disney Publishing Worldwide
ISSUE May 3, 1999
CATEGORY Portrait Spread

■ 399
PUBLICATION ESPN
DESIGN DIRECTOR Peter Yates
ART DIRECTOR Yvette L. Francis
DESIGNER Reyes Meléndez
PHOTO EDITOR Kristina Snyder
PHOTOGRAPHER Per Gustavson
PUBLISHER Disney Publishing Worldwide
ISSUE October 4, 1999
CATEGORY Portrait Spread

■ 400
PUBLICATION ESPN
DESIGN DIRECTOR Peter Yates
ART DIRECTOR Yvette L. Francis
DESIGNERS Peter Yates, Henry Lee
PHOTO EDITORS Kristina Snyder, Nik Kleinberg
PHOTOGRAPHERS Mary Ellen Mark, Isabel Snyder, Piotr Sikora, John Huet
PUBLISHER Disney Publishing Worldwide
ISSUE December 27, 1999
CATEGORY Portrait Story

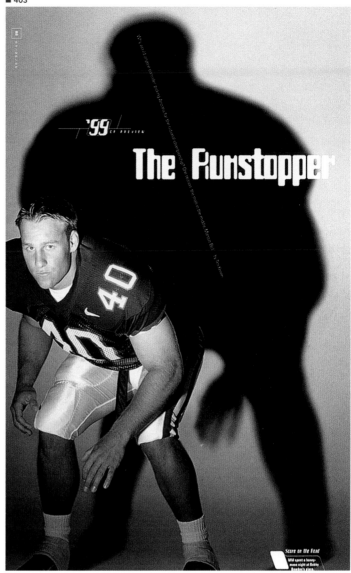

photography ■ MERIT

■ 401
PUBLICATION ESPN
DESIGN DIRECTOR F. Darrin Perry
ART DIRECTOR Peter Yates
DESIGNER F. Darrin Perry
PHOTO EDITOR Nik Kleinberg
PHOTOGRAPHER Jeff Sciortino
PUBLISHER Disney Publishing Worldwide
ISSUE May 3, 1999
CATEGORY Portrait Single Page

■ 402
PUBLICATION ESPN
DESIGN DIRECTOR F. Darrin Perry
ART DIRECTOR Peter Yates
DESIGNER F. Darrin Perry
PHOTO EDITOR Nik Kleinberg
PHOTOGRAPHER Gregory Heisler
PUBLISHER Disney Publishing Worldwide
ISSUE August 9, 1999
CATEGORY Portrait Single Page

■ 403
PUBLICATION ESPN
DESIGN DIRECTOR F. Darrin Perry
ART DIRECTOR Peter Yates
DESIGNER Chris Rudzik
PHOTO EDITOR John Toolen
PHOTOGRAPHER Yariu Milchan
PUBLISHER Disney Publishing Worldwide
ISSUE September 6, 1999
CATEGORY Portrait Single Page

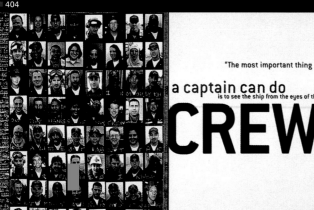

"The most important thing **a captain can do** is to see the ship from the eyes of the **CREW."**

"The best interest of the **PATIENT** is the only interest to be considered."

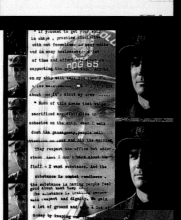

YOU EXPECT TO BE AWED BY THE VIEW

EACH AFTERNOON, IN A TINY WORKROOM ON THE 12TH FLOOR OF THE MAYO CLINIC, THE BATTLE AGAINST CANCER BEGINS WITH AN ARGUMENT. AT 1 P.M., SUPPORT STAFFERS AT THE WORLD-FAMOUS **FROM THE CURRENT CASELOAD.**

The Agenda

The Agenda

"There's a war for talent going on, and we're right in the middle of it."
Andy Esparza

404
PUBLICATION Fast Company
ART DIRECTOR Patrick Mitchell
DESIGNER Gretchen Smelter
PHOTO EDITOR Alicia Jylkka
PHOTOGRAPHER Frank W. Ockenfels 3
PUBLISHER Fast Company
ISSUE April 1999
CATEGORY Reportage Story

405
PUBLICATION Fast Company
ART DIRECTOR Patrick Mitchell
DESIGNER Gretchen Smelter
PHOTO EDITOR Alicia Jylkka
PHOTOGRAPHER Burk Uzzle
PUBLISHER Fast Company
ISSUE April 1999
CATEGORY Reportage Story

406
PUBLICATION Fast Company
ART DIRECTOR Patrick Mitchell
DESIGNER Emily Crawford
PHOTO EDITOR Alicia Jylkka
PHOTOGRAPHER Antonin Kratochvil
PUBLISHER Fast Company
ISSUE December 1999
CATEGORY Portrait Spread

Jeff Daniel

ENGINES OF DEMOCRACY

"WE'RE **CREATING** A WHOLE NEW

indus-try

THAT CAN IMPROVE PEOPLE'S LIVES."

Roger Martin

"When you're building Business school 2.0, you don't start from scratch."

photography ■ MERIT

PUBLICATION Fast Company
ART DIRECTOR Patrick Mitchell
DESIGNERS Patrick Mitchell, Emily Crawford
PHOTO EDITOR Alicia Jylkka
PHOTOGRAPHER Fredrik Brodén
PUBLISHER Fast Company
ISSUE December 1999
CATEGORY Portrait Spread

PUBLICATION Fast Company
ART DIRECTOR Patrick Mitchell
DESIGNER Gretchen Smelter
PHOTO EDITOR Alicia Jylkka
PHOTOGRAPHER Catherine Ledner
PUBLISHER Fast Company
ISSUE April 1999
CATEGORY Reportage Spread

PUBLICATION Fast Company
ART DIRECTOR Patrick Mitchell
DESIGNER Emily Crawford
PHOTO EDITOR Alicia Jylkka
PHOTOGRAPHER Kate Swan
PUBLISHER Fast Company
ISSUE December 1999
CATEGORY Portrait Spread

PUBLICATION Fast Company
ART DIRECTOR Patrick Mitchell
DESIGNER Gretchen Smelter
PHOTO EDITOR Alicia Jylkka
PHOTOGRAPHER Mary Ellen Mark
PUBLISHER Fast Company
ISSUE October 1999
CATEGORY Reportage Story

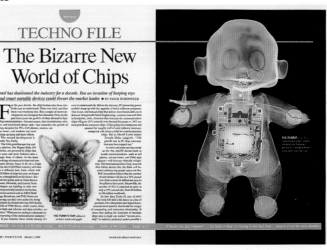

■ 414

■ 415

COURTNEY SLOANE
HAS HER FINGER ON THE
PULSE OF DESIGN
IN AND BEYOND THE MUSIC
INDUSTRY.

COURTNEY ROCKS

BY JULIE MOLINE

■ 416

ALL ABOUT EVA

BY EVE M. KAHN

■ 417

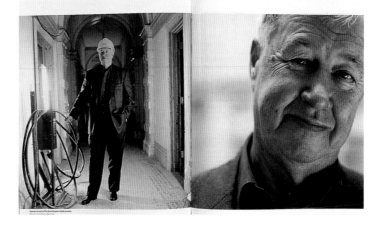

Unfinished Business

by Michelle Ogundehin

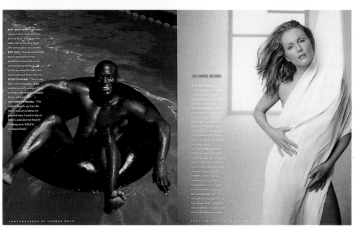

■ 414

PUBLICATION InStyle
ART DIRECTOR Paul Roelofs
DESIGNER Paul Roelofs
PHOTO EDITORS Laurie Kratochvil, Maureen Griffin
PHOTOGRAPHERS Matthew Rolston, Andrew Eccles, Isabel Snyder, George Lange, Brigitte LaCombe, Art Streiber, Albert Watson, George Holz, Mark Liddell, Carlo Dalla Chiesa, Robert Trachtenberg
PUBLISHER Time Inc.
ISSUE September 1999
CATEGORY Portrait Story

■ 415

PUBLICATION Interiors
ART DIRECTOR Paul Carlos
DESIGNER Paul Carlos
PHOTO EDITOR Mackenzie Green
PHOTOGRAPHER Brigitte LaCombe
PUBLISHER BPI Communications
ISSUE September 1999
CATEGORY Portrait Spread

■ 416

PUBLICATION Interiors
ART DIRECTOR Paul Carlos
DESIGNER Paul Carlos
PHOTO EDITOR Mackenzie Green
PHOTOGRAPHER Brigitte Lacombe
PUBLISHER BPI Communications
ISSUE September 1999
CATEGORY Portrait Spread

■ 417

PUBLICATION Interiors
ART DIRECTOR Paul Carlos
DESIGNER Paul Carlos
PHOTO EDITOR Mackenzie Green
PHOTOGRAPHER Graham MacIndoe
PUBLISHER BPI Communications
ISSUE November 1999
CATEGORY Portrait Spread

Snowstorms in beach weather?

Stranger things have happened.

Okay, maybe not.

Freak of Nature

PHOTOGRAPHY BY KELLY KLEIN

love that body

That's what we want you to do, and that's what we want you to say when you're naked. Jane Larkworthy does the inner/outer body beautiful thing.

PHOTOGRAPHY BY FREDERIK LIEBERATH

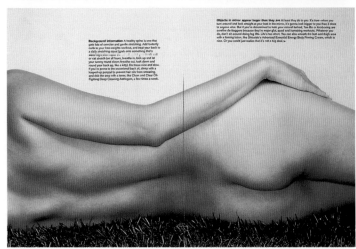

■ 418
PUBLICATION Jane
ART DIRECTOR Johan Svensson
DESIGNER Amy Demas
PHOTO EDITOR Cary Estes Leitzes
PHOTOGRAPHER Kelly Klein
PUBLISHER Fairchild Publications
ISSUE February 1999
CATEGORY Fashion/Beauty Story

■ 419
PUBLICATION Jane
ART DIRECTOR Johan Svensson
DESIGNER Amy Demas
PHOTO EDITOR Cary Estes Leitzes
PHOTOGRAPHER Frederik Lieberath
PUBLISHER Fairchild Publications
ISSUE November 1999
CATEGORY Fashion/Beauty Story

photography ■ MERIT

■ 420
PUBLICATION Jane
ART DIRECTOR Johan Svensson
DESIGNER Amy Demas
PHOTO EDITOR Cary Estes Leitzes
PHOTOGRAPHER Regan Cameron
PUBLISHER Fairchild Publications
ISSUE March 1999
CATEGORY Fashion/Beauty Story

■ 421
PUBLICATION Joe
CREATIVE DIRECTOR Lloyd Ziff
DESIGNER Michael Mrak
PHOTO EDITOR Julie Claire
PHOTOGRAPHER Geof Kern
PUBLISHER Time Inc. Custom Publishing
CLIENT Starbucks
ISSUE Vol. 1, No. 1 1999
CATEGORY Photo Illustration

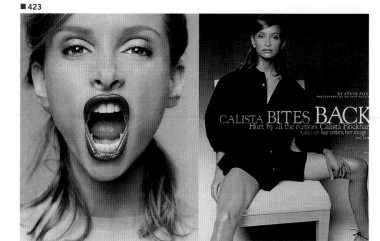

queens of **mean**

claire trevor

coleen gray

CALISTA BITES BACK
Hurt by all the rumors, Calista Flockhart takes on her critics, her image and food

ann savage

claire trevor

f

PEOPLE STARE
WHEN SHE WALKS THROUGH

That's proof she's anorexic!"
without any money!

audrey totter
evelyn keyes

*restaurant and nobody's taking
my picture and I get depressed"*

marie windsor
jane greer

■422
PUBLICATION Los Angeles
CREATIVE DIRECTOR David Armario
DESIGNERS David Armario, Myla Sorensen
PHOTO EDITORS Lisa Thackaberry, Michelle Hauf
PHOTOGRAPHER Matthew Rolston
PUBLISHER Fairchild Publications
ISSUE March 1999
CATEGORY Portrait Story

■423
PUBLICATION Los Angeles
CREATIVE DIRECTOR David Armario
DESIGNERS David Armario, Myla Sorensen
PHOTO EDITORS Lisa Thackaberry, Michelle Aaja
PHOTOGRAPHER Matthew Rolston
PUBLISHER Fairchild Publications
ISSUE June 1999
CATEGORY Portrait Story

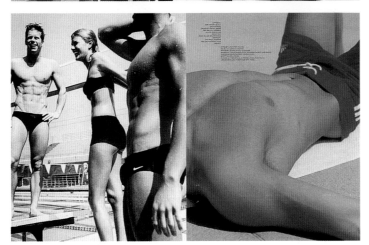

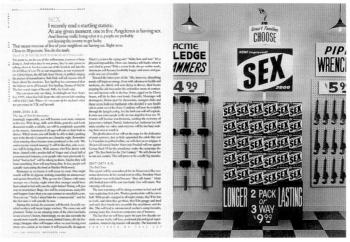

WOMEN IN UNIFORM

Minimalist chic, maximum ease: Look for sleek, streamlined clothes that make getting dressed every day a no-brainer. photographs by riccardo tinelli

photography ■ MERIT

■ 424
PUBLICATION Los Angeles
CREATIVE DIRECTOR David Armario
DESIGNERS David Armario, Myla Sorensen
PHOTO EDITORS Lisa Thackaberry, Michelle Aaja
PHOTOGRAPHER Pablo Alfaro
PUBLISHER Fairchild Publications
ISSUE July 1999
CATEGORY Fashion/Beauty Story

■ 425
PUBLICATION Los Angeles
CREATIVE DIRECTOR David Armario
DESIGNERS David Armario, Myla Sorensen
PHOTO EDITORS Lisa Thackaberry, Michelle Hauf
PHOTOGRAPHER Dan Winters
PUBLISHER Fairchild Publications
CATEGORY Photo Illustration

■ 426
PUBLICATION Mademoiselle
CREATIVE DIRECTOR Cynthia Searight
DESIGN DIRECTOR Lisa Shapiro
DESIGNERS Cynthia Searight, Lisa Shapiro
PHOTO EDITOR Carla Popenfus
PHOTOGRAPHER Riccardo Tinelli
PUBLISHER Condé Nast Publications, Inc.
ISSUE March 1999
CATEGORY Fashion/Beauty Spread

■ 427
PUBLICATION Martha Stewart Living
DESIGN DIRECTOR Eric A. Pike
ART DIRECTOR Claudia Bruno
DESIGNERS Claudia Bruno, Ayesha Patel, Susan Spungen
PHOTO EDITOR Heidi J. Posner
PHOTOGRAPHER Victoria Pearson
PUBLISHER Martha Stewart Living Omnimedia
ISSUE May 1999
CATEGORY Still Life/Interiors Story

■ 428
PUBLICATION Martha Stewart Weddings
ART DIRECTOR Ellen Burnie
DESIGNERS Ellen Burnie, Wendy Kromer,
Page Marchese Norman, Wendy Sidewater
PHOTO EDITOR Heidi J. Posner
PHOTOGRAPHER Grant Peterson
PUBLISHER Martha Stewart Living Omnimedia
ISSUE Winter 1999
CATEGORY Still Life/Interiors Story

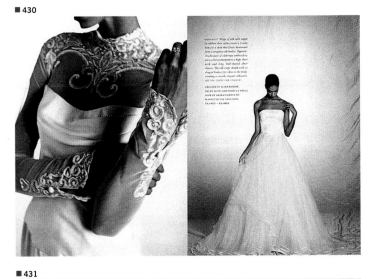

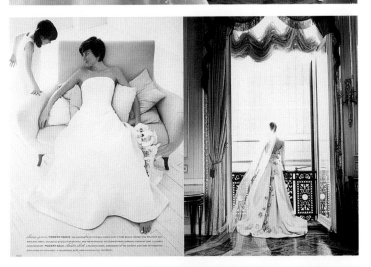

■ 429
PUBLICATION Martha Stewart Weddings
ART DIRECTOR Ellen Burnie
DESIGNERS Ellen Burnie, Helen Lund
PHOTO EDITOR Heidi J. Posner
PHOTOGRAPHER Susan Salinger
PUBLISHER Martha Stewart Living Omnimedia
ISSUE Summer 1999
CATEGORY Still Life/Interiors Story

■ 430
PUBLICATION Martha Stewart Weddings
ART DIRECTOR Ellen Burnie
DESIGNERS Ellen Burnie, Helen Lund, Rebecca Thuss
PHOTO EDITOR Heidi J. Posner
PHOTOGRAPHER Bobby Fisher
PUBLISHER Martha Stewart Living Omnimedia
ISSUE Winter 1999
CATEGORY Still Life/Interiors Spread

■ 431
PUBLICATION Money
ART DIRECTOR Syndi C. Becker
DESIGNER MaryAnn Salvato
PHOTO EDITOR Shawn Vale
PHOTOGRAPHER Brian Velenchenko
PUBLISHER Time Inc.
ISSUE January 1999
CATEGORY Portrait Spread

■432
PUBLICATION Men's Journal
ART DIRECTOR Michael Lawton
DESIGNER Michael Lawton
PHOTO EDITOR MC Marden
PHOTOGRAPHER Elizabeth L. Gilbert
PUBLISHER Wenner Media
ISSUE November 1999
CATEGORY Portrait Story

■433
PUBLICATION Men's Journal
ART DIRECTOR Michael Lawton
DESIGNER Robert Perino
PHOTO EDITOR MC Marden
PHOTOGRAPHER Elizabeth L. Gilbert
PUBLISHER Wenner Media
ISSUE November 1999
CATEGORY Reportage Single Page

■434
PUBLICATION Men's Journal
ART DIRECTOR Michael Lawton
DESIGNER Michael Lawton
PHOTO EDITOR MC Marden
PHOTOGRAPHER Elizabeth L. Gilbert
PUBLISHER Wenner Media
ISSUE November 1999
CATEGORY Reportage Story

■435
PUBLICATION Men's Journal
ART DIRECTOR Michael Lawton
DESIGNERS Thomas Alberty,
 Michael Lawton
PHOTO EDITOR Casey Tierney
PHOTOGRAPHER Keoki Flagg
PUBLISHER Wenner Media
ISSUE December 1999
CATEGORY Reportage Single Page

A DIFFERENT REALITY

THESE AFRICAN TALISMANS OF TRANSFORMATION PROVIDE ENTREE TO THE UNSEEN.   PHOTOGRAPHY BY RON TARVER

ECHEHONAL MASK, IVORY COAST

SCULPTURE REPRESENTING THE DUALITY OF HUMAN NATURE, ZAIRE

YORUBA ALTAR PIECE, NIGERIA

SENUFO RHYTHM POUNDER, IVORY COAST (TOP), SONGYE MASK, ZAIRE (BOTTOM)

AKUA DOLL, GHANA

THE SKY LINE
FAR OUT

Brasília, the futuristic capital of Brazil, which sits in the middle of nowhere, has become a retro icon.

BY PAUL GOLDBERGER / PHOTOGRAPHS BY ROBERT POLIDORI

■ 436

PUBLICATION Philadelphia Inquirer Magazine
ART DIRECTORS Chrissy Dunleavy, Susan Syrnick
DESIGNER Chrissy Dunleavy
PHOTOGRAPHER Ron Tarver
ISSUE February 7, 1999
CATEGORY Still Life/Interiors Story

■ 437

PUBLICATION The New Yorker
PHOTO EDITOR Elisabeth Biondi
PHOTOGRAPHER Robert Polidori
PUBLISHER Condé Nast Publications, Inc.
ISSUE March 8, 1999
CATEGORY Reportage Story

173

photography ■ MERIT

EXILE AND RETURN

Kosovar Albanian refugees fled Slobodan Milosevic's Serbian "cleansers" and began arriving in Macedonia in March, only to find that most Macedonians did not want them there, either. Local officials confined this group for hours in extreme heat in a bus between the border and the Brazhane refugee camp.

Upon returning to Kosovo, ethnic Albanian refugees often found that the towns and villages they had left behind had been vandalized beyond recognition. A crossroads in downtown Djakovica after the Serbian withdrawal, in June.

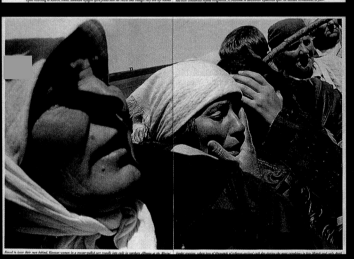

Forced to leave their own behind, Kosovar women in a tractor-pulled cart trundle into exile in northern Albania at the Morini border crossing, where tens of thousands of refugees arrived each day during the main exodus in late March and early April.

Top: Kosovar refugees in Macedonia and Albania included an old woman, her wrists broken by Serbs, who died by the road, and is Kosovo, celebrations in Prizren. Bottom: British paratroopers in Pristina greet Kosovar survivors and arrest Kosovo Liberation Army

HISTORY always seems to go either too fast or too slow...

[body text continues]

THE BIRDMAN

Tony Hawk—part Michael Jordan, part Evel Knievel—is the star of a multimillion-dollar industry that still can't shake its outlaw image.

BY MARK LEVINE

CARLSBAD, CALIFORNIA, which is situated along a hundred-and-twenty-mile strip of coast between San Diego and Los Angeles, is a town where the impulse to slip up-right on a fast-moving piece of wood has spawned two closely related but rivalrous tribes—the surfers and the skateboarders...

PHOTOGRAPH BY MARTIN SCHOELLER

The Hawks at home: the skateboarder is a master of gravity-defying maneuvers.

ANNALS OF ENTERTAINMENT

CREATIVE DIFFERENCES

David Lynch wanted to make a TV series unlike any other. The network said it was eager to get beyond the formulas of prime-time programming. What could go wrong?

BY TAD FRIEND

IT was a mild March night in Hollywood, near the end of the shoot for "Mulholland Drive," a two-hour pilot that David Lynch was filming for ABC...

ONE day last August, David Lynch drove his 1971 Mercedes to Century City to pitch "Mulholland Drive" to Jamie Tarses, the president—until her resignation last week—of ABC Entertainment...

In the studio, David Lynch decides carrying duties about television. "With all the commercials and his terrible pictures and pictures..."

438

PUBLICATION The New Yorker
PHOTO EDITOR Elisabeth Biondi
PHOTOGRAPHER Gilles Peress
PUBLISHER Condé Nast Publications, Inc.
ISSUE July 19, 1999
CATEGORY Reportage Story

439

PUBLICATION The New Yorker
PHOTO EDITOR Elisabeth Biondi
PHOTOGRAPHER Martin Schoeller
PUBLISHER Condé Nast Publications, Inc.
ISSUE July 26, 1999
CATEGORY Portrait Spread

440

PUBLICATION The New Yorker
PHOTO EDITOR Elisabeth Biondi
PHOTOGRAPHER Martin Schoeller
PUBLISHER Condé Nast Publications, Inc.

REVELATIONS

A work in progress.

PHOTOGRAPHS BY RICHARD AVEDON

Don McCullin's

INDIA

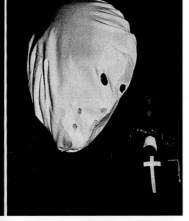

photography ■ MERIT

■441

PUBLICATION The New Yorker
PHOTO EDITOR Elisabeth Biondi
PHOTOGRAPHER Richard Avedon
PUBLISHER Condé Nast Publications, Inc.
ISSUE November 29, 1999
CATEGORY Portrait Story

■442

PUBLICATION Photo District News
ART DIRECTOR Darren Ching
DESIGNERS Ryan Burke, Tahir Hemphill, Dan Flint
PHOTO EDITOR Mackenzie Green
PHOTOGRAPHER Alexandra Boulat
PUBLISHER VNU/USA
ISSUE May 1999
CATEGORY Reportage Spread

■443

PUBLICATION Photo District News
ART DIRECTOR Darren Ching
DESIGNERS Ryan Burke, Tahir Hemphill
PHOTO EDITOR Mackenzie Green
PHOTOGRAPHER Don McCullin
PUBLISHER VNU/USA
ISSUE September 1999
CATEGORY Reportage Spread

the lucky one

A family's
battle with
AIDS becomes
a story of
separation
and survival
Photographs by
Randy Olson

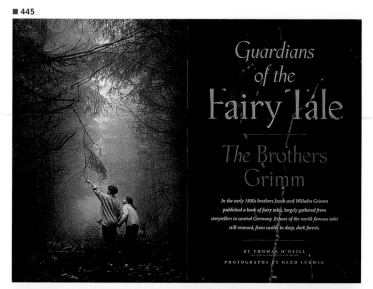

Guardians of the Fairy Tale

The Brothers Grimm

In the early 1800s brothers Jacob and Wilhelm Grimm
published a book of fairy tales, largely gathered from
storytellers in central Germany. Echoes of the world-famous tales
still resound, from castles to deep, dark forests.

BY THOMAS O'NEILL

PHOTOGRAPHS BY GERD LUDWIG

"Oh, you dear children, who has brought you here? Do come in, and stay with me. No harm shall happen to you." She took them both by the hand, and led them into her little house. Then good food was set before them, milk and pancakes,

In a moment, numbers of little earth-men came forth, and asked what the King's daughter

■ 444
PUBLICATION Mother Jones
CREATIVE DIRECTOR Rhonda Rubinstein
ART DIRECTORS Benjamin Shaykin, Cal Joy
PHOTO EDITOR Maren Levinson
PHOTOGRAPHER Randy Olson
PUBLISHER Foundation for National Progress
ISSUE May/June 1999
CATEGORY Reportage Story

■ 445
PUBLICATION National Geographic
DESIGN DIRECTOR Constance H. Phelps
DESIGNER David Whitmore
PHOTO EDITOR Susan Welchman
PHOTOGRAPHER Gerd Ludwig
PUBLISHER National Geographic Society
ISSUE December 1999
CATEGORY Reportage Story

ANTS AND PLANTS
FRIENDS AND FOES
Article and photographs by MARK W. MOFFETT

Evolution
in the
Revolution
CUBA

By JOHN J. PUTMAN
Photographs by DAVID ALAN HARVEY

A CLOSE-KNIT BUNCH

STICKY SITUATION

■ 446
PUBLICATION National Geographic
DESIGN DIRECTOR Constance H. Phelps
DESIGNER Lisa Lytton
PHOTO EDITOR Kathy Moran
PHOTOGRAPHER Mark W. Moffett
PUBLISHER National Geographic Society
ISSUE May 1999
CATEGORY Reportage Story

■ 447
PUBLICATION National Geographic
DESIGN DIRECTOR Constance H. Phelps
DESIGNER Constance H. Phelps
PHOTO EDITOR John Echave
PHOTOGRAPHER David Alan Harvey
PUBLISHER National Geographic Society
ISSUE June 1999
CATEGORY Reportage Story

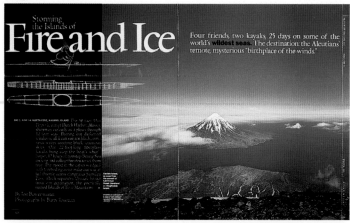

Storming the Islands of
Fire and Ice

Four friends, two kayaks, 25 days on some of the world's **wildest seas.** The destination: the Aleutians' remote, mysterious "birthplace of the winds."

By Joe Bowermaster
Photographs by Barry Tessman

"There are no roads, no villages, and no trails in the inner gorge—only the river hurtling through a lost world that visitors say feels utterly removed from time and space. It would be hard to find another place where nature manifests itself on such a vast, raw scale."

We paddle away from tidal rips where currents passing over shallows create powerful standing waves like **rapids on a river.**

On the 100th anniversary of the Army-Navy rivalry, the military Super Bowl still has spit, polish and firepower

The WAR GAME

PHOTOGRAPHS BY BILL CRAMER
TEXT BY MAXIMILLIAN POTTER

herbert

islands in the sky

kagamil

uliaga

chuginadak

carlisle

For the first time on our trip the wind dies. Completely. It lasts an hour, and **it feels all wrong.**

Scott McGuire looks north to Kagamil Island from Skiff Cove on Chuginadak.

■ 448

PUBLICATION National Geographic Adventure
DESIGN DIRECTOR Tom Bentkowski
ART DIRECTOR Sam Serebin
DESIGNERS Eve Binder, Tom Bentkowski
PHOTO EDITOR MC Marden
PHOTOGRAPHER Barry Tessman
PUBLISHER National Geographic Society
ISSUE Winter 1999
CATEGORY Reportage Story

■ 449

PUBLICATION National Geographic Adventure
DESIGN DIRECTOR Tom Bentkowski
ART DIRECTOR Sam Serebin
DESIGNERS Sam Serebin, Tom Bentkowski
PHOTO EDITOR Nell Hupman
PHOTOGRAPHER Ian Baker
PUBLISHER National Geographic Society
ISSUE Spring 1999
CATEGORY Reportage Spread

■ 450

PUBLICATION Philadelphia
ART DIRECTOR Tim Baldwin
DESIGNER John Goryl
PHOTOGRAPHER Bill Cramer
PUBLISHER Metrocorp Publishing
ISSUE December 1999
CATEGORY Portrait Spread

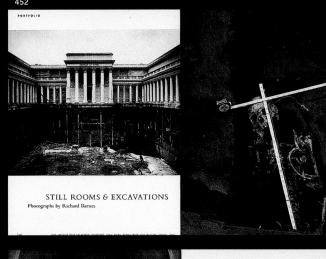

PORTFOLIO

STILL ROOMS & EXCAVATIONS
Photographs by Richard Barnes

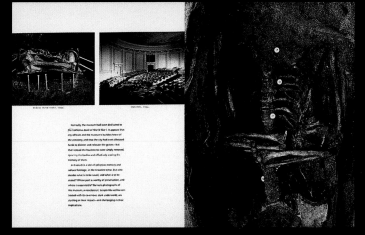

■ 451
PUBLICATION NewWest
CREATIVE DIRECTOR Steven Ralph Jerman
DESIGNER Steven Ralph Jerman
PHOTO EDITOR Steven Ralph Jerman
PHOTOGRAPHER Michael McRae
STUDIO Jerman Design Incorporated
PUBLISHER Sandmark Publishing Co.
ISSUE August 1999
CATEGORY Reportage Story

■ 452
PUBLICATION Orion
CREATIVE DIRECTOR Hans Teensma
DESIGN DIRECTOR Katie Craig
PHOTO EDITOR Hadas Dembo
PHOTOGRAPHER Richard Barnes
STUDIO Impress, Inc.

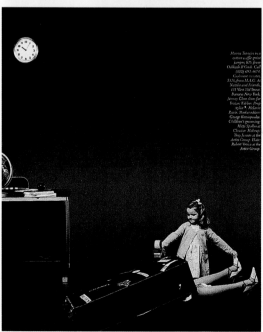

■ 453
PUBLICATION The New York Times Magazine
ART DIRECTOR Janet Froelich
DESIGNER Claude Martel
PHOTOGRAPHER Robert Trachtenberg
PHOTO STYLIST Elizabeth Stewart
PUBLISHER The New York Times
ISSUE February 28, 1999
CATEGORY Fashion/Beauty Story

■ 454
PUBLICATION The New York Times Magazine
ART DIRECTORS Janet Froelich, Joele Cuyler
DESIGNERS Joele Cuyler, Ignacio Rodriguez
PHOTO EDITORS Kathy Ryan, Jody Quon
PHOTOGRAPHER Malerie Marder
PUBLISHER The New York Times
ISSUE May 16, 1999
CATEGORY Portrait Story

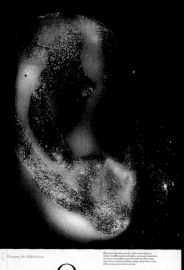

The Next Clinton

The politics of being a First Lady, a potential senator — and a Clintonian above all. By James Bennet

Photograph by Chuck Close

Hillary, Herself

'The possibility of partisan or political attacks does not deter me,' she said, referring to a possible Senate campaign. 'That is not anything that would prevent me' — and here she started laughing — 'after having been through what we've been through, from deciding to run for office.'

Mapping the Millennium

Inside Out

Genetic Self-Portrait by Gary Schneider

Text by John Noble Wilford

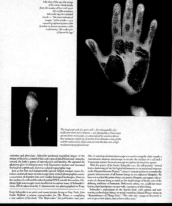

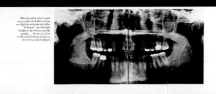

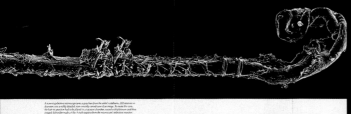

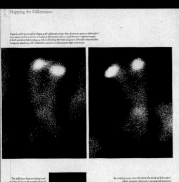

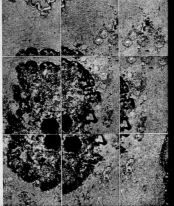

■ 455

PUBLICATION The New York Times Magazine
ART DIRECTORS Janet Froelich, Joele Cuyler
DESIGNERS Joele Cuyler, Ignacio Rodriguez
PHOTO EDITORS Kathy Ryan, Sarah Harbutt
PHOTOGRAPHER Gary Schneider
PUBLISHER The New York Times
ISSUE October 17, 1999
CATEGORY Reportage Story

■ 456

PUBLICATION The New York Times Magazine
ART DIRECTOR Janet Froelich
DESIGNER Claude Martel
PHOTO EDITOR Kathy Ryan
PHOTOGRAPHER Chuck Close
PUBLISHER The New York Times
ISSUE May 30, 1999
CATEGORY Portrait Story

photography ■ MERIT

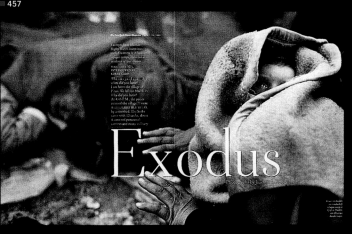

Exodus

Photographs by Joachim Ladefoged

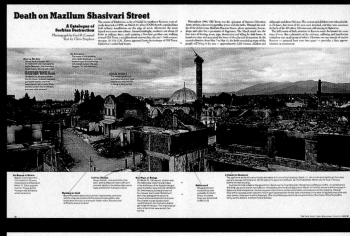

Death on Mazllum Shasivari Street

A Catalogue of Serbian Destruction

Photographs by Fred R. Conrad
Text by Chris Stephen

'We Know These Faces'
By Cynthia Ozick

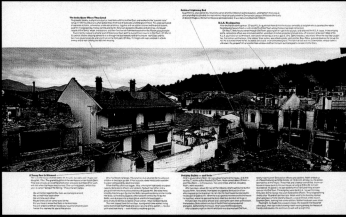

The country has spent the years since Communism spiraling downward. Who is to blame? That's becoming a highly charged question in American politics.
By John Lloyd
Photographs by Anthony Suau

The Russian Devolution

Going Domestic in Taipei

THE HUMAN HABITAT

Newlyweds relish setting up their first homes …

Photographs by Chien-Chi Chang
Text by Dennis Engbarth

W

Living Large in Poland

THE HUMAN HABITAT

… into full-fledged mansions.

Photographs by Tomasz Tomaszewski
Text by Mark Schapiro

T

Country Living in India

THE HUMAN HABITAT

A farmhouse isn't always a red-barn affair.

Photographs by Dilip Mehta
Text by Celia W. Dugger

T

Making the Most of It in Tennessee

THE HUMAN HABITAT

Creating a home …

Photographs by Mike Smith
Text by Mike Perry

A

'The Peony Pavilion' is finally coming to New York, and with it, China's blossoming star, Qian Yi.

Painting a Princess

Text by James R. Oestreich   Photographs by Andrew Eccles

If the opera is an international success, Qian hopes that the Shanghai Bureau of Culture will relent and let it tour China.

photography ■ MERIT

■ 460
PUBLICATION The New York Times Magazine
ART DIRECTOR Janet Froelich
DESIGNER Catherine Gilmore-Barnes
PHOTO EDITOR Kathy Ryan
PHOTOGRAPHERS Chien Chi Chang, Tomasz Tomaszewski, Dilip Mehta, Mike Smith
PUBLISHER The New York Times
ISSUE March 7, 1999
CATEGORY Reportage Story

■ 461
PUBLICATION The New York Times Magazine
ART DIRECTOR Janet Froelich
DESIGNER Catherine Gilmore-Barnes
PHOTO EDITOR Kathy Ryan
PHOTOGRAPHER Andrew Eccles
PUBLISHER The New York Times
ISSUE July 4, 1999
CATEGORY Portrait Story

The Aura
Of the Aura

JOEL-PETER WITKIN

THE PLAGUE YEARS
Decimation, via the Black Death and AIDS.

East Timor's Aftermath
A rare look at the faces and horrors of a deadly blood feud.

One militia member claims that high-ranking militiamen – the ones with guns – were given alcohol and a vial of liquid, which made them fearless and crazed.

Narrate
Or
Die   Why Scheherazade keeps on talking.

■ 462
PUBLICATION The New York Times Magazine
ART DIRECTOR Janet Froelich
DESIGNER Jennifer Gilman
PHOTO EDITOR Kathy Ryan
PHOTOGRAPHER Henry Leutwyler
PUBLISHER The New York Times
ISSUE June 27, 1999
CATEGORY Portrait Spread

■ 463
PUBLICATION The New York Times Magazine
ART DIRECTORS Janet Froelich, Joele Cuyler
DESIGNERS Joele Cuyler, Ignacio Rodriguez
PHOTO EDITORS Kathy Ryan, Sarah Harbutt
PHOTOGRAPHER Joel-Peter Witkin
PUBLISHER The New York Times
ISSUE September 19, 1999
CATEGORY Portrait Single Page

■ 464
PUBLICATION The New York Times Magazine
ART DIRECTOR Janet Froelich
DESIGNER Catherine Gilmore-Barnes
PHOTO EDITOR Kathy Ryan
PHOTOGRAPHER Philip Blenkinsop
PUBLISHER The New York Times
ISSUE October 24, 1999
CATEGORY Reportage Story

■ 465
PUBLICATION The New York Times Magazine
ART DIRECTORS Janet Froelich, Joele Cuyler
DESIGNERS Joele Cuyler, Ignacio Rodriguez
PHOTO EDITORS Kathy Ryan, Sarah Harbutt
PHOTOGRAPHER Dan Winters
PUBLISHER The New York Times
ISSUE April 18, 1999
CATEGORY Portrait Spread

Ten years after
the revolution,
Solidarity's key
strategist is
friends with his
old enemies
and enemies with
his old friends.

The Accommodations of Adam Michnik | BY ROGER COHEN

No one said
post-Communism
was going to be
easy.

Steve Martin, In Revision

How the Jerk became a man of letters. By RJ Smith

Photograph by NORMAN JEAN ROY

After the Fall

The former Enemy

Polish society has mostly benefited from the change in system.

Jerzy Urban

After the Fall

Victorious but Not Necessarily Content

The Dissidents

INTERVIEWS BY Franta Harris

PHOTOGRAPHS BY Rankin

'I didn't have illusions about a clean revolution.'

Laszlo Rajk | DISSIDENT

TRICKLE-DOWN CIVIL RIGHTS

WITH HIS WALL STREET PROJECT, JESSE JACKSON
IS FINDING THAT BIG BUSINESS IS EASIER TO MOVE THAN
THE DEMOCRATIC PARTY, SOUTHERN SHERIFFS OR
EVEN THE DECATUR, ILL., SCHOOL BOARD. BUT CAN HE
REALLY HELP THE WORKING POOR BY RUBBING
ELBOWS WITH C.E.O.'S?

BY GEORGE PACKER

PHOTOGRAPH BY NORMAN JEAN ROY

The Dissidents

You hear women saying that things are worse, but it isn't true.

Jirina Siklova | DISSIDENT, PH.D.

I see the Commies,
I see the clever guys
doing well.

Lech Walesa | POLAND

photography ■ MERIT

■ 466

PUBLICATION The New York Times Magazine
ART DIRECTOR Janet Froelich
DESIGNER Catherine Gilmore-Barnes
PHOTO EDITOR Kathy Ryan
PHOTOGRAPHERS Steve Pyke, Rankin
PUBLISHER The New York Times
ISSUE November 7, 1999
CATEGORY Portrait Story

■ 467

PUBLICATION The New York Times Magazine
ART DIRECTOR Janet Froelich
DESIGNER Catherine Gilmore-Barnes
PHOTO EDITOR Kathy Ryan
PHOTOGRAPHER Norman Jean Roy
PUBLISHER The New York Times
ISSUE August 8, 1999
CATEGORY Portrait Spread

■ 468

PUBLICATION The New York Times Magazine
ART DIRECTOR Janet Froelich
DESIGNER Joele Cuyler
PHOTO EDITOR Kathy Ryan
PHOTOGRAPHER Norman Jean Roy
PUBLISHER The New York Times
ISSUE December 12, 1999
CATEGORY Portrait Spread

cultural ties

"Afro-couture" is how editorial stylist Roberto Nardozzi describes his inspiration for this month's geometric styles. "African tribes always accessorize their hair in elaborate ways, the trick is knowing when to stop before the look becomes too costumey," says Nardozzi.

CLIP ART

EDITORIAL HAIRSTYLIST NICOLAS JURNJACK FULFILLS HIS LONG-STANDING DREAM OF TURNING HAIR CLIPPINGS FROM THE SALON FLOOR INTO ART WITH THE LOOKS ON THESE PAGES.
PHOTOGRAPHY BY DIDIER MALIGE

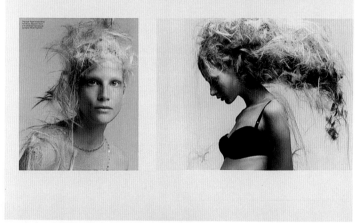

■ 469
PUBLICATION Salon News
DESIGN DIRECTOR Jean Griffin
ART DIRECTOR Victoria Maddocks
PHOTOGRAPHER Roberto D'Este
PUBLISHER Fairchild Publications
ISSUE July 1999
CATEGORY Fashion/Beauty Story

■ 470
PUBLICATION Salon News
DESIGN DIRECTOR Jean Griffin
ART DIRECTOR Martin Perrin
PHOTOGRAPHER Didier Milige
PUBLISHER Fairchild Publications
ISSUE October 1999
CATEGORY Fashion/Beauty Story

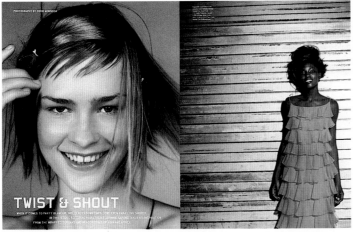

TWIST & SHOUT

beauty andthebeach

FOR EVERY SUMMER QUANDARY, THERE'S A CHIC, SIMPLE SOLUTION. BY SUZANNE B. GLEASON

fast food

BETTER THAN TAKEOUT,
THESE SUPER-EASY
SUPPERS ARE REAL
CONVENIENCE FOOD

Photographs by Mark Thomas

photography ■ MERIT

■ 471

PUBLICATION Salon News
DESIGN DIRECTOR Jean Griffin
ART DIRECTOR Martin Perrin
PHOTOGRAPHER Eddie Monsoon
PUBLISHER Fairchild Publications
ISSUE December 1999
CATEGORY Fashion/Beauty Story

■ 472

PUBLICATION Shape
CREATIVE DIRECTOR Kathy Nenneker
ART DIRECTOR Yvonne Duran
DESIGNER Lisa Leconte
PHOTO EDITOR Melissa O'Brien
PHOTOGRAPHER Fiorenzo Borghi
PUBLISHER Weider Publications, Inc
ISSUE May 1999
CATEGORY Fashion/Beauty Spread

■ 473

PUBLICATION Woman's Day
CREATIVE DIRECTOR Brad Pallas
ART DIRECTORS Kai-Ping Chao, Kenneth Nadel
DESIGNER Kai-Ping Chao
PHOTO EDITOR Keri Pampuch
PHOTOGRAPHER Mark Thomas
PUBLISHER Hachette Filipacchi Magazines, Inc.
ISSUE September 1999
CATEGORY Still Life/Interiors Spread

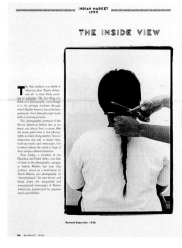

THE INSIDE VIEW

TOM FIELDS

THE TRAIL OF TEARS

ZIG
JACKSON

CENTER
OF ATTENTION

class of 99

This is not just a list of smart people, though many of the people profiled here are smart. These are not the greatest minds of our time or the ones who make the world spin on a different axis because of some greater selflessness or high concept of revolution. What they are is bright, funny and shrewd, wicked, weird and sometimes colossally dumb. In short, they are the internet—the best and worst of us. Here, *Shift* looks at the people and events that are shaping the net and defining its eccentricities
by Matthew McKinnon, Richard Bingham and Maryam Sanati

■ 474
PUBLICATION Santa Fean
ART DIRECTOR Paula Eastwood
DESIGNER Paula Eastwood
PHOTOGRAPHERS Tom Fields, Zig Jackson
ISSUE August 1999
CATEGORY Portrait Story

■ 475
PUBLICATION Walking
ART DIRECTOR Lisa A. Sergi
PHOTOGRAPHER Susie Cushner
PUBLISHER RD Publications, Inc.
ISSUE March/April 1999
CATEGORY Still Life/Interiors Spread

■ 476
PUBLICATION Shift
CREATIVE DIRECTOR Carmen Dunjko
ART DIRECTOR Malcolm Brown
DESIGNERS Carmen Dunjko, Malcolm Brown
PHOTO EDITOR Bree Seeley
PHOTOGRAPHER Chris Buck
PUBLISHER Normal Net Inc.
ISSUE November 1999
CATEGORY Photo Illustration

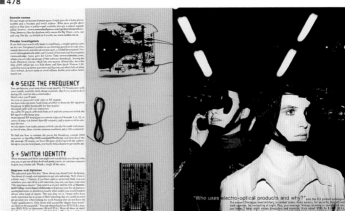

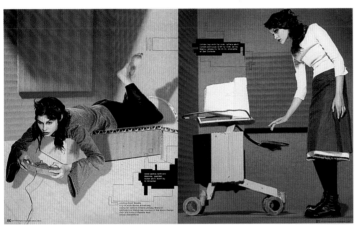

photography ■ MERIT

■ 477
PUBLICATION Shift
CREATIVE DIRECTOR Carmen Dunjko
ART DIRECTOR Malcolm Brown
DESIGNERS Carmen Dunjko, Christine Stephens, Malcolm Brown
PHOTO EDITOR Bree Seeley
PHOTOGRAPHER Chris Nicholls
PUBLISHER Normal Net Inc.
ISSUE September 1999
CATEGORY Photo Illustration

■ 478
PUBLICATION Shift
CREATIVE DIRECTOR Carmen Dunjko
ART DIRECTOR Malcolm Brown
DESIGNERS Carmen Dunjko, Malcolm Brown
PHOTO EDITOR Bree Seeley
PHOTOGRAPHERS Jerome Albertini, Sandy Nicholson
PUBLISHER Normal Net Inc.
ISSUE Summer 1999
CATEGORY Photo Illustration

■479
PUBLICATION Rolling Stone
ART DIRECTOR Fred Woodward
DESIGNER Siung Tjia
PHOTO EDITOR Rachel Knepfer
PHOTOGRAPHER David LaChapelle
PUBLISHER Straight Arrow Publishers
ISSUE January 15, 1999
CATEGORY Portrait Story

■480
PUBLICATION Rolling Stone
ART DIRECTOR Fred Woodward
DESIGNERS Fred Woodward,
Siung Tjia
PHOTO EDITOR Rachel Knepfer
PHOTOGRAPHER Mark Seliger
PUBLISHER Straight Arrow Publishers
ISSUE February 18, 1999
CATEGORY Portrait Spread

■481
PUBLICATION Rolling Stone
ART DIRECTOR Fred Woodward
DESIGNERS Fred Woodward,
Gail Anderson
PHOTO EDITOR Rachel Knepfer
PHOTOGRAPHER Mark Seliger
PUBLISHER Straight Arrow Publishers
ISSUE March 4, 1999
CATEGORY Portrait Spread

■482
PUBLICATION Rolling Stone
ART DIRECTOR Fred Woodward
DESIGNER Siung Tjia
PHOTO EDITOR Rachel Knepfer
PHOTOGRAPHER Mark Seliger
PUBLISHER Straight Arrow Publishers
ISSUE March 15, 1999
CATEGORY Portrait Spread

A Rising Tide of Tears

Who will safeguard the human rights and dignity of the 1.5 million displaced civilians of Kosovo? Who will lead them home?

Photographs by SEBASTIÃO SALGADO

{ Text by *Chuck Sudetic* }

ROLLING STONE, JUNE 24, 1999 · 49

THE TEARS OF THE MOTHERS, *the empty eyes of the young widows, the wood smoke of the camps, the children running barefoot through the spring mud – the world has witnessed these scenes before.*

'AN AFFRONT TO HUMANITY': *Milosevic's Operation Horseshoe has uprooted ninety percent of Kosovo's 1.7 million Albanians.*

■483
PUBLICATION Rolling Stone
ART DIRECTOR Fred Woodward
DESIGNERS Fred Woodward, Gail Anderson
PHOTO EDITOR Rachel Knepfer
PHOTOGRAPHER Sebastião Salgado
PUBLISHER Straight Arrow Publishers
ISSUE June 24, 1999
CATEGORY Reportage Story
    A MERIT Portrait Single Page

■484
PUBLICATION Rolling Stone
ART DIRECTOR Fred Woodward
DESIGNER Siung Tjia
PHOTO EDITOR Rachel Knepfer
PHOTOGRAPHERS Jean-Baptiste Mondino,
Fred Woodward, Martin Schoeller, Kurt Markus
PUBLISHER Straight Arrow Publishers
ISSUE June 10, 1999
CATEGORY Portrait Story
    A, B, C MERIT Portrait Spread

A Sadness *at the* Heart *of the* World

FORTY DAYS *with the endangered tribes of the Brazilian rain forest* ◀◀◀

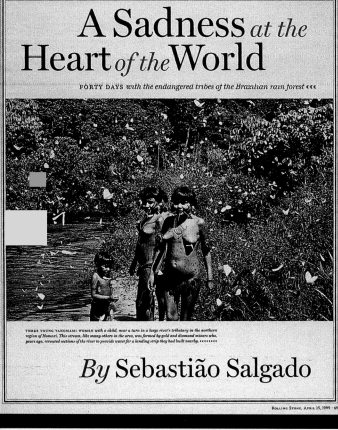

THREE YOUNG YANOMAMI WOMEN *with a child, near a turn in a large river's tributary in the northern region of Homozi. This stream, like many others in the area, was formed by gold and diamond miners who, years ago, rerouted sections of the river to provide water for a landing strip they had built nearby.* ◀◀◀◀◀◀◀

By Sebastião Salgado

ROLLING STONE, APRIL 15, 1999 · 69

ONE OF THE MOST POTENT SYMBOLS for the native tribes in the Amazon River valley, the most threatening omen that their way of life will soon disappear, is the road. Because once a road is set into the forest, once the lanes are surveyed, the trees cleared, the soil leveled and paved over, then come the trucks, the noise, the trash, the disease and, in the end, still-wider roads. And before the steam settles over the first freshly paved roads, the cultures of the indigenous people are forever altered. ◀ LAST FALL, I spent forty

THE YANOMAMI *look like a hybrid of the primitive and modern worlds. Girls wear banana-leaf bras with jeans; men who once went naked wear khaki shorts.* ◀◀◀

■ 485
PUBLICATION Rolling Stone
ART DIRECTOR Fred Woodward
DESIGNER Gail Anderson
PHOTO EDITOR Rachel Knepfer
PHOTOGRAPHER Sebastião Salgado
PUBLISHER Straight Arrow Publishers
ISSUE April 15, 1999
CATEGORY Reportage Story

BY FRED SCHRUERS

TOM PETTY
The Rolling Stone Interview

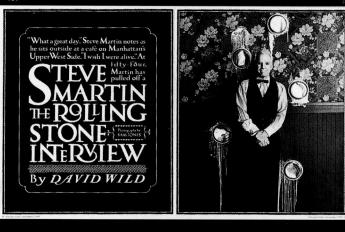

"What a great day," Steve Martin notes as he sits outside at a café on Manhattan's Upper West Side. "I wish I were alive." At fifty-four, Martin has pulled off a

STEVE MARTIN THE ROLLING STONE INTERVIEW

Photographs by SAM JONES

By DAVID WILD

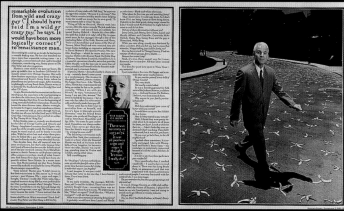

remarkable evolution from wild and crazy guy ◀ I should have said I'm a wild *or* crazy guy," he says. "It would have been more logically correct" to renaissance man.

■ 486
PUBLICATION Rolling Stone
ART DIRECTOR Fred Woodward
DESIGNERS Fred Woodward, Siung Tjia
PHOTO EDITOR Rachel Knepfer
PHOTOGRAPHER Kurt Markus
PUBLISHER Straight Arrow Publishers
ISSUE July 8, 1999
CATEGORY Portrait Spread

■ 487
PUBLICATION Rolling Stone
ART DIRECTOR Fred Woodward
DESIGNERS Fred Woodward, Gail Anderson
PHOTO EDITORS Rachel Knepfer, Fiona McDonagh
PHOTOGRAPHER Sam Jones
PUBLISHER Straight Arrow Publishers
ISSUE September 2, 1999
CATEGORY Portrait Story
A MERIT Portrait Spread

"ALL THE NEWS THAT FITS"

RS 811

CHANGIN' TIMES

"It's like seeing a black guy doing country & western, know what I'm saying?"

— Dr. Dre on Eminem

PHOTOGRAPH BY DAVID LACHAPELLE

ROLLING STONE, APRIL 29, 1999 · 15

A

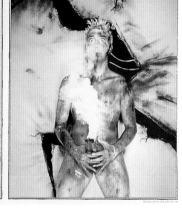

EMINEM BLOWS UP

BY ANTHONY BOZZA

PHOTOGRAPHS BY DAVID LACHAPELLE

By ERIKA FORTGANG

THE GIRL IN THE TREE

For a year and a half, JULIA BUTTERFLY has made her home twenty stories above ground in an endangered California redwood. Is she the new face of the environmental movement?

Photographs by Dan Winters

photographs by mark seliger

photography ■ MERIT

■ 488

PUBLICATION Rolling Stone
ART DIRECTOR Fred Woodward
DESIGNER Fred Woodward
PHOTO EDITOR Rachel Knepfer
PHOTOGRAPHER David LaChapelle
PUBLISHER Straight Arrow Publishers
ISSUE January 29, 1999
CATEGORY Portrait Story
    A MERIT Portrait Spread

■ 489

PUBLICATION Rolling Stone
ART DIRECTOR Fred Woodward
DESIGNERS Fred Woodward, Siung Tjia
PHOTO EDITOR Rachel Knepfer
PHOTOGRAPHER Dan Winters
PUBLISHER Straight Arrow Publishers
ISSUE July 8, 1999
CATEGORY Reportage Spread

■ 490

PUBLICATION Rolling Stone
ART DIRECTOR Fred Woodward
DESIGNER Siung Tjia
PHOTO EDITOR Rachel Knepfer
PHOTOGRAPHER Mark Seliger
PUBLISHER Straight Arrow Publishers
ISSUE September 2, 1999
CATEGORY Portrait Single Page

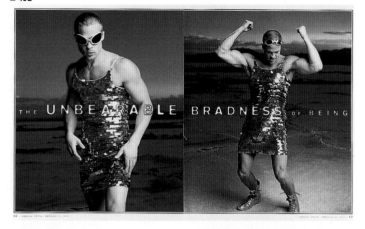

■ 491
PUBLICATION Rolling Stone
ART DIRECTOR Fred Woodward
DESIGNERS Fred Woodward, Gail Anderson
PHOTO EDITORS Rachel Knepfer, Fiona McDonagh
PHOTOGRAPHER Mark Seliger
PUBLISHER Straight Arrow Publishers
ISSUE October 14, 1999
CATEGORY Portrait Spread

■ 492
PUBLICATION Rolling Stone
ART DIRECTOR Fred Woodward
DESIGNERS Fred Woodward, Siung Tjia
PHOTO EDITOR Rachel Knepfer
PHOTOGRAPHER Mark Seliger
PUBLISHER Straight Arrow Publishers
ISSUE October 28, 1999
CATEGORY Portrait Spread

■ 493
PUBLICATION Rolling Stone
ART DIRECTOR Fred Woodward
DESIGNERS Fred Woodward, Siung Tjia
PHOTO EDITOR Rachel Knepfer
PHOTOGRAPHER Mark Seliger
PUBLISHER Straight Arrow Publishers
ISSUE October 28, 1999
CATEGORY Portrait Spread

■ 494
PUBLICATION Rolling Stone
ART DIRECTOR Fred Woodward
DESIGNERS Fred Woodward, Ken DeLago
PHOTO EDITOR Rachel Knepfer
PHOTOGRAPHER Kurt Markus
PUBLISHER Straight Arrow Publishers
ISSUE November 11, 1999
CCATEGORY Portrait Story
    A **MERIT** Portrait Spread

SON OF A PREACHER MAN

Meet Jay Bakker, son of Jim and Tammy Faye. His dad preached prosperity. His preaches punk rock. His mom wore too much eyeliner. So has he.

By Katherine Marsh
Photographed by Mary Ellen Mark

Above: Father and son, July '99. Below: Tammy Faye, Jay, Jim and Tammy Sue, circa 1985.

Nice & Naughty
By David Lipsky

Christina Ricci takes on her image as an angry, fun, hazardously sexy teen who will say anything

"On her anorexia: "I wanted people to take care of me. I loved it when I got skinny enough to bug stuff in the publicist's section."

495

PUBLICATION Rolling Stone
ART DIRECTOR Fred Woodward
DESIGNERS Fred Woodward, Gail Anderson
PHOTO EDITOR Rachel Knepfer
PHOTOGRAPHER Peggy Sirota
PUBLISHER Straight Arrow Publishers
ISSUE December 9, 1999
CATEGORY Portrait Story
MERIT Portrait Spread

496

PUBLICATION Rolling Stone
ART DIRECTOR Fred Woodward
DESIGNER Siung Tjia
PHOTO EDITOR Rachel Knepfer
PHOTOGRAPHER Mary Ellen Mark
PUBLISHER Straight Arrow Publishers
ISSUE September 16, 1999
CATEGORY Portrait Story
MERIT Portrait Spread

photography ■ MERIT

By Mim Udovitch

THE DEVIL IN MISS JOLIE

Hollywood's next great bombshell is the tattooed love goddess known as Angelina Jolie. She's played vixens, temptresses and a doomed, drug-addicted supermodel. And for some reason, people think she's dark

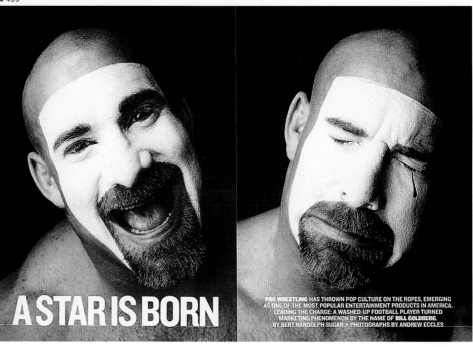

A STAR IS BORN

PRO WRESTLING HAS THROWN POP CULTURE ON THE ROPES, EMERGING AS ONE OF THE MOST POPULAR ENTERTAINMENT PRODUCTS IN AMERICA. LEADING THE CHARGE: A WASHED-UP FOOTBALL PLAYER TURNED MARKETING PHENOMENON BY THE NAME OF BILL GOLDBERG. BY BERT RANDOLPH SUGAR • PHOTOGRAPHS BY ANDREW ECCLES

■ 497

PUBLICATION Rolling Stone
ART DIRECTOR Fred Woodward
DESIGNER Siung Tjia
PHOTO EDITOR Rachel Knepfer
PHOTOGRAPHER Mark Seliger
PUBLISHER Straight Arrow Publishers
ISSUE August 19, 1999
CATEGORY Portrait Spread

■ 498

PUBLICATION Rolling Stone
ART DIRECTOR Fred Woodward
DESIGNER Fred Woodward
PHOTO EDITOR Rachel Knepfer
PHOTOGRAPHER Mary Ellen Mark
PUBLISHER Straight Arrow Publishers
ISSUE February 18, 1999
CATEGORY Portrait Story

■ 499

PUBLICATION P.O.V.
DESIGN DIRECTOR Florian Bachleda
DESIGNERS Florian Bachleda, Pino Impastato
PHOTOGRAPHER Andrew Eccles
PUBLISHER B.Y.O.B./Freedom Ventures, Inc.
ISSUE May 1999
CATEGORY Portrait Spread

■ 500

Charles Schwab
THE OLD BOY NETWORK

They're retired, they're stock-obsessed, and they're turning discount brokers' offices into geriatric clubhouses. Don't these guys have anything better to do? (Uh, no.)
BY STEPHEN THOMAS

PHOTOGRAPHS BY JASON SCHMIDT

JACK POMERANTZ USED TO CARRY A BEEPER AND A PHONE. HE DOESN'T NEED THEM ANYMORE. 'I KNOW WHERE TO FIND HIM,' SAYS HIS WIFE.

AT ONE WATERHOUSE OFFICE, REGULARS WERE LUNCHING IN THE LOUNGE AND GETTING PERSONAL CALLS ROUTED THROUGH THE MAIN SWITCHBOARD; A CHIROPRACTOR EVEN HELD DE FACTO OFFICE HOURS.

■ 501

IT'S LONELY AT THE BOTTOM

THE DISMAL MARKET FOR SMALL-CAP STOCKS ISN'T JUST HURTING PORTFOLIOS — IT'S TAKING A HUMAN TOLL AS WELL.

BY KEN BROWN, ROGER LOWENSTEIN AND LANDON THOMAS JR.

PHOTOGRAPH BY ANTONIN KRATOCHVIL

■ 502

1,000 WORDS

Swing's the Thing

■ 503

by Beth Weinhouse

10
simple steps for a healthier new year

RESOLUTIONS THAT YOUR WHOLE FAMILY WILL FIND EASY TO MAKE—AND KEEP

PHOTOGRAPHS BY NOLA LOPEZ

■ 500

PUBLICATION SmartMoney
ART DIRECTOR Amy Rosenfeld
DESIGNER Donna Agajanian
PHOTO EDITORS Alison Morley, Jamie Watts
PHOTOGRAPHER Jason Schmidt
PUBLISHER Dow Jones & Hearst Corp.
ISSUE May 1999
CATEGORY Portrait Story

■ 501

PUBLICATION SmartMoney
ART DIRECTOR Amy Rosenfeld
DESIGNER Donna Agajanian
PHOTO EDITORS Alison Morley, Jamie Watts
PHOTOGRAPHER Antonin Kratochvil
PUBLISHER Dow Jones & Hearst Corp.
ISSUE May 1999
CATEGORY Portrait Spread

■ 502

PUBLICATION Stanford
ART DIRECTOR Bambi Nicklen
PHOTOGRAPHER Glenn Matsumuva
PUBLISHER Stanford University
ISSUE March/April 1999
CATEGORY Reportage Spread

■ 503

PUBLICATION Target the Family
CREATIVE DIRECTOR Terry Ross Koppel
ART DIRECTOR Hitomi Sato
DESIGNER Jennifer Muller
PHOTO EDITOR Maya Kaimal
PHOTOGRAPHER Nola Lopez
PUBLISHER Time Inc. Custom Publishing
ISSUE Winter 1999
CATEGORY Fashion/Beauty Spread

■ 504

Leading Off

Shaqqing Up

■ 505

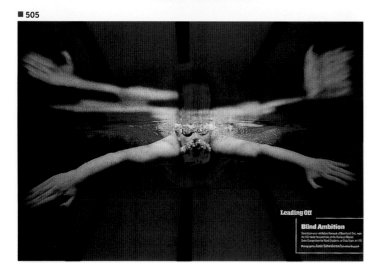

Leading Off

Blind Ambition

■ 506

Leading Off

Eye Drop

■ 507

■ 504
PUBLICATION Sports Illustrated
CREATIVE DIRECTOR Steven Hoffman
DESIGNER Jodi L. Napolitani
PHOTOGRAPHER John W. McDonough
PUBLISHER Time Inc.
ISSUE March 1, 1999
CATEGORY Reportage Spread

■ 505
PUBLICATION Sports Illustrated
CREATIVE DIRECTOR Steven Hoffman
DESIGNER Jodi L. Napolitani
PHOTOGRAPHER Jamie Schwaterow
PUBLISHER Time Inc.
ISSUE May 3, 1999
CATEGORY Reportage Spread

■ 506
PUBLICATION Sports Illustrated
CREATIVE DIRECTOR Steven Hoffman
DESIGNER Jodi L. Napolitani
PHOTOGRAPHER Bob Martin
PUBLISHER Time Inc.
ISSUE June 14, 1999
CATEGORY Reportage Spread

■ 507
PUBLICATION Sports Illustrated
CREATIVE DIRECTOR Steven Hoffman
DESIGNER Devin Pedzwater
PHOTOGRAPHERS Hy Peskin,
Walter Ioss Jr., Chris Cole,
Ronald Modra
PUBLISHER Time Inc.
ISSUE July 26, 1999
CATEGORY Reportage Story

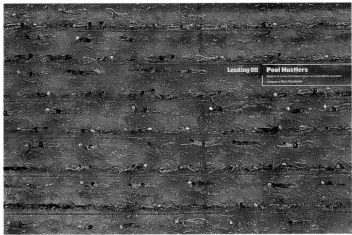

NOVEMBER 14,
1998 No flag was thrown on this tackle of Nebraska's Eric Crouch by Kansas State's Travis Ochs.

PHOTOGRAPH BY
CRAIG HACKER

photography ■ MERIT

■ 508
PUBLICATION Sports Illustrated
CREATIVE DIRECTOR Steven Hoffman
DESIGNER Al Young
PHOTOGRAPHER Heinz Kluetmeier
PUBLISHER Time Inc.
ISSUE August 16, 1999
CATEGORY Reportage Spread

■ 509
PUBLICATION Sports Illustrated
CREATIVE DIRECTOR Steven Hoffman
DESIGNER Al Young
PHOTOGRAPHER Jeff Burke
PUBLISHER Time Inc.
ISSUE November 29, 1999
CATEGORY Reportage Spread

■ 510
PUBLICATION Sports Illustrated
CREATIVE DIRECTOR Steven Hoffman
DESIGNER Devin Pedzwater
PHOTOGRAPHER Sam Forencich
PUBLISHER Time Inc.
ISSUE July 26, 1999
CATEGORY Reportage Spread

■ 511
PUBLICATION Sports Illustrated
CREATIVE DIRECTOR Steven Hoffman
DESIGNER Devin Pedzwater
PHOTOGRAPHER Craig Hacker
PUBLISHER Time Inc.
ISSUE July 26, 1999
CATEGORY Reportage Single Page

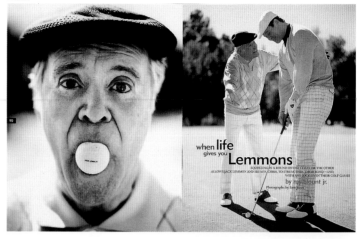

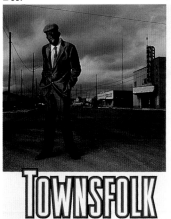

TOWNSFOLK

A TAVERN KEEPER IN VAN HORN, THE BIRDMAN OF PORT O'CONNOR:
FIFTEEN TEXANS WHO GIVE THEIR COMMUNITY ITS CHARACTER.

PHOTOGRAPHS BY MICHAEL O'BRIEN

Photographs by Charles Ommanney

His First Steps

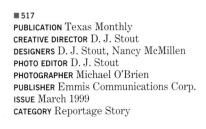

■ 517
PUBLICATION Texas Monthly
CREATIVE DIRECTOR D. J. Stout
DESIGNERS D. J. Stout, Nancy McMillen
PHOTO EDITOR D. J. Stout
PHOTOGRAPHER Michael O'Brien
PUBLISHER Emmis Communications Corp.
ISSUE March 1999
CATEGORY Reportage Story

■ 518
PUBLICATION Texas Monthly
CREATIVE DIRECTOR D. J. Stout
DESIGNERS D. J. Stout, Nancy McMillen
PHOTO EDITOR D. J. Stout
PHOTOGRAPHER Charles Ommanney
PUBLISHER Emmis Communications Corp.
ISSUE June 1999
CATEGORY Reportage Story

photography ■ MERIT

AL
PACINO

AT THE PLANT

US REPORT

LITTLE BIG MAN

For someone who has sued his parents and gone from star to security guard, former 'Diff'rent Strokes' kid Gary Coleman seems surprisingly at peace

■ 519
PUBLICATION Us
ART DIRECTOR Rina Migliaccio
DESIGNER Joshua Liberson
PHOTO EDITOR Jennifer Crandall
PHOTOGRAPHER Mark Seliger
PUBLISHER Us Magazine Co., L.P.
ISSUE December 1999
CATEGORY Portrait Spread

■ 520
PUBLICATION Us
ART DIRECTOR Richard Baker
DESIGNER Peter Cury
PHOTO EDITOR Jennifer Crandall
PHOTOGRAPHER Len Irish
PUBLISHER Us Magazine Co., L.P.
ISSUE February 1999
CATEGORY Portrait Spread

■ 521
PUBLICATION Us
ART DIRECTOR Rina Migliaccio
DESIGNER Rina Migliaccio
PHOTO EDITOR Jennifer Crandall
PHOTOGRAPHER Geof Kern
PUBLISHER Us Magazine Co., L.P.
ISSUE September 1999
CATEGORY Fashion/Beauty Story

■ 522
PUBLICATION Us
ART DIRECTOR Richard Baker
DESIGNER Rina Migliaccio
PHOTO EDITOR Jennifer Crandall
PHOTOGRAPHER Sam Jones
PUBLISHER Us Magazine Co., L.P.
ISSUE January 1999
CATEGORY Portrait Spread

■ 523
PUBLICATION The Village Voice
DESIGN DIRECTOR Ted Keller
ART DIRECTOR Minh Uong
DESIGNER Stacy Wakefield
PHOTO EDITOR Meg Handler
PHOTOGRAPHER Andrew Lichtenstein
PUBLISHER VV Publishing Corp.
ISSUE October 12, 1999
CATEGORY Reportage Spread

■ 524
PUBLICATION Working Woman
CREATIVE DIRECTOR Heidi Volpe
ART DIRECTOR Greg Concha
DESIGNER Heidi Volpe
PHOTO EDITOR Martha Maristany
PHOTOGRAPHER David Michael Kennedy
PUBLISHER Working Woman Network.com
ISSUE October 1999
CATEGORY Portrait Spread

■ 525
PUBLICATION Premiere
ART DIRECTOR Richard Baker
DESIGNER Chalkley Calderwood Pratt
PHOTO EDITOR Nancy Jo Iacoi
PHOTOGRAPHER Chris Buck
PUBLISHER Hachette Filipacchi Magazines, Inc.
ISSUE October 1999
CATEGORY Portrait Spread

■ 526
PUBLICATION President's Choice Magazine
ART DIRECTOR Carol Moskot
DESIGNER Carol Moskot
PHOTOGRAPHER Colin Faulkner
ISSUE March 1999
CATEGORY Still Life/Interiors Spread

photography ■ MERIT

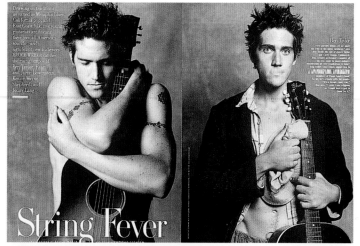

String Fever

"I've lost my voice a couple times now," says Jonny Lang. "I'm not as young as I used to be."

■ 527
PUBLICATION Vanity Fair
DESIGN DIRECTOR David Harris
ART DIRECTOR Gregory Mastrianni
PHOTO EDITORS Susan White, Lisa Berman, Abby Moskowitz
PHOTOGRAPHER Bruce Weber
PUBLISHER Condé Nast Publications, Inc.
ISSUE January 1999
CATEGORY Portrait Story

■ 528
PUBLICATION Vanity Fair
DESIGN DIRECTOR David Harris
ART DIRECTOR Gregory Mastrianni
PHOTO EDITORS Susan White, Lisa Berman
PHOTOGRAPHER Annie Leibovitz
PUBLISHER Condé Nast Publications, Inc.
ISSUE April 1999
CATEGORY Portrait Spread

■ 529
PUBLICATION Vanity Fair
DESIGN DIRECTOR David Harris
ART DIRECTOR Gregory Mastrianni
PHOTO EDITORS Susan White, Lisa Berman, SunHee Grinnell
PHOTOGRAPHER Michael O'Neill
PUBLISHER Condé Nast Publications, Inc.
ISSUE April 1999
CATEGORY Portrait Spread

■ 530
PUBLICATION Vanity Fair
DESIGN DIRECTOR David Harris
ART DIRECTOR Gregory Mastrianni
PHOTO EDITORS Susan White, Lisa Berman, Kathyrn MacLeod
PHOTOGRAPHER Annie Leibovitz
PUBLISHER Condé Nast Publications, Inc.
ISSUE April 1999
CATEGORY Portrait Spread

Through the Stardust

Return from Planet Pee-wee

photography ■ MERIT

■ 531
PUBLICATION Vanity Fair
DESIGN DIRECTOR David Harris
ART DIRECTOR Gregory Mastrianni
PHOTO EDITORS Susan White, Lisa Berman, Ron Beinner
PHOTOGRAPHER David LaChapelle
PUBLISHER Condé Nast Publications, Inc.
ISSUE April 1999
CATEGORY Portrait Spread

■ 532
PUBLICATION Vanity Fair
DESIGN DIRECTOR David Harris
ART DIRECTOR Gregory Mastrianni
PHOTO EDITORS Susan White, Lisa Berman, Ron Beinner
PHOTOGRAPHER David LaChapelle
PUBLISHER Condé Nast Publications, Inc.
ISSUE September 1999
CATEGORY Portrait Story

■ 533
PUBLICATION Vanity Fair
DESIGN DIRECTOR David Harris
ART DIRECTOR Gregory Mastrianni
PHOTO EDITORS Susan White, Lisa Berman, Jeannie Rhodes,
Geraldine Agoncillo, Kathryn MacLeod
PHOTOGRAPHER Annie Leibovitz
PUBLISHER Condé Nast Publications, Inc.
ISSUE May 1999
CATEGORY Portrait Story

■ 534
PUBLICATION Vanity Fair
DESIGN DIRECTOR David Harris
ART DIRECTOR Gregory Mastrianni
PHOTO EDITORS Susan White, Lisa Berman, Ron Beinner
PHOTOGRAPHER David LaChapelle
PUBLISHER Condé Nast Publications, Inc.
ISSUE December 1999
CATEGORY Portrait Spread

Canoodling with Julia

"I don't think I realized that the cost of fame is that it's open season on *every moment* of your life."

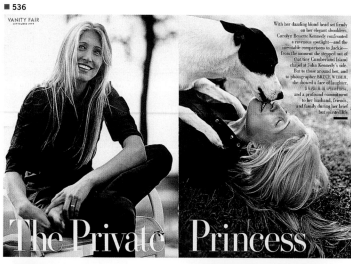

The Private Princess

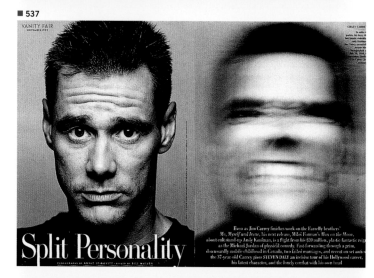

Split Personality

"It's a wonderful thing to get an Oscar. But I really don't like the idea of kissing people to get it."

■ 535
PUBLICATION Vanity Fair
DESIGN DIRECTOR David Harris
ART DIRECTOR Gregory Mastrianni
PHOTO EDITORS Susan White, Lisa Berman, SunHee Grinnell
PHOTOGRAPHER Mario Testino
PUBLISHER Condé Nast Publications, Inc.
ISSUE June 1999
CATEGORY Portrait Story

■ 536
PUBLICATION Vanity Fair
DESIGN DIRECTOR David Harris
ART DIRECTOR Gregory Mastrianni
PHOTO EDITORS Susan White, Lisa Berman, Jeannie Rhodes
PHOTOGRAPHER Bruce Weber
PUBLISHER Condé Nast Publications, Inc.
ISSUE September 1999
CATEGORY Portrait Story

■ 537
PUBLICATION Vanity Fair
DESIGN DIRECTOR David Harris
ART DIRECTOR Gregory Mastrianni
PHOTO EDITORS Susan White, Lisa Berman, Geraldine Agoncillo, Kathryn MacLeod
PHOTOGRAPHER Annie Leibovitz
PUBLISHER Condé Nast Publications, Inc.
ISSUE November 1999
CATEGORY Portrait Story

■ 538
PUBLICATION Vanity Fair
DESIGN DIRECTOR David Harris
ART DIRECTOR Gregory Mastrianni
PHOTO EDITORS Susan White, Lisa Berman,
SunHee Grinnell, Kathryn MacLeod
PHOTOGRAPHER Annie Leibovitz
PUBLISHER Condé Nast Publications, Inc.
ISSUE December 1999
CATEGORY Portrait Spread

■ 539
PUBLICATION Vanity Fair
DESIGN DIRECTOR David Harris
ART DIRECTOR Gregory Mastrianni
PHOTO EDITORS Susan White, Lisa Berman,
SunHee Grinnell, Kathryn MacLeod
PHOTOGRAPHER Annie Leibovitz
PUBLISHER Condé Nast Publications, Inc.
ISSUE December 1999

■ 540
PUBLICATION Vanity Fair
DESIGN DIRECTOR David Harris
ART DIRECTOR Gregory Mastrianni
PHOTO EDITORS Susan White, Lisa Berman, Jeannie Rhodes
PHOTOGRAPHER Annie Leibovitz
PUBLISHER Condé Nast Publications, Inc.
ISSUE October 1999
CATEGORY Portrait Single Page

■ 541
PUBLICATION Vanity Fair
DESIGN DIRECTOR David Harris
ART DIRECTOR Gregory Mastrianni
PHOTO EDITORS Susan White, Lisa Berman,
Geraldine Agoncillo, Kathryn MacLeod
PHOTOGRAPHER Annie Leibovitz
PUBLISHER Condé Nast Publications, Inc.
ISSUE July 1999
CATEGORY Portrait Single Page

MOTHER COURAGE

Jerry Hall and her and
Mick Jagger's
son Gabriel, photographed on
November 23, 1998,
for Annie Leibovitz's new
book, Women.

photography ■ MERIT

THE DEUCE
Photographs taken by William Butterworth and Andrew Garn in New York City, 1979–85.
Text by Guy Gonzales

Once upon a time, N.Y.C.'s 42nd Street was the only place to lose the ill-street blues—but those days are gone. One sex-industry survivor takes a nostalgic look back at the G-stringed gyrations of a lost generation.

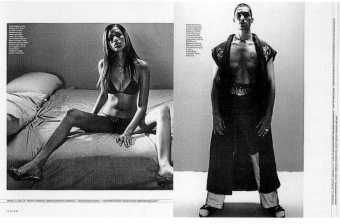

■ 542
PUBLICATION Vibe
DESIGN DIRECTOR Dwayne Shaw
PHOTO EDITOR George Pitts
PHOTOGRAPHERS William Butterworth, Andrew Garn
PUBLISHER Miller Publishing Group
ISSUE April 1999
CATEGORY Reportage Story

■ 543
PUBLICATION Vibe
ART DIRECTOR Brandon Kavulla
DESIGNER Brandon Kavulla
PHOTO EDITOR George Pitts
PHOTOGRAPHER Marc Baptiste
PUBLISHER Miller Publishing Group
ISSUE August 1999
CATEGORY Fashion/Beauty Story

the PROFESSIONAL

WRITER. SINGER. PRODUCER. ARRANGER. PLAYER. BRIAN MCKNIGHT IS A MUSICIAN'S MUSICIAN. SO AMY *LINDEN* HAS TO WONDER, WHY DOES THIS HIGHLY TRAINED MASTER AT HIS CRAFT LIKE BARRY MANILOW SO MUCH?

PHOTOGRAPHED BY ROBERT MAXWELL AUGUST 17, 1999, CHELSEA, NEW YORK CITY

MCKNIGHT SMILES EAR-TO-EAR, BASKING IN BIG '80S MEMORIES OF THE COWBOY-HATTED LEAD GUITARIST. "THAT'S WHAT I'M SAYING, RICHIE SAMBORA ON TOP OF THE MOUNTAIN, KILLING IT! BRINGS OUT THE WHITE BOY IN ME!"

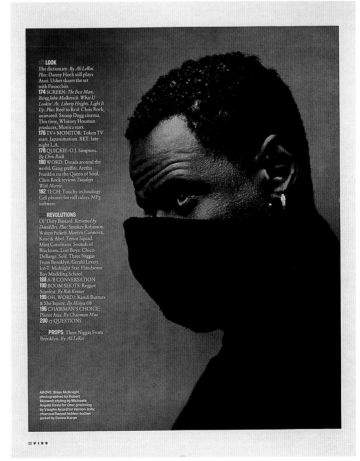

LOOK
The dictionary. By Ali LeRoi.
Plus: Danny Hoch still plays
Atari. Usher shares the set
with Pinocchio.
174 SCREEN: The Best Man.
Being John Malkovich. What U
Lookin' At. Liberty Heights. Light It
Up. Plus: Reel to Real: Chris Rock,
animated. Snoop Dogg cinema.
This time, Whitney Houston
produces, Monica stars.
176 TV+ MONITOR: Token TV
stars. Japanimation. BET: late-
night L.A.
178 QUICKIE: O.J. Simpson.
By Chris Rock
180 WORD: Dreads around the
world. Gang graffiti. Aretha
Franklin on the Queen of Soul.
Chris Rock reviews Tuesdays
With Morrie.
182 TECH: Touchy technology.
Cell phones for ruff riders. MP3
software.

REVOLUTIONS
Ol' Dirty Bastard. Reviewed by
David Bry. Plus: Smokey Robinson.
Wilson Pickett. Marilyn Cannova.
Kane & Abel. Terror Squad.
Mint Condition. Sounds of
Blackness. Lost Boyz. Chico
DeBarge. Solé. Three Niggas
From Brooklyn. Gerald Levert.
Ice-T. Midnight Star. Handsome
Boy Modeling School.
188 A/B CONVERSATION
190 BOOM SHOTS: Reggae.
Sunfest. By Rob Kenner.
195 OH, WORD!: Kandi Burruss
& She'kspere. By Minya Oh
196 CHAIRMAN'S CHOICE:
Planet Asia. By Chairman Mao
200 17 QUESTIONS

PROPS: Three Niggas From
Brooklyn. By Ali LeRoi.

ABOVE: Brian McKnight photographed by Robert Maxwell; styling by Michaela Angela Davis for One; grooming by Vaughn Acord for Vernon Jolly; charcoal flannel hidden-button jacket by Donna Karan.

32 VIBE

■ 544
PUBLICATION Vibe
ART DIRECTOR Brandon Kavulla
DESIGNER Meegan Barnes
PHOTO EDITOR George Pitts
PHOTOGRAPHER Alexei Hay
PUBLISHER Miller Publishing Group
ISSUE August 1999
CATEGORY Fashion/Beauty Story

■ 545
PUBLICATION Vibe
DESIGN DIRECTOR Robert Newman
PHOTO EDITOR George Pitts
PHOTOGRAPHER Robert Maxwell
PUBLISHER Miller Publishing Group
ISSUE November 1999
CATEGORY Portrait Story

photography ■ MERIT

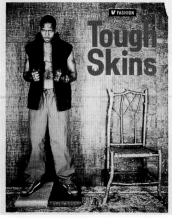

Tough Skins

What's the sexiest look for fall? Men in fur. Here, eight cool cats show off the hottest trend for the casually chic next century.

THE GYP SIES

The ultimate urban bohemians at home in their gypsy camp in Milan. They dress fresh in handwoven and quilted clothing, live off the land, travel in packs of family and friends. They always keep it moving.

■ 546
PUBLICATION Vibe
DESIGN DIRECTOR Robert Newman
PHOTO EDITOR George Pitts
PHOTOGRAPHER Barron Claiborne
PUBLISHER Miller Publishing Group
ISSUE December 1999
CATEGORY Fashion/Beauty Story

■ 547
PUBLICATION Vibe
DESIGN DIRECTOR Robert Newman
DESIGNER Robert Newman
PHOTO EDITOR George Pitts
PHOTOGRAPHER Davide Cernuschi
PUBLISHER Miller Publishing Group
ISSUE November 1999
CATEGORY Fashion/Beauty Story

illustration

N E V E R   S A Y   D I E

THIRTEEN YEARS AGO, a prominent UCLA gerontologist named Roy Walford was invited to appear on *Good Morning America.* One of the nation's leading experts on "caloric restriction," the only anti-aging theory that had been proven to increase longevity in mammals, Walford had just written a book called *The 120-Year Diet,* which detailed how decades of research on habitually underfed lab animals could be applied to humans.

As it happened, the guest who preceded him on the show that day was Shirley Mac-Laine, who was promoting her latest daffy memoir. Observing the friendly, attentive way in which his hosts discussed the actress's encounters with reincarnated spirits—"They didn't question her in depth and swallowed everything she said," Walford recalls—the esteemed scientist figured he had nothing to fear. But once he settled into a chair opposite Charles Gibson, Walford found himself fielding spitballs instead of softballs.

"Because I had a book about life extension, they simply couldn't believe it, or me," Walford says. "They thought I was a quack or something, that you really couldn't maintain that anybody could live that long."

What a difference a new millennium makes. As Los Angeles stares down the barrel of the 21st century, the news bubbling

With millions of baby boomers expected to live into their 90s in the coming century—the under-30 crowd could routinely break 100—how will a city as youth-obsessed as L.A. cope? Will "80 is the new 70" be the new catch phrase? Will Tom Ford design muumuus? Will CBS be hip? One thing's for sure: With nobody getting any younger, getting old is bound to get chic

BY LISA LEFF

ILLUSTRATIONS BY BRIAN CRONIN

FEBRUARY 25 1964

CASSIUS CLAY BEATS SONNY LISTON

A Lot More Than Lip Service

by Richard Hoffer
illustration by Owen Smith

HE'D HAVE better fights, create greater spectacle, make more history, practice another religion, have another name, become a so-called traitor to his country, transform himself into its conscience and light an Olympic torch. So there was a lot more news in him than this. But in February 1964, when he was 22, Cassius Clay helped set the tone for a decade (at least) when he toppled Sonny Liston in one of sport's most important upsets.

Maybe the '60s would have been tumultuous without Clay's wild personality. Probably the times, they were a-changin' anyway. But give Clay—later Muhammad Ali, of course—credit for being a magical character who in the course of a spectacular boxing career somehow made us reconsider politics, war, race and religion. Poetry, too.

The spell in which he held us was cast that night in Miami Beach, when he dared challenge Liston, an unsavory personality but the establishment nonetheless. Clay, despite his Olympic gold in 1960 and his obvious charisma, was a huge underdog. Liston, the champion after a couple of unsettling knockouts of Floyd Patterson, was considered indomitable. He fit in with America's principal value at the time: Bigger is better. He was a 9-to-1 favorite at one point and the expert opinion was that the ringside physician had better have some postmortem experience.

Clay talked the talk, then fought the fight, delivering a six-round pounding to the supposedly invincible Liston.

1918 SEPTEMBER 11

THE RED SOX WIN THE WORLD SERIES

A Bird's-eye View in Beantown

by Leigh Montville
Illustration by Kadir Nelson

OCTOBER 7 1945

DON HUTSON STARS FOR THE PACKERS

A Talent Ahead of His Time

by Peter King
Illustration by Roberto Parada

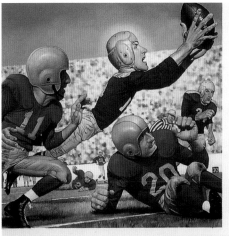

AUGUST 1-9 1936

JESSE OWENS DOMINATES THE BERLIN OLYMPICS

Flying in the Face of the Führer

by Phil Taylor
Illustration by C.F. Payne

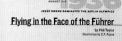

■ 549
PUBLICATION Sports Illustrated
CREATIVE DIRECTOR Steven Hoffman
DESIGNER Linda Root
ILLUSTRATORS Owen Smith, Kadir Nelson, Roberto Parada, C. F. Payne
PUBLISHER Time Inc.
ISSUE November 29, 1999
CATEGORY Story

illustration ■ SILVER

213

Movies

By Owen Gleiberman

1 Movie of the Year

Man on the Moon

Comedian, mass-media joker, walking personality crisis: Andy Kaufman was all of these things, and the joy of *Man on the Moon* is the way that screenwriters Scott Alexander and Larry Karaszewski and director Milos Forman transform Kaufman's dance of life and performance into a dizzying and maniacally funny celebration of American showbiz. Jim Carrey's eerie, virtuosic impersonation doesn't tell us who Kaufman was inside, exactly, yet it captures the delirious thrill he took in making every moment a charade, perpetually playing someone else in order to play with your head. He was Latka Gravas and Elvis Presley, wanton woman wrestler and man on the moon—a sweet, spectral nerd forever split off from his scabrous, lounge-demon id, Tony Clifton. With a couple of decades' hindsight, the movie reassembles Kaufman into a cracked prophet of the Entertainment Age, a wild-man prankster who created his own form of hocus-pocus guerrilla theater. The teasing upshot is that only someone who was *this* disconnected, this much of a stranger even to himself, could have gone to such fearless and demented lengths to connect with an audience. In its celebration of Andy Kaufman's obsessive desire to burst the fourth wall, to leave you laughing with your jaw on the floor, *Man on the Moon*, more than *The Truman Show* or *Being John Malkovich*, emerges as a great, exhilarating fable for the era of virtual identity.

illustration by Mark Ulriksen

2 TOPSY-TURVY
Miraculously, Mike Leigh's merry, haunting, ebullient epic about Gilbert and Sullivan seems to wipe away every period piece you've seen. It's as if you'd climbed into a time machine and landed in the hidden heart of Victorian London, a world of civilized high spirits in which the courtliness of even the most trivial encounter becomes at once delectable and deeply enigmatic—a playful cover for the sensuality beneath. (Here, it's the mind and body that are topsy-turvy.) The film understands that William S. Gilbert (Jim Broadbent), the dour clockwork lyricist, trapped in his mathematical absurdism, and Sir Arthur Sullivan (Allan Corduner), the blissed-out composer-conductor imp, weren't creating high art. But as it follows a crucial moment late in their careers, when the famous duo part ways, reunite, and then—in what may be the most intimate and rapturous backstage theater chronicle ever filmed—create and stage *The Mikado*, the movie becomes a transcendent celebration of the English soul, of a lost empire founded on the beauty of order.

3 BOYS DON'T CRY
What made Teena Brandon, a wayward loner drifting through rural Nebraska in the early '90s, want to pass herself off as a rough-and-tumble young man named Brandon Teena? The answer is assuredly "psychosexual," but the galvanizing power of Kimberly Peirce's starkly lyrical first feature is that it dramatizes this daredevil role reversal in the American badlands as a blind quest for freedom—as the story of a girl driven to own a boy's experience in a man's world. The extraordinary

ENTERTAINMENT WEEKLY 117

Music

By David Browne

1 Album of the Year

The Ego Has Landed

Robbie Williams (Capitol)

illustration by Edmund Guy

Video

By Ty Burr

1 Video of the Year

The Wizard of Oz DVD

(Warner, G)

Internet

By Noah Robischon

1 Phenom of the Year

Digital Music

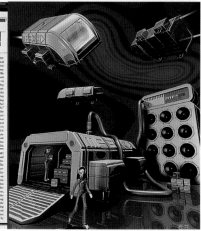

■ 550

PUBLICATION Entertainment Weekly
DESIGN DIRECTOR Geraldine Hessler
ART DIRECTOR John Walker
DESIGNER Jennifer Procopio
ILLUSTRATORS Faiyaz Jafri, Edmund Guy, Anita E. Kunz, Daniel Adel, Mark Ulriksen
PUBLISHER Time Inc.
ISSUE December 24-31, 1999
CATEGORY Story

BRIAN CRONIN IS AN ILLUSTRATOR FROM IRELAND, NOW LIVING IN NEW YORK. HIS WORK CAN BE SEEN IN THE MAY / JUNE ISSUE OF PRINT MAGAZINE.

illustration ■ SILVER

■ 551
PUBLICATION National Post
ART DIRECTOR Leanne M. Shapton
DESIGNER Leanne M. Shapton
ILLUSTRATOR Brian Cronin
PUBLISHER Southam Inc.
ISSUE June 1, 1999
CATEGORY Spread

MARILYN MANSON by Steve Brodner

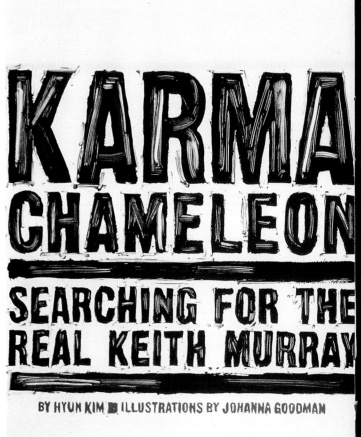

KARMA CHAMELEON

SEARCHING FOR THE REAL KEITH MURRAY

BY HYUN KIM ■ ILLUSTRATIONS BY JOHANNA GOODMAN

114 | BLAZE

illustration ■ SILVER

■ 552
PUBLICATION Rolling Stone
ART DIRECTOR Fred Woodward
DESIGNER Gail Anderson
ILLUSTRATOR Steve Brodner
PUBLISHER Straight Arrow Publishers
ISSUE December 30, 1999
CATEGORY Spread

■ 553
PUBLICATION Blaze
ART DIRECTOR Arem K. Duplessis
DESIGNER Arem K. Duplessis
ILLUSTRATOR Johanna Goodman
PUBLISHER Vibe/Spin Ventures
ISSUE January 1999
CATEGORY Spread

Valuation: // The Amazon Conundrum / By John Fried /

Are they talking about the same company? Amazon is either retailing's future or a failed bid to rewrite the market's rules.

For growth in its franchise and its market value, Amazon.com has set the standard for every E-commerce operation. Formed in 1994 by polymath Jeff Bezos in the proverbial garage in Seattle, Amazon has exploded out of nowhere into a household-name retailer with a projected $1.4 billion in 1999 revenue. The growth of Amazon's market capitalization, currently around $20 billion, is even more spectacular. Since its initial public offering in May 1997, Amazon.com stock (Nasdaq: AMZN; recent price, $66) has climbed more than 4,000 percent and at one point was up more than 7,000 percent. Initially offered at a split-adjusted price of $1.50 a share, it has traded near $110 (adjusted for subsequent splits), and at the height of last winter's Internet buying panic, it was nothing for its price to swing 20 percent in a single session. Like most other Internet stocks, Amazon has recently fallen sharply off its highs, but the argument over its value rages on. The stock remains one of the market's most actively traded issues, with an average of 9.4 million shares changing hands each day. » For many investors, a bet on Amazon is a proxy

Illustration by Brian Cronin

■ 554
PUBLICATION Worth
ART DIRECTOR Philip Bratter
DESIGNERS Deanna Lowe, Jorge Colombo, Sarah Garcea
ILLUSTRATOR Brian Cronin
PUBLISHER Worth Media
ISSUE November 1999
CATEGORY Spread

■ 555
PUBLICATION The New York Times
ART DIRECTOR Jerelle Kraus
ILLUSTRATOR Ralph Steadman
PUBLISHER The New York Times
ISSUE August 13, 1999
CATEGORY Single Page

E1

FRIDAY, AUGUST 13, 1999

Weekend MOVIES PERFORMING ARTS

The New York Times

Finding the Saint
In a Musical Devil

S AY this for Leon Botstein: he has never shirked a challenge. As president of Bard College, conductor, and now the music director of the American Symphony Orchestra, Mr. Botstein has over the last decade evolved a valuable and lively event, the Bard Music Festival, heaping discussions atop performances, all centered on a single composer, for two overflowing weekends in the summer and a Saturday in the fall.

The festival, which begins tonight in Annandale-on-Hudson, N.Y., has attracted a following that, though modest, has remained loyal through not only "easy" times (Haydn, Brahms, Tchaikovsky, Strauss) but also more strenuous ones, like a season devoted to Charles Ives.

Now Mr. Botstein applies what some may consider the acid test: Arnold Schoenberg, who is, in times grown Romantically soft, routinely blamed for every musical sin of the 20th century. (And there have been many.)

Schoenberg, as copious discussions at the festival will undoubtedly make clear, was many things: waning Romantic as well as archmodernist, formative influence as well as rugged individualist, musical saint as well as sinner.

Every composer benefits from excellent performances. Much of Schoenberg's music *requires* them in order to make its effect. And although his works have not been recorded as extensively as those of many another composer, most have been well served on disk. So the classical music critics of The New York Times are taking the opportunity to embellish Mr. Botstein's good efforts by steering listeners to a few sure things: favorite recordings of Schoenberg's music. Their comments are on page 5.

At a time when Schoenberg's good name seems to need all the redemption it can get, a fair hearing of performances like these, whether live or on record, surely makes the strongest possible case.

JAMES R. OESTREICH

Concerts, page 4; critics' favorite CD's, page 5.

Illustrations by Ralph Steadman for The New York Times

THEATER REVIEW

A Radio Freud Meets Her Match

By BEN BRANTLEY

Psychopaths, like small children, have an endearing way of blurting out embarrassing truths that no one else dare utter. Toward the long-awaited end of "Voices in the Dark," the thrill-free thriller by John Pielmeier that opened last night at the Longacre Theater, the play's resident homicidal maniac weighs in with a most astute critical judgment as he considers the gore around him: "Oh, what a mess!" Bless him. Someone had to say it.

By that point, "Voices in the Dark," which stars a very valiant Judith Ivey as an imperiled radio talk show host, has managed to throw in elements from just about every shivery woman-in-jeopardy plot of the last six or seven decades. It has evoked, to its detriment, everything from old-fashioned telephone-centered shockers like "Sorry, Wrong Number" and

VOICES IN THE DARK

There has even been nervous violin music (by Robert Waldman) à la Bernard Herrmann's score for "Psycho."

Still to come is the sequence in which Ms. Ivey's character quaintly tries to defang her predator by summoning his alternate personality, just as those good doctors did with Joanne Woodward in "The Three Faces of Eve." But this psycho isn't buying. "You want to integrate me?" he asks. "Well, I'm going to disintegrate you."

Once again, he is right on target. Integration, whether of plot ends or of humor and suspense, just isn't going to happen in this play. It's like the overcooked veal stew that is prepared onstage and which may or may not include some extra meat from the eviscerated body in the Jacuzzi. Nobody, maniacs

"Midnight Lace" to carnage-in-the-woods movies like "Friday the 13th."

Continued on Page 4

Nicole Bengiveno/The New York Times
Judith Ivey in John Pielmeier's "Voices in the Dark," which opened last night at the Longacre Theater.

INSIDE

FILM REVIEW 1 4
That's show-biz: "Bowfinger," starring Steve Martin and Eddie Murphy.

FILM REVIEW 1 8
Reckless: Claire Danes in "Brokedown Palace."

AT THE MOVIES 1 6
"The Blair Witch Project" as Internet phenomenon.

FILM REVIEW 2 4
"Detroit Rock City."

illustration ■ SILVER

The New York Times
Book Review

March 7, 1999 $1.25

This Man Is an Island

In 'Throwim Way Leg,' a scientist in New Guinea meets ways of life extinct elsewhere.

Reviewed by
D. J. R. Bruckner **13**

'The Times of My Life,'
Max Frankel's autobiography
Reviewed by Ward Just **7**

Robert B. Reich on Thomas
Geoghegan's paralyzed citizen **8**

DUGALD STERMER

1993, Tupac in '94, Nas in '95, and Queen Latifah in '96–have all been entertainer, whom the author won't name, invited him to go gun shopping in Brooklyn six years ago. The artist had

"These rappers get targeted because they're like walking ATMs."

caught with guns in their vehicles. And when they weren't stashing guns in their cars while they drove, it seems celebrities were trying to take their weapons onto planes. Over the past seven years, Martin Lawrence, Eddie Van Halen, Christian Slater, Harry Connick Jr., and Keith "Guru" Elam of Gang Starr all tried to take guns through airport security. The high-profile weapons arrests have practically created a crime category of its own: Stars Busted While Packing.

But while *any* celebrity might make headlines after a weapons charge, more often than not, it's young black rappers who are splashed across the front page. For every Eddie Van Halen arrested with a gun, it seems there are nearly half a dozen Bustas or ODBs getting chauffeured in the back of squad cars for the same offense. "We're finding that many young rappers are still involving themselves with the hoodlum life," says New York Police Department Lieut. Eric Adams, cofounder of the New York-based 100 Blacks in Law Enforcement. "Those who don't are considered sellouts."

Undoubtedly, some rappers *do* flash their firearms to solidify their status as hard rocks on the hip hop landscape. It only takes a glance through the racks of a record store to see that for artists like Scarface, Ice-T, and Mobb Deep, guns are a near obsession. They rhyme about weapons, pose with them on their album covers, and some even name themselves after their favorites–as did Mack 10, Peter Gunz, and Smif-N-Wessun (who, in response to complaints from the gun company Smith & Wesson, changed their name to Da Cocoa Brovaz two years ago).

"At some level, guns are fashion accessories," says Nelson George, critic and author of *Hip Hop America* (Viking, 1998). "They're cool things to have. A lot of rappers go to gun clubs, practice at the range. Guns have always been a part of America as sort of a style thing."

George recounts how a prominent

recently been robbed and wanted a gun for protection. But when they got to the store, George says, the entertainer got caught up in the "romance" of high-power weaponry.

"He wanted a Glock with a laser sight and all the toys," George says. "On one hand, he had been rolled on–it was a bad experience–and he wanted to feel more comfortable and safe. On the other hand, he didn't want a .22. He wanted a really big, scary, sexy gun. He wanted a gun that, when he pulled it out, he wouldn't have to shoot."

George's shopping companion may have wanted his Glock just for

"We're finding that many young rappers are still involving themselves with the hoodlum life," says New York Police Department Lieut. Eric Adams.

show, but many artists insist that guns aren't about image, they're about protection.

According to Method Man, many artists arm themselves to keep from getting ganked. "We're targets, man, and people don't understand," he says. "I mean, our lives are in danger. If I got a gun, it's for protection. You have motherfuckers who love your music and would *still* rob your ass. Like, 'I'm sorry, dude. I love your music–but times is hard.'"

And when times is hard, who better to rob than someone who makes his living brag-

"He wanted a really big, scary, sexy gun. He wanted a gun that, when he pulled it out, he wouldn't have to shoot."

ging on record about all the cars, jewels, and clothes he owns? Especially if he tops it off with lyrics that seem to invite confrontation. "I dare you," barks Black Rob on his recent Bad Boy hit of the same name, "to come against me."

"You make these claims on records and people want to test you," says Brand Nubian MC Sadat X.

Bill Stephney, president and CEO

necticut," he says. "These kids are going back to Lefrak, [Queens] and Bushwick, [Brooklyn] and East Orange, [New Jersey]. And they don't get some special treatment because they're there. They get targeted because they're like walking ATMs, essentially."

Sure enough, the list of rappers stuck for their paper and personal effects reads like the *Billboard* top 20: Foxy Brown, Ice Cube, and Suge Knight have all had their homes broken into. Tupac Shakur was shot five times and stripped of $40,000 worth of jewelry in a robbery at a Manhattan recording studio in 1994. And just this past January, Guru got jacked

for his cell phone and a $6,000 diamond Rolex outside of a Richmond Hill, Queens recording studio.

"People see someone out on the street," says Sadat X. "Maybe driving a nice car or having jewelry, and a lot of times it's just a mentality, '*Let's roll on him*!'" Sadat says because they see themselves as targets, close to 80 percent of the rappers he knows carry weapons.

That adds up to a lot of guns. Especially when you include not just rappers but also their bodyguards, drivers, hanger-ons, and friends. It's

rumored that shortly before he was murdered in 1997, Biggie armed himself and about 40 of his boys when they traveled to a Los Angeles-area arena to do a show. Sources say Brooklyn's favorite son was trying to stave off a threat of violence from a local gang who had gotten upset when the rapper refused to pay off members for "protection" during his concert. Stories of real gangstas extorting performers, and

even label executives, for funds are often whispered about among industry insiders. One record exec who used to walk the line between ill and legal says, "A lot of ex-dope dealers feel like it's safer to threaten artists and get money from them than it is to be getting their hands dirty with crack."

Of course, when it comes to being gun happy, rappers have plenty in common with the rest of America. As of July 1998, there were more than 235 million firearms in the United States–almost as many as there are people living in America.

The difference is that the majority of gun owners in the country don't have constant run-ins with the law. Rappers are part of a select group particularly vulnerable to getting stopped by cops: young black men.

Following numerous, highly publicized complaints from around the country, police departments in states such as Pennsylvania, Florida, California, and Maryland are being investigated by various civil rights groups for "profiling"–that is, stopping vehicles and searching them based on the race of the driver. And in New Jersey, in 1994, a group of 19 black drivers filed a joint motion claiming they had been illegally targeted, stopped, searched, and arrested by troopers on the New Jersey Turnpike. New Jersey Superior Court Judge Robert E. Francis ruled in favor of the defendants, and said that profiling was indeed "tolerated [and] encouraged" by state police. New Jersey is now appealing the decision.

"Black males *are* being targeted," says Columbia University professor Michael Eric Dyson, author of *Race Rules* (Vintage, 1997). "Not only are they arrested at a higher percentage than whites, but they are tagged in a justice system that follows them the rest of their lives."

Still, law-enforcement agents argue that it's the rappers themselves who are

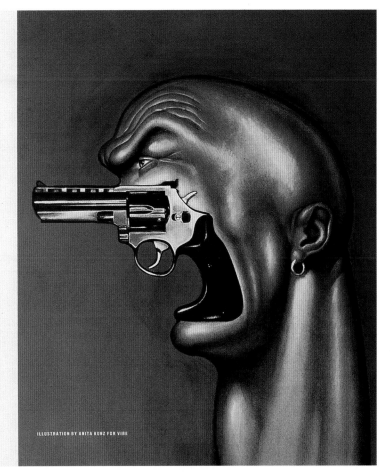

ILLUSTRATION BY ANITA KUNZ FOR VIBE

122 **VIBE**

■ 556
PUBLICATION The New York Times Book Review
ART DIRECTOR Steven Heller
ILLUSTRATOR Dugald Stermer
PUBLISHER The New York Times
ISSUE March 7, 1999
CATEGORY Single Page

■ 557
PUBLICATION Vibe
DESIGN DIRECTOR Dwayne Shaw
ART DIRECTOR Brandon Kavulla
ILLUSTRATOR Anita E. Kunz
PUBLISHER Miller Publishing Group
ISSUE April 1999
CATEGORY Spread

illustration ■ SILVER

CHANEL AT HOME PLATE

This is the story
of my Chanel suit,
and how it has
lived my life so far.

BY HILLARY JOHNSON
ILLUSTRATED BY JULIETTE BORDA

The Monogamous Investor
To contemplate and nurture, or to pull the trigger over and over?

BY REGINA BARRECA
ILLUSTRATED BY BENOÎT

My suit's unlived life.

A male friend asked
me one night at dinner,
"What is the whole
Chanel thing about?"

[SPECIAL REPORT]

GUARD
DOG *supreme*

Want better security?
Then stop leaving the keys in your front door

BY TOM PARKER

Someday I'm going to
buy a boat and cruise
around the world. Or
maybe just up to Alaska.

My
Spaceship Earth
Uniform.

Must Have Been A Dream

by Calvin Hubbartown

■ 558
PUBLICATION Equity
ART DIRECTOR Deanna Lowe
DESIGNERS Jorge Colombo, Deanna Lowe
ILLUSTRATOR Juliette Borda
PUBLISHER Worth Media
ISSUE Fall 1999
CATEGORY Story
  A MERIT Single Page
  B MERIT Single Page
  C MERIT Single Page

■ 559
PUBLICATION Equity
ART DIRECTOR Deanna Lowe
DESIGNER Deanna Lowe
ILLUSTRATOR Benoît
PUBLISHER Worth Media
ISSUE Spring 1999
CATEGORY Spread

■ 560
PUBLICATION Electronic Business
DESIGN DIRECTOR John Sizing
ILLUSTRATOR Pol Turgeon
STUDIO JS Publication Design
PUBLISHER Cahners Business
Information
ISSUE May 1999
CATEGORY Spread

■ 561
PUBLICATION ESPN
DESIGN DIRECTOR F. Darrin Perry
ART DIRECTOR Peter Yates
ILLUSTRATOR PJ Loughran
PUBLISHER Disney Publishing
Worldwide
ISSUE January 25, 1999
CATEGORY Spread

THE TRUTH ABOUT DOGS

by STEPHEN BUDIANSKY

Recent explorations into the field of canine genetics are changing the way we think about man's best friend—"man's best parasite" may be more like it—and could help us repair the damage done by a century of inbreeding

BOOKS

A Cataclysm of Thought

In 1905 Albert Einstein, a twenty-six-year-old clerk, published five epochal papers. One was later awarded a Nobel Prize. Reading them today, our reviewer is thrilled by their genius

by Alan Lightman

EINSTEIN'S MIRACULOUS YEAR: Five Papers That Changed the Face of Physics
edited by John Stachel.
Princeton University Press.
216 pages, $19.95.

■ 562
PUBLICATION The Atlantic Monthly
ART DIRECTOR Robin Gilmore-Barnes
ILLUSTRATOR Mark Ulriksen
PUBLISHER The Atlantic Monthly
ISSUE January 1999
CATEGORY Story

■ 563
PUBLICATION The Atlantic Monthly
ART DIRECTORS Robin Gilmore-Barnes, Betsy Urrico
ILLUSTRATOR Hanoch Piven
PUBLISHER The Atlantic Monthly
ISSUE January 1999
CATEGORY Single Page

gluttony 2

I can't believe I ate the whole thing

by ALISON ARNETT

Continued on Page 29

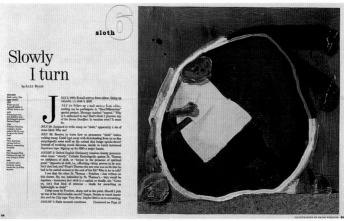

sloth 6

Slowly I turn

by ALEX BEAM

Continued on Page 33

ESSAYS BY FIVE
NEW ENGLAND
WRITERS

NEW BEGINNINGS

At the threshold ∞ By Stephen McCauley

greed 7

What's mine is mine

by JOHN YEMMA

anger 3

It's a mad, mad, mad, mad world

by DAVID M. SHRIBMAN

Continued on Page 36

envy 1

It's not easy being green

by JOSEPH P. KAHN

Continued on Page 15

■ 564
PUBLICATION The Boston Globe Magazine
DESIGN DIRECTOR Lucy Bartholomay
ART DIRECTOR Catherine Aldrich
ILLUSTRATOR Thomas Fuchs
PUBLISHER The Globe Newspaper Co.
ISSUE October 3, 1999
CATEGORY Spread

■ 565
PUBLICATION The Boston Globe Magazine
ART DIRECTOR Catherine Aldrich
DESIGNER Catherine Aldrich
ILLUSTRATOR Philippe Lardy
PUBLISHER The Globe Newspaper Co.
ISSUE January 3, 1999
CATEGORY Spread

■ 566
PUBLICATION The Boston Globe Magazine
DESIGN DIRECTOR Lucy Bartholomay
ART DIRECTORS Catherine Aldrich, Jane Martin
ILLUSTRATORS Simone Adels, Tom La Duke
PUBLISHER The Globe Newspaper Co.
ISSUE October 3, 1999
CATEGORY Spread

■ 567
PUBLICATION The Boston Globe Magazine
DESIGN DIRECTOR Lucy Bartholomay
ART DIRECTORS Catherine Aldrich, Jane Martin
ILLUSTRATOR David Wheeler
PUBLISHER The Globe Newspaper Co.
ISSUE October 3, 1999
CATEGORY Spread

■ 568
PUBLICATION The Boston Globe Magazine
DESIGN DIRECTOR Lucy Bartholomay
ART DIRECTORS Catherine Aldrich, Jane Martin
ILLUSTRATOR Brian Cronin
PUBLISHER The Globe Newspaper Co.
ISSUE October 3, 1999
CATEGORY Spread

■ 569
PUBLICATION The Boston Globe Magazine
ART DIRECTOR Catherine Aldrich
DESIGNER Catherine Aldrich
ILLUSTRATOR Anita E. Kunz
PUBLISHER The Globe Newspaper Co.
ISSUE December 1999
CATEGORY Spread

BRANDED

By Matthew Heller

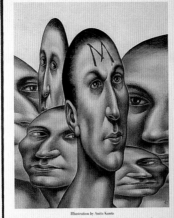

Illustration by Anita Kunz

DROP POUNDS ALL OVER TOWN

BY JAMIE JEBIN, R.D.

AT THE DRIVE-THRU WINDOW

THE VIEW FROM L.A.
Our dumb-blonde image is, like, so over. Deal with it

BY DEBORAH MICHEL
ILLUSTRATIONS BY BENOÎT

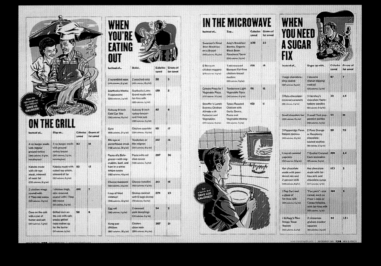

IN THE KITCHEN
AT THE MINIMART
IN YOUR BARCALOUNGER

Health
HOW TO LIVE FOREVER

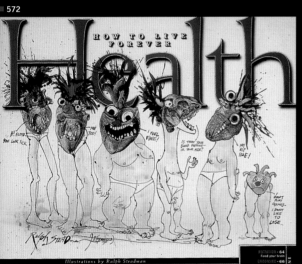

Illustrations by Ralph Steadman

CLINIC | By Rebecca Voelker

The Ticker Test
How does your heart measure up?

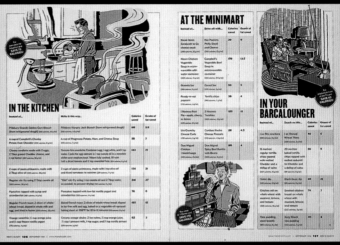

WHEN YOU'RE EATING OUT
IN THE MICROWAVE
WHEN YOU NEED A SUGAR FIX
ON THE GRILL

570
PUBLICATION California Lawyer
DESIGN DIRECTOR Louise Kollenbaum
DESIGNER Louise Kollenbaum
ILLUSTRATOR Anita E. Kunz
PUBLISHER Daily Journal Corp.
ISSUE October 1999
CATEGORY Spread

571
PUBLICATION Los Angeles
CREATIVE DIRECTOR David Armario
DESIGNERS David Armario, Myla Sorensen
ILLUSTRATOR Benoît
PUBLISHER Fairchild Publications
ISSUE February 1999
CATEGORY Spread

572
PUBLICATION Men's Journal
ART DIRECTOR Michael Lawton
DESIGNER Michael Lawton
ILLUSTRATOR Ralph Steadman
PUBLISHER Wenner Media
ISSUE March 1999
CATEGORY Single Page

573
PUBLICATION Men's Health
ART DIRECTOR Jeanine Melnick
ILLUSTRATOR Jonathan Carlson
PUBLISHER Rodale Inc.
ISSUE September 1999
CATEGORY Story

ILLUSTRATION MERIT

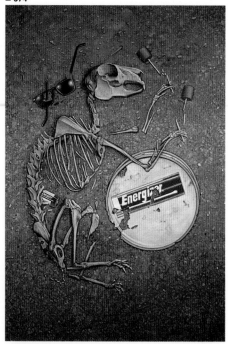

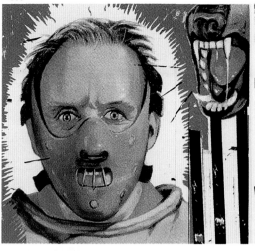

HannibalLecter
has been missing in action
for the last 10 years. Now
America's favorite cannibal is
back in HANNIBAL Thomas
Harris's long-awaited sequel to
THE SILENCE OF THE LAMBS
and everyone in Hollywood
is gearing up
for a feeding
frenzy.

by Chris Nashawaty

THE HUNGRY

Illustration by Tavis Coburn

Fall MOVIE Preview

Illustration by TAVIS COBURN

TWINKLE, TWINKLE, NOT-SO-LITTLE STAR

Illustration by DANIEL ADEL

★★★ The World Wrestling Federation
may have 'STONE COLD' STEVE AUSTIN and
'BADD ASS' Billy Gunn, but the *truly* bone-
crunching, back-slamming action takes place
in a much tougher arena: HOLLYWOOD.
This year the competition has been especially
BRUTAL—at least for space in these pages—
with producers like Rollickin' Scott Rudin
and Jerry 'the Rock' Bruckheimer rising to
title contenders, while stars like Kevin (It'll
Cost Ya) Costner and BRAD 'NOT SUCH A HIT'
PITT took it on the chin. Even 1999's
championship-belt winner—SUMNER 'HE'LL
CARVE YOUR HEADSTONE' REDSTONE—
needed help from a new tag-team partner
(Mel 'Bad Karma' Karmazin), slip
into some boxer shorts, and get ready to
rummmmble, as EW referees its 10th
year of celebrity death matches. Among the
HEAVYWEIGHTS to pin your hopes on:
FIGHTIN' MICHAEL CRICHTON, Hammerin'
Cameron Diaz, Mike 'the Zipper' De Luca,
To Helen and Back Hunt, MAIMIN' MATT
DAMON, and HARRISON 'NO COMPARISON'
FORD. ★★★ And, oh yeah, MADONNA.

POWER MANIA

Sumner REDSTONE
and Mel KARMAZIN
CHAIRMAN·CEO·REIGNING MEDIA CHAMP; PRESIDENT-COO, VIACOM INC.

POWER MANIA

FALLING

PRETTY (TOUGH) WOMEN

POWER MOVES

BUILT FORD TOUGH   Random Hearts aside, Harrison is still a top contender for the $100 million box office ring

Illustration by EDMUND GUY

580
PUBLICATION Entertainment Weekly
DESIGN DIRECTOR John Korpics
DESIGNER Liliane Vilmenay
ILLUSTRATOR Tavis Coburn
PUBLISHER Time Inc.
ISSUE May 7, 1999
CATEGORY Spread

581
PUBLICATION Entertainment Weekly
DESIGN DIRECTOR Geraldine Hessler
ART DIRECTOR Geraldine Hessler
DESIGNER George McCalman
ILLUSTRATOR Tavis Coburn
PUBLISHER Time Inc.
ISSUE August 20-7, 1999
CATEGORY Spread

582
PUBLICATION Entertainment Weekly
DESIGN DIRECTOR Geraldine Hessler
ART DIRECTOR John Walker
DESIGNER Ellene Standke
ILLUSTRATOR Daniel Adel
PUBLISHER Time Inc.
ISSUE October 29, 1999
CATEGORY Spread

583
PUBLICATION Entertainment Weekly
DESIGN DIRECTOR Geraldine Hessler
ART DIRECTOR John Walker
DESIGNER Ellene Standke
ILLUSTRATORS Tavis Coburn,
C. F. Payne, Edmund Guy,
Anita E. Kunz
PUBLISHER Time Inc.
ISSUE October 29, 1999
CATEGORY Story

ILLUSTRATION MERIT

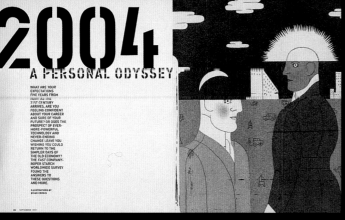

2004
A PERSONAL ODYSSEY

WHAT ARE YOUR
EXPECTATIONS
FIVE YEARS FROM
NOW? AS THE
21ST CENTURY
ARRIVES, ARE YOU
FEELING CONFIDENT
ABOUT YOUR CAREER
AND SURE OF YOUR
FUTURE? OR DOES THE
PROSPECT OF EVER-
MORE-POWERFUL
TECHNOLOGY AND
NEVER-ENDING
CHANGE LEAVE YOU
WISHING YOU COULD
RETURN TO THE
SIMPLER DAYS OF
THE OLD ECONOMY?
THE FAST COMPANY-
ROPER STARCH
WORLDWIDE SURVEY
FOUND THE
ANSWERS TO
THESE QUESTIONS
AND MORE.

ILLUSTRATIONS BY
BRIAN CRONIN

ideas.com

CONTEXT INTEGRATION IS A FAST-GROWING COMPANY WITH LOTS OF BRIGHT IDEAS—
AND A WEB-BASED KNOWLEDGE NETWORK TO TEST, TRACK, CAPTURE, AND SHARE THOSE
IDEAS, SAYS ITS KNOWLEDGE MANAGER. "WE THINK THIS IS A BETTER WAY TO WORK,"
SO DO ITS CLIENTS, WHICH INCLUDE SOME OF THE BIGGEST NAMES ON WALL STREET AND
IN THE ENTERTAINMENT BUSINESS. BY CHUCK SALTER ILLUSTRATIONS BY JOHN HERSEY

FC
ROPER STARCH
SURVEY

It was every consultant's nightmare.
He was on his own, and he was stumped.
A major mutual-fund organization had
placed an urgent call

FIVE YEARS FROM NOW WHEN YOU LOOK
BACK AT TODAY'S ENVIRONMENT, WHAT WILL YOU SAY?

REPORT
FROM THE FUTURE

The E-Lance Economy

BY KATHARINE MIESZKOWSKI
ILLUSTRATIONS BY CHIP WASS

MONEY & INVESTING

Certified Public Accomplice

Would you buy a mutual fund or an insurance policy from your CPA? GE, MetLife and AXA are betting you will. But you might not want to think twice.

ILLUSTRATION MERIT

■ 588
PUBLICATION Fast Company
ART DIRECTOR Patrick Mitchell
DESIGNER Patrick Mitchell
ILLUSTRATOR Tavis Coburn
PUBLISHER Fast Company
ISSUE October 1999
CATEGORY Story

■ 589
PUBLICATION Fortune Small Business
ART DIRECTOR Traci Churchill
DESIGNER Traci Churchill
ILLUSTRATOR Maira Kalman
PUBLISHER Time Inc.
ISSUE April 1999
CATEGORY Spread

■ 590
PUBLICATION Forbes
CREATIVE DIRECTOR Robert Mansfield
DESIGNER Steve Ramos
ILLUSTRATOR Brian Cronin
PUBLISHER Forbes Inc.
ISSUE November 15, 1999
CATEGORY Spread

■ 591
PUBLICATION Gentlemen's Quarterly
DESIGN DIRECTOR Arem K. Duplessis
ART DIRECTOR George Moschlades
DESIGNER Valerie Fong
ILLUSTRATOR Zohar Lazar
PUBLISHER Condé Nast Publications, Inc.
ISSUE December 1999
CATEGORY Spread

CURSES, FOILED AGAIN

All it takes is a ticked-off goat owner, and your whole sports team is cursed.

BASEBALL PLAYERS can be remarkably superstitious lunch. They hop over base lines on their way to the outfield, refuse to change underwear during a hitting streak, stop for the same soda at the same 7-Eleven every day. It has to do with thinking they're in control, the belief that somehow the individual can influence the metaphysical. ¶ But some things in baseball are beyond the scope of the individual, more powerful than mere superstitious routine, so entrenched that they hover over entire franchises like black clouds, even on a perfect summer day. They are evil curses, conceived by simple circumstances but reinforced by years of misery. Why they are reserved primarily for the national pastime is a matter for debate. Most likely, it's a product of baseball's long history and ardent mythology, along with some of the most chronically depressed franchises in organized sports. These are their stories.

BY BRAD HERZOG

DAD WAS A GOLFER

A son recalls with fondness his father's exuberance for the game, and the steadfast respect for the beauty that are an example for all.

BY CHUCK HOGAN

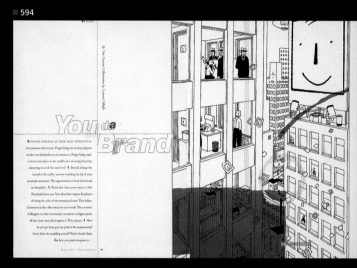

You da Brand

THE CURSE OF THE BAMBINO

A local rooter lamented, "I figure the Red Sox is ruined."

THE CURSE OF THE BILLY GOAT

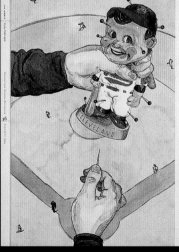

Cleveland's suffering was so constant that it merited an entire movie.

THE CURSE OF ROCKY COLAVITO

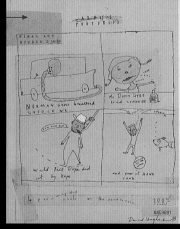

Fatal Attraction

WHAT IF EVERYTHING YOU KNOW ABOUT ASSET ALLOCATION is wrong?

For many financial planners, allocating clients' assets has become the focus of what they do, and what they earn. Do they really know what they're doing?

By William Jahnke
Illustration By David Hughes

592
PUBLICATION Navigator
ART DIRECTOR Susan L. Bogle
DESIGNER Susan L. Bogle
ILLUSTRATOR Barry Blitt
PUBLISHER Pace Communications
CLIENT Holiday Inn Express
ISSUE June/July 1999
CATEGORY Story

593
PUBLICATION Golf Journal
ART DIRECTOR Donna Panagakos
ILLUSTRATOR Allen Garns
PUBLISHER United States
Golf Association
ISSUE June 1999
CATEGORY Spread

594
PUBLICATION Hemispheres
CREATIVE DIRECTOR Jaimey Easler
ILLUSTRATOR Laurent Cilluffo
PUBLISHER Pace Communications
CLIENT United Airlines
ISSUE May 1999
CATEGORY Spread

595
PUBLICATION Investment Advisor
CREATIVE DIRECTOR Dorothy A. Jones
ILLUSTRATOR David Hughes
PUBLISHER Investment Advisor Group
ISSUE April 1999
CATEGORY Spread

Inquirer Magazine

Welcome to the future

What's ahead in
Longevity
Demography
Business
Leisure
Spirituality
Technology
Ethics

A SPECIAL
DOUBLE ISSUE

Welcome to the future

Illustrations by Philippe Lardy

THE FUTURE

By studying trends and statistics, futurists make forecasts
about the decades to come. And what they have to say tells
us a lot about then — and now. By Tanya Barrientos

Longevity

LONGEVITY

All of us, as individuals and as a nation, will grow older
and grayer. And life may stretch further into the distance than
anyone ever contemplated. By Michael Vitez

Demography

DEMOGRAPHY

America will change its complexion.
What is less clear is how strong the pull to assimilate will be — and
what it will mean to be "white." By Michael Sokolove

WHY CLICK IS MARRYING MORTAR

*Yahoo buy Disney? DoubleClick buy Young & Rubicam?
It's time for dot coms to start dreaming such dreams.*

By Bill Roberts

by Jon R. Luoma

The chemical revolution ushered in a world of changes.
Many of them, it's becoming clear, are in our bodies.

system failure

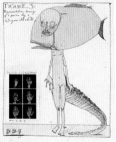

**Sperm problems are an ominous "red flag" for male
reproductive health. Declining sperm counts
are matched by soaring rates of testicular cancer.**

ILLUSTRATION

MERIT

■ 596
PUBLICATION Inquirer Magazine
ART DIRECTORS Chrissy Dunleavy, Susan Syrnick
DESIGNER Chrissy Dunleavy
ILLUSTRATOR Philippe Lardy
PUBLIHSER Philadelphia Inquirer
ISSUE December 19-26, 1999
CATEGORY Story

■ 597
PUBLICATION Internet World
ART DIRECTOR Scott Gormley
DESIGNER Pat Prince
ILLUSTRATOR Christoph Niemann
PUBLISHER Penton Media, Inc.
ISSUE November 15, 1999
CATEGORY Spread

■ 598
PUBLICATION Mother Jones
CREATIVE DIRECTOR Rhonda Rubinstein
ART DIRECTORS Benjamin Shaykin, Cal Joy
ILLUSTRATOR David Hughes
PUBLISHER Foundation for National Progress
ISSUE July/August 1999
CATEGORY Story

work YOUR brain

HOW TO
IDENTIFY NATURAL
BRAIN STYLES
LOGICAL
EMOTIONAL
CONCEPTUAL
ANALYTICAL
TO IMPROVE YOUR
PERFORMANCE
AND SALES

BY DANA RAY

Knowers love logic – not personal warmth or bonding.

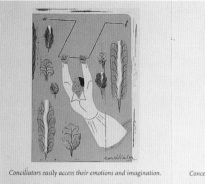

Conciliators easily access their emotions and imagination.

Conceptors are creative, inventive and entrepreneurial.

Deliberators excel at processing and analyzing information.

19 easy ways to enjoy a healthier diet

Here's a simple—and delicious—eating plan that is certain to nourish both body and soul.

By Maggie Keresey
Illustrations by
Frederique Bertrand

MAKE THE MOST OF YOUR MEMORY

By Phyllis Schneider
Illustrations By
Martin Jarrie

Occasional forgetfulness doesn't necessarily signal trouble. For most people, it's a normal—if annoying—part of life.

Rose's Turn

In his role as a new correspondent on '60 Minutes II,' Charlie Rose has arrived — but makes you nostalgic for everything you never knew you liked about him.

By Rebecca Johnson

■ 599
PUBLICATION Selling Power
ART DIRECTOR Colleen McCudden
DESIGNER Colleen McCudden
ILLUSTRATOR Brian Cronin
PUBLISHER Personal Selling Power
ISSUE October 1999
CATEGORY Story

■ 600
PUBLICATION New Choices:
Living Even Better After 50
ART DIRECTOR Jackie Jordan
DESIGNER Jackie Jordan
ILLUSTRATOR Frédérique Bertrand
PUBLISHER The Reader's Digest
Association, Inc.
ISSUE September 1999
CATEGORY Spread

■ 601
PUBLICATION New Choices:
Living Even Better After 50
ART DIRECTOR Jackie Jordan
DESIGNER Jackie Jordan
ILLUSTRATOR Martin Jarrie
PUBLISHER The Reader's Digest
Association, Inc.
ISSUE December 1999
CATEGORY Spread

■ 602
PUBLICATION
The New York Times Magazine
ART DIRECTOR Janet Froelich
DESIGNER Claude Martel
ILLUSTRATOR Steve Brodner
PUBLISHER The New York Times
ISSUE March 21, 1999
CATEGORY Spread

■ 603
PUBLICATION
The New York Times Magazine
ART DIRECTOR Janet Froelich
DESIGNER Claude Martel
ILLUSTRATOR Margaret Keane
STYLIST Elizabeth Stewart
PUBLISHER The New York Times
ISSUE May 23, 1999
CATEGORY Story

■ 604
PUBLICATION
The New York Times Magazine
ART DIRECTOR Janet Froelich
DESIGNER Claude Martel
ILLUSTRATOR Steve Brodner
PUBLISHER The New York Times
ISSUE July 18, 1999
CATEGORY Spread

■ 605
PUBLICATION
The New York Times Magazine
ART DIRECTORS Janet Froelich,
Joele Cuyler
DESIGNERS Joele Cuyler,
Ignacio Rodriguez
ILLUSTRATOR Carroll Dunham
PUBLISHER The New York Times
ISSUE September 19, 1999
CATEGORY Spread

■ 606
PUBLICATION
The New York Times Magazine
ART DIRECTOR Janet Froelich
DESIGNER Nancy Harris
ILLUSTRATOR Dynamic Duo Studio
PUBLISHER The New York Times
ISSUE November 21, 1999
CATEGORY Spread

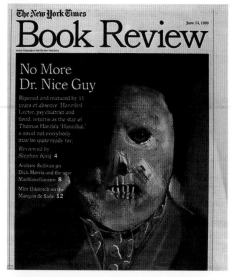

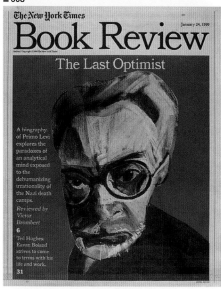

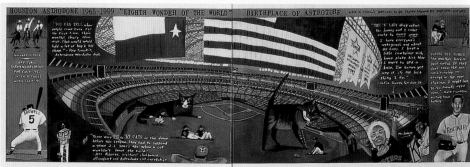

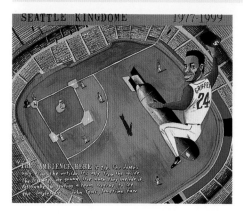

■ 607
PUBLICATION The New York Times Book Review
ART DIRECTOR Steven Heller
ILLUSTRATOR Marshall Arisman
PUBLISHER The New York Times
ISSUE June 13, 1999
CATEGORY Single Page

■ 608
PUBLICATION The New York Times Book Review
ART DIRECTOR Steven Heller
ILLUSTRATOR Andrea Ventura
PUBLISHER The New York Times
ISSUE January 24, 1999
CATEGORY Single Page

■ 609
PUBLICATION The New York Times Book review
ART DIRECTOR Steven Heller
ILLUSTRATOR Andy Rash
PUBLISHER The New York Times
ISSUE February 28, 1999
CATEGORY Single Page

■ 610
PUBLICATION The New Yorker
ART DIRECTOR Christine Curry
ILLUSTRATOR Mark Ulriksen
PUBLISHER Condé Nast Publications, Inc.
ISSUE September 13, 1999
CATEGORY Story

■ 611
PUBLICATION The New Yorker
ART DIRECTOR Françoise Mouly
ILLUSTRATOR Mike Hodges
PUBLISHER Condé Nast Publications, Inc.
ISSUE May 10, 1999
CATEGORY Single Page

LICENSED TO KILL

The pay: excellent. The hours: flexible. The perks: busting down doors, beating people senseless and shooting them dead. Harmon Leon joins the ranks of the world's most lawless lawmen: bounty hunters. Illustration by Paul Corio

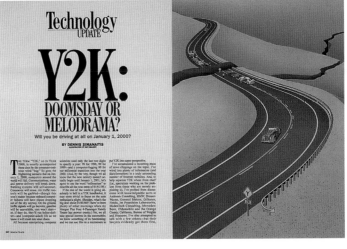

Technology UPDATE

Y2K: DOOMSDAY OR MELODRAMA?

Will you be driving at all on January 1, 2000?

BY DENNIS SIMANAITIS

■ 613

MY MAFIA MOLL

BY HERBERT GOLD • ILLUSTRATION BY OWEN SMITH

■ 616

TELEPHONE TANTRUMS. POISON-PEN LETTERS. WEB SITES DESIGNED FOR NO OTHER REASON THAN REVENGE.

rage against the machine

AMERICAN CONSUMERS ARE BECOMING MORE AND MORE OBSESSED ABOUT GETTING EVEN WITH COMPANIES THAT HAVE DONE THEM WRONG. BUT IS WAGING A LIFETIME BATTLE OVER AN ESPRESSO MAKER WORTH IT?

BY CLIFTON LEAF AND LISA KALIS

■ 614

6 family-tested strategies for potty-training success

No More Diapers!

By Stephanie Wood

ILLUSTRATIONS BY AJ GARCES

■ 617

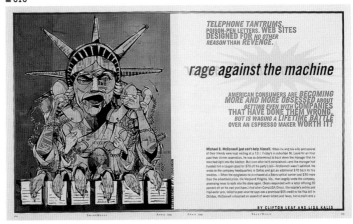

Leading Off

Black Battlers

■ 612
PUBLICATION P.O.V.
DESIGN DIRECTOR Florian Bachleda
DESIGNER Pino Impastato
ILLUSTRATOR Paul Corio
PUBLISHER B.Y.O.B./Freedom Ventures, Inc.
ISSUE April 1999
CATEGORY Spread

■ 613
PUBLICATION Modern Maturity
CREATIVE DIRECTOR Cynthia J. Friedman
ART DIRECTOR Cynthia J. Friedman
ILLUSTRATOR Owen Smith
PUBLISHER AARP
ISSUE May 1999
CATEGORY Spread

■ 614
PUBLICATION Parenting
ART DIRECTOR Susan Dazzo
DESIGNER James Lung
ILLUSTRATOR A. J. Garces
PUBLISHER Time Inc.
ISSUE March 1999
CATEGORY Spread

■ 615
PUBLICATION Road & Track
ART DIRECTOR Richard M. Baron
DESIGNER Richard M. Baron
ILLUSTRATOR Guy Billout
PUBLISHER Hachette Filipacchi Magazines, Inc.
ISSUE May 1999
CATEGORY Spread

■ 616
PUBLICATION SmartMoney
ART DIRECTOR Amy Rosenfeld
DESIGNER Donna Agajanian
ILLUSTRATOR PJ Loughran
PUBLISHER Dow Jones & Hearst Corp.
ISSUE April 1999
CATEGORY Spread

■ 617
PUBLICATION Sports Illustrated
CREATIVE DIRECTOR Steven Hoffman
DESIGNER Ed Truscio
ILLUSTRATOR Kadir Nelson
PUBLISHER Time Inc.
ISSUE August 30, 1999
CATEGORY Story

ILLUSTRATION MERIT

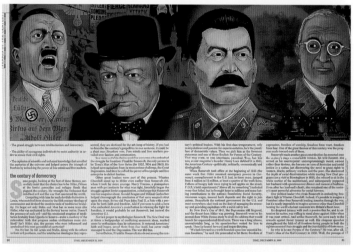

■ 618
PUBLICATION UCLA Magazine
DESIGN DIRECTOR Charles Hess
DESIGNERS Dana Barton, Jackie Morrow
ILLUSTRATOR Zohar Lazar
STUDIO C. Hess Design
PUBLISHER UCLA
ISSUE Spring 1999
CATEGORY Spread

■ 619
PUBLICATION TV Guide
DESIGN DIRECTOR Maxine Davidowitz
DESIGNER Mike Dawson
ILLUSTRATOR Juliette Borda
PUBLISHER TV Guide Inc.
ISSUE October 23, 1999
CATEGORY Spread

■ 620
PUBLICATION Time
DESIGN DIRECTOR Arthur Hochstein
ART DIRECTOR Sharon Okamoto
ILLUSTRATOR David Bowers
PUBLISHER Time Inc.
ISSUE December 31, 1999
CATEGORY Spread

■ 621
PUBLICATION Time
DESIGN DIRECTOR Arthur Hochstein
ART DIRECTOR Sharon Okamoto
ILLUSTRATOR Edel Rodriguez
PUBLISHER Time Inc.
ISSUE December 31, 1999
CATEGORY Story

THE MILLENNIUM — 12th century

(c. 1138-1193)
saladin
The Kurdish adventurer proved to the Crusaders that God had no trouble favoring an "infidel"

RUNNERS-UP

(1882-1945)
franklin delano roosevelt
He raised the edifice of the American Century by restoring a nation's promise of plenty and by intervening to save a world enveloped in darkness
By Doris Kearns Goodwin

THE MILLENNIUM — 13th century

genghis khan (c.1167-1227)
The world conqueror swept through Asia like an apocalypse and set in motion forces more powerful than the sword

(1879-1955)
albert einstein
He was the pre-eminent scientist in a century dominated by science. The touchstones of the era—the Bomb, the Big Bang, quantum physics and electronics—all bear his imprint
By Frederic Golden

PERSON OF THE CENTURY

THE MILLENNIUM — 19th century

thomas edison
(1847-1931)
His inventions not only reshaped modernity but also promised a future bounded only by creativity

RUNNERS-UP

(1869-1948)
mohandas gandhi
In an age of empire and military might, he proved that the powerless had power and that force of arms would not forever prevail against force of spirit
By Johanna McGeary

ILLUSTRATION MERIT ■

THE MILLENNIUM — 18th century

thomas jefferson
(1743-1826)
A political visionary's "expression of the American mind" still inspires revolution around the world

■ 622
PUBLICATION Time
DESIGN DIRECTOR Arthur Hochstein
ART DIRECTOR Sharon Okamoto
ILLUSTRATORS Chang Pak, Kinuko Craft, C. F. Payne, Amy Guip
PUBLISHER Time Inc.
ISSUE December 31, 1999
CATEGORY Story

■ 623
PUBLICATION Time
DESIGN DIRECTOR Arthur Hochstein
ART DIRECTOR Sharon Okamoto
ILLUSTRATOR Tim O'Brien
PUBLISHER Time Inc.
ISSUE December 31, 1999
CATEGORY Story

Is the government out to get the OL' DIRTY BASTARD? Is the Ol' Dirty Bastard the second coming of Christ? Is the Ol' Dirty Bastard cracked out or cracking up? *Sacha Jenkins* looks high and low for the man behind the masks and wonders, Can he be saved?

LOOKING FOR JESUS

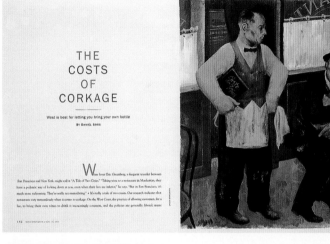

THE COSTS OF CORKAGE

West is best for letting you bring your own bottle

BY DANIEL SOGG

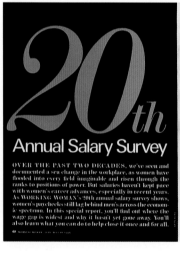

20th
Annual Salary Survey

OVER THE PAST TWO DECADES, we've seen and documented a sea change in the workplace, as women have flooded into every field imaginable and risen through the ranks to positions of power. But salaries haven't kept pace with women's career advances, especially in recent years. As WORKING WOMAN's 20th annual salary survey shows, women's paychecks still lag behind men's across the economic spectrum. In this special report, you'll find out where the wage gap is widest and why it hasn't yet gone away. You'll also learn what you can do to help close it once and for all.

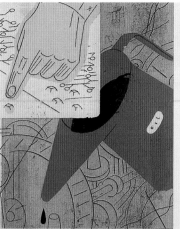

When new technologies come into wide use, creating scores of new businesses and immense fortunes in the process, those at the center of the action can be expected to manifest a certain expansiveness that verges on irrational exuberance. So it's not terribly surprising that technology executives, economists, and professional investors sometimes seem to be vying with one another to come up with the most sweeping terms to describe the present moment. Stephen Waite, a money manager who runs the high-performance Warburg Pincus Global Telecommunications Fund, likens the current era to the years immediately following Gutenberg's invention of movable type. "Four years after Gutenberg," he asks, "would you know where the publishing industry was going? Would you want to invest in it anyway?" Not to be outdone, Nuala Beck, a Toronto-based economist specializing in the high-tech economy, says, "The only moment I can compare to the present day is when the Middle Ages gave way to the Renaissance." After such grand claims, Rebecca Patton, a former

each discontinuous innovation produces a whirlwind of revenue growth, but it also destroys companies even as it creates others—heard anything from burroughs or smith corona lately?

howard hughes,
the mogul, entrepreneur, and inventor, was psychotic and drugged, dying in mexico.

PUBLICATION Vibe
DESIGN DIRECTOR Robert Newman
DESIGNER Brandon Kavulla
ILLUSTRATOR Edmund Guy
PUBLISHER Miller Publishing Group
ISSUE December 1999
CATEGORY Spread

PUBLICATION Wine Spectator
ART DIRECTOR David A. Bayer
DESIGNER Philip Ficks
ILLUSTRATOR Gérard DuBois
PUBLISHER M. Shanken Communications Inc.
ISSUE November 15, 1999
CATEGORY Spread

PUBLICATION Working Woman
CREATIVE DIRECTOR Heidi Volpe
ART DIRECTOR Greg Concha
DESIGNER Heidi Volpe
ILLUSTRATOR Anita E. Kunz
PUBLISHER Working Woman Network.com
ISSUE July/August 1999
CATEGORY Spread

PUBLICATION Worth
ART DIRECTOR Philip Bratter
DESIGNER Sarah Garcea
ILLUSTRATOR Brian Cronin
PUBLISHER Worth Media
ISSUE April 1999
CATEGORY Story

PUBLICATION Worth
ART DIRECTOR Philip Bratter
DESIGNER Anton Ioukhnovets
ILLUSTRATOR Barry Blitt
PUBLISHER Worth Media
ISSUE June 1999
CATEGORY Spread

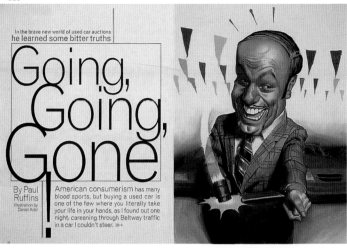

In the brave new world of used car auctions
he learned some bitter truths

Going, Going, Gone

By Paul Ruffins
Illustration by Daniel Adel

American consumerism has many blood sports, but buying a used car is one of the few where you literally take your life in your hands, as I found out one night, careening through Beltway traffic in a car I couldn't steer. ➤

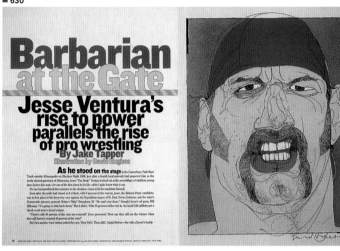

Barbarian at the Gate

Jesse Ventura's rise to power parallels the rise of pro wrestling

By Jake Tapper
Illustration by David Hughes

As he stood on the stage at the Canterbury Park Race Track outside Minneapolis on Election Night 1998, just after a fourth local network had projected him as the newly elected governor of Minnesota, Jesse "The Body" Ventura locked out at the assemblage of chaffinch young faces before him and—for one of the first times in his life—didn't quite know what to say.

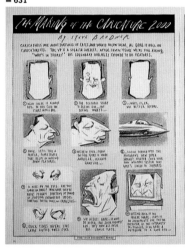

What Every CEO
Needs To Know About

Electronic Business
A SURVIVAL GUIDE

ILLUSTRATION MERIT

■ 629
PUBLICATION The Washington Post Magazine
ART DIRECTOR Kelly Doe
DESIGNER Kelly Doe
ILLUSTRATOR Daniel Adel
PUBLISHER The Washington Post Co.
ISSUE February 21, 1999
CATEGORY Spread

■ 630
PUBLICATION The Washington Post Magazine
ART DIRECTOR Kelly Doe
DESIGNER David Herbick
ILLUSTRATOR David Hughes
PUBLISHER The Washington Post Co.
ISSUE May 9, 1999
CATEGORY Spread

■ 631
PUBLICATION The Washington Post Magazine
ART DIRECTOR Kelly Doe
DESIGNER Kelly Doe
ILLUSTRATOR Steve Brodner
PUBLISHER The Washington Post Co.
ISSUE June 27, 1999
CATEGORY Story

■ 632
PUBLICATION BusinessWeek E.Biz
DESIGN DIRECTOR Mitch Shostak
ART DIRECTOR Viviana Bromberg
ILLUSTRATOR Glenn Mitsui
STUDIO Shostak Studios Inc.
PUBLISHER The MacGraw-Hill Companies, Inc.
ISSUE March 22, 1999
CATEGORY Spread or Single Page

■ 633
PUBLICATION LA Weekly
ART DIRECTOR Bill Smith
ILLUSTRATOR Geoff Grahn
PUBLISHER Stern Publishing
ISSUE February 26, 1999
CATEGORY Single Page

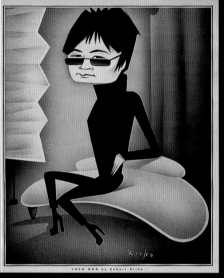

634
PUBLICATION Rolling Stone
ART DIRECTOR Fred Woodward
DESIGNER Gail Anderson
ILLUSTRATOR Drew Friedman
PUBLISHER Straight Arrow Publishers
ISSUE December 12, 1999
CATEGORY Spread

635
PUBLICATION Rolling Stone
ART DIRECTOR Fred Woodward
DESIGNER Gail Anderson
ILLUSTRATOR Robert Risko
PUBLISHER Straight Arrow Publishers
ISSUE December 30, 1999
CATEGORY Single Page

636
PUBLICATION Rolling Stone
ART DIRECTOR Fred Woodward
DESIGNER Gail Anderson
ILLUSTRATOR Vivienne Flesher
PUBLISHER Straight Arrow Publishers
ISSUE November 11, 1999
CATEGORY Single Page

637
PUBLICATION Rolling Stone
ART DIRECTOR Fred Woodward
DESIGNER Gail Anderson
ILLUSTRATOR Gary Baseman
PUBLISHER Straight Arrow Publishers
ISSUE November 25, 1999
CATEGORY Single Page

638
PUBLICATION Fortune
ART DIRECTOR Margery Peters
DESIGNER Ann Decker
PHOTO EDITORS Scott Thode, William Nabers
PHOTOGRAPHERS Margot Hartford,
Andy Freeberg, Laurie Steiner, Brian Smale,
Scott Thode, Jay Blakesberg, Wyatt
McSpadden, Allen Kennedy, Tom Sobolik,
Katherine Lambert, Asia Kepka, Gail Albert
Halaban, Rex Rystedt, Rafael Fuchs,
Michael O'Neill, Jonathan Saunders
INFORMATION GRAPHICS EDITOR Linda Eckstein
PUBLISHER Time Inc.
ISSUE September 27, 1999
CATEGORY Information Graphics

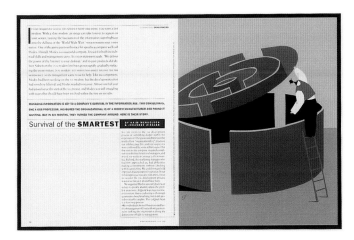

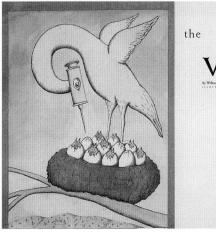

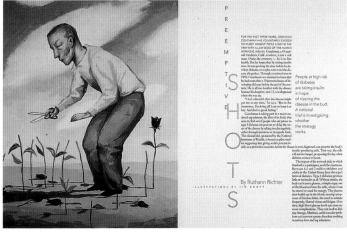

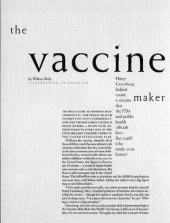

ILLUSTRATION MERIT ■

■ 645

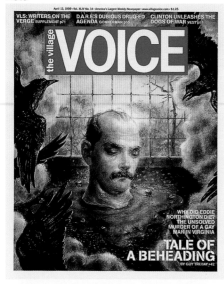

■ 647

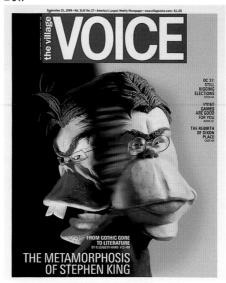

■ 649

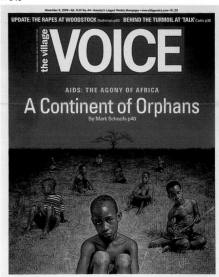

■ 646

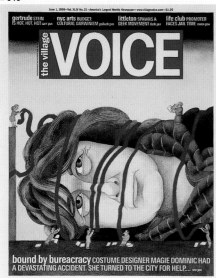

■ 648

■ 650

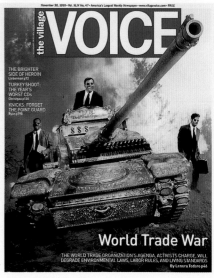

■ 645
PUBLICATION The Village Voice
DESIGN DIRECTOR Ted Keller
ART DIRECTOR Minh Uong
DESIGNER Stacy Wakefield
ILLUSTRATOR Thomas Woodruff
PUBLISHER VV Publishing Corp.
ISSUE April 13, 1999
CATEGORY Single Page

■ 646
PUBLICATION The Village Voice
DESIGN DIRECTOR Ted Keller
ART DIRECTOR Minh Uong
DESIGNER Stacy Wakefield
ILLUSTRATOR Etienne Delessert
PUBLISHER VV Publishing Corp.
ISSUE June 1, 1999
CATEGORY Single Page

■ 647
PUBLICATION The Village Voice
DESIGN DIRECTOR Ted Keller
ART DIRECTOR Minh Uong
DESIGNER Stacy Wakefield
ILLUSTRATOR David O'Keefe
PUBLISHER VV Publishing Corp.
ISSUE September 21, 1999
CATEGORY Single Page

■ 648
PUBLICATION The Village Voice
DESIGN DIRECTOR Ted Keller
ART DIRECTOR Minh Uong
DESIGNER Stacy Wakefield
ILLUSTRATORS Stanley Martucci, Cheryl Greisback
PUBLISHER VV Publishing Corp.
ISSUE October 12, 1999
CATEGORY Single Page

■ 649
PUBLICATION The Village Voice
DESIGN DIRECTOR Ted Keller
ART DIRECTOR Minh Uong
DESIGNER Stacy Wakefield
ILLUSTRATOR Patrick Faricy
PUBLISHER VV Publishing Corp.
ISSUE November 9, 1999
CATEGORY Single Page

■ 650
PUBLICATION The Village Voice
DESIGN DIRECTOR Ted Keller
ART DIRECTOR Minh Uong
DESIGNER Stacy Wakefield
ILLUSTRATOR David Seeley
PUBLISHER VV Publishing Corp.
ISSUE November 30, 1999
CATEGORY Single Page

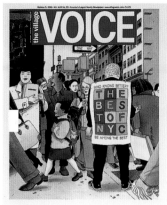

A

B

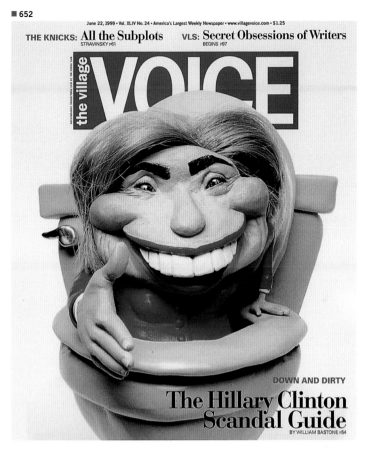

THE HILLARY CLINTON **CHEAT SHEET**

a guide to the scandals and issues that could stall her senate run

BY WILLIAM BASTONE
ILLUSTRATION BY GARY AAGAARD

■ 652
PUBLICATION The Village Voice
DESIGN DIRECTOR Ted Keller
ART DIRECTOR Minh Uong
DESIGNER Stacy Wakefield
ILLUSTRATOR David O'Keefe
PUBLISHER VV Publishing Corp.
ISSUE June 22, 1999
CATEGORY Single Page

■ 653
PUBLICATION The Village Voice
DESIGN DIRECTOR Ted Keller
ART DIRECTOR Minh Uong
DESIGNER Stacy Wakefield
ILLUSTRATOR Gary Aagaard
PUBLISHER VV Publishing Corp.
ISSUE June 22, 1999
CATEGORY Spread

■ 651
PUBLICATION The Village Voice
DESIGN DIRECTOR Ted Keller
ART DIRECTOR Minh Uong
DESIGNER Stacy Wakefield
ILLUSTRATOR Jorge Colombo
PUBLISHER VV Publishing Corp.
ISSUE October 5, 1999
CATEGORY Story
    A MERIT Single Page
    B MERIT Single Page

ILLUSTRATION MERIT ■

■ 654

■ 654
PUBLICATION The Washington Post/
Health Section
ART DIRECTOR
Stacie Harrison Reistetter
ILLUSTRATOR Ingo Fast
ISSUE August 3, 1999
CATEGORY Story

■ 655

■ 655
PUBLICATION The Washington Post/
Health Section
ART DIRECTOR
Stacie Harrison Reistetter
ILLUSTRATOR Cynthia von Buehler
ISSUE August 24, 1999
CATEGORY Story

■ 656

■ 656
PUBLICATION The Washington Post/
Health Section
ART DIRECTOR
Stacie Harrison Reistetter
ILLUSTRATOR Mark Ulriksen
ISSUE November 16, 1999
CATEGORY Story

■ 657

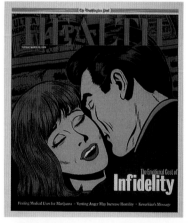

■ 657
PUBLICATION The Washington Post/
Health Section
ART DIRECTOR
Stacie Harrison Reistetter
ILLUSTRATOR Mark Zingarelli
ISSUE March 30, 1999
CATEGORY Story

658–659 (The American Lawyer spreads)

CLARENCE DARROW (1857–1938)
BY GEOFFREY COWAN

A Man For Some Seasons

The Darrow legend once inspired generations of young idealists. Stripped of his mythic stature, Clarence Darrow is now a man we worship less but identify with more.

ILLUSTRATION BY MARK ULRIKSEN

RALPH NADER (1934–)
BY T.R. GOLDMAN

The Lone Ranger

Fueled by single-minded determination and a well-developed sense of outrage, Ralph Nader created the modern consumer law movement.

ILLUSTRATION BY C.F. PAYNE

660 (Weekend Post)

Weekend POST

SATURDAY, MARCH 6, 1999

The Sport of Geeks

Don't tell them it's only a game

A BRIEF HISTORY OF GAMING

RECOMMENDED BY 9 OUT OF 10 GEEKS

'SOMETIMES I END UP GIVING THE GAMES AWAY BECAUSE I'M TOO ADDICTED IT'S SORT OF A PROBLEM'

BY JONATHAN KAY

SPAWN OF THE ATARI

TOMB RAIDER · PONG · PAC MAN · HALF-LIFE · SPACE INVADERS · WORMS 2 · ZORK

A GENERATION OF EXECUTIVE MEN IS ADDICTED TO VIDEO GAMES. IS COMPUTER ENTERTAINMENT THE NEW COCAINE?

ON FRIDAY I PLAYED STARCRAFT WITH SOME FRIENDS. THEN I WENT ONLINE AND FOUND SOME PEOPLE TO PLAY WORMS 2 FOR A COUPLE OF HOURS. THEN, I PLAYED HALF-LIFE FOR AN HOUR BEFORE GOING TO BED. THE SUN WAS STARTING TO COME UP — AND MY WHOLE DAY WAS SHOT. – BRUCE BOYDEN

658
PUBLICATION The American Lawyer
ART DIRECTOR Joan Ferrell
DESIGNER Joan Ferrell
ILLUSTRATOR Mark Ulriksen
PUBLISHER American Lawyer Media
ISSUE December 1999
CATEGORY Spread

659
PUBLICATION The American Lawyer
ART DIRECTOR Joan Ferrell
DESIGNER Joan Ferrell
ILLUSTRATOR C. F. Payne
PUBLISHER American Lawyer Media
ISSUE December 1999
CATEGORY Spread

660
PUBLICATION Weekend Post
ART DIRECTOR Friederike N. Gauss
DESIGNERS Friederike N. Gauss, Thea Partdrige
ILLUSTRATOR Gary Baseman
PUBLISHER National Post Southam Inc.
ISSUE March 6, 1999
CATEGORY Story

THE WALL STREET JOURNAL FRIDAY, SEPTEMBER 10, 1999 W5

SPORTS

Move Over, Rocky Balboa

Our Reporter Dons Gloves, Lands Jabs, Stays Up; Plus, She's A Girl!

By Wynter Spence

When we shook hands before the match, I thought, 'Maybe we could be friends.' Seeing her stare at me now, face distorted by her own mouthpiece, I don't think so.

Music 33 · Television/Radio 39
Art/Architecture 41 · Guide 44

Arts & Leisure Part Two

The New York Times

SUNDAY, OCTOBER 31, 1999   33

The Thrill of Discovering an Unheard Sound

By JON GARELICK

There were vivid encounters with Creole music in New Orleans and with a recording by somebody named Mingus in the 1970's.

Jon Garelick is associate arts editor of The Boston Phoenix.

Continued on Page 34

Arts & Leisure

The New York Times

Sunday, January 17, 1999

Ellington At 100: Reveling in Life's Majesty

Weekend

MOVIES PERFORMING ARTS

The New York Times

FRIDAY, JANUARY 22, 1999

Uncorking Elgar's Essence

Critics suggest Elgar's CD's, page 4.

Last Exit: Hurtling Down the Road to Ruin

By JANICE MASLIN

Circuits

The New York Times

THURSDAY, DECEMBER 30, 1999

This New Year's Eve, Technology Will Drop the Ball

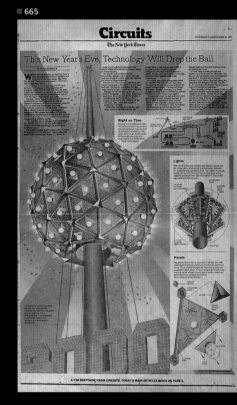

Right on Time

Lights

Panels

A Y2K KEEPSAKE FROM CIRCUITS. TODAY'S MAIN ARTICLES BEGIN ON PAGE 2.

661
PUBLICATION The Wall Street Journal Weekend Journal
ART DIRECTOR Stephen Fay
DESIGNERS Daniel Smith, Andrew Horton
ILLUSTRATOR Eric Palma
PUBLISHER Dow Jones & Co., Inc.
ISSUE September 10, 1999
CATEGORY Single Page

662
PUBLICATION The New York Times
ART DIRECTOR Michael Valenti
DESIGNER Michael Valenti
ILLUSTRATOR Wesley A. Bedrosian
PUBLISHER The New York Times
ISSUE October 31, 1999
CATEGORY Single Page

663
PUBLICATION The New York Times
ART DIRECTOR Michael Valenti
ILLUSTRATOR Mark Ulriksen
PUBLISHER The New York Times
ISSUE January 17, 1999
CATEGORY Single Page

664
PUBLICATION The New York Times
ART DIRECTOR Jerelle Kraus
ILLUSTRATOR Larry Rivers
PUBLISHER The New York Times
ISSUE January 22, 1999
CATEGORY Single Page

665
PUBLICATION The New York Times
DESIGNER John Papasian
ILLUSTRATOR John Papasian
PUBLISHER The New York Times
ISSUE December 30, 1999
CATEGORY Information Graphics

■ 666
PUBLICATION The Wall Street Journal
DESIGN DIRECTOR Joe Dizney
DESIGNER Joe Dizney
ILLUSTRATOR Joe Ciardiello
PUBLISHER Dow Jones & Co., Inc.
ISSUE December 16, 1999
CATEGORY Single Page

■ 667
PUBLICATION The Wall Street Journal Reports
DESIGN DIRECTOR Greg Leeds
ART DIRECTOR Vera Naughton
ILLUSTRATOR Melinda Beck
PUBLISHER Dow Jones & Co., Inc.
ISSUE June 14, 1999
CATEGORY Single Page

■ 668
PUBLICATION The Boston Globe
DESIGN DIRECTOR Dan Zedek
ART DIRECTOR Janet L. Michaud
DESIGNER Janet L. Michaud
ILLUSTRATOR Chuck Pyle
PUBLISHER The Globe Newspaper Co.
ISSUE July 10, 1999
CATEGORY Single Page

■ 669
PUBLICATION The Boston Globe
DESIGN DIRECTOR Dan Zedek
ART DIRECTOR Janet L. Michaud
DESIGNER Janet L. Michaud
ILLUSTRATOR Chuck Pyle
PUBLISHER The Globe Newspaper Co.
ISSUE July 13, 1999
CATEGORY Single Page

■ 670
PUBLICATION The Boston Globe
DESIGN DIRECTOR Dan Zedek
ART DIRECTOR Susan Levin
DESIGNER Susan Levin
ILLUSTRATOR Rico Lins
PUBLISHER The Globe Newspaper Co.
ISSUE October 3, 1999
CATEGORY Single Page

■ 671
PUBLICATION Vanity Fair
DESIGN DIRECTOR David Harris
ART DIRECTOR Gregory Mastrianni
ILLUSTRATOR Robert Risko
PUBLISHER Condé Nast Publications, Inc.
ISSUE May 1999
CATEGORY Single Page

ILLUSTRATION MERIT ■

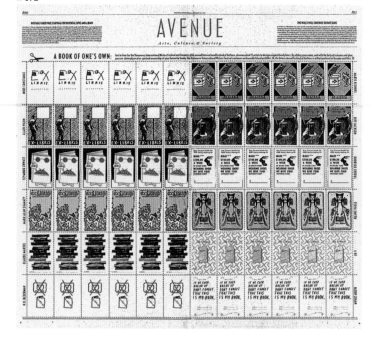

■ 672
PUBLICATION National Post
ART DIRECTOR Leanne M. Shapton
DESIGNER Leanne M. Shapton
ILLUSTRATORS Mike Constable, Alain Pilon, Maris Bishofs, Jeff Jacuson, Seymour Chwast, Rodrigo Corral, Mark Alan Stamaty, Fiona Smyth, Claude Martel, R.O. Blechman, Jason Logan
PUBLISHER Southam Inc.
ISSUE October 22, 1999
CATEGORY Single Page

■ 673
PUBLICATION National Post
ART DIRECTOR Leanne M. Shapton
DESIGNER Leanne M. Shapton
ILLUSTRATOR Emmanuel Pierre
PUBLISHER Southam Inc.
ISSUE August 9, 1999
CATEGORY Single Page

■ 674
PUBLICATION National Post
ART DIRECTOR Leanne M. Shapton
ILLUSTRATOR Jonathon Rosen
PUBLISHER Southam Inc.
ISSUE December 15, 1999
CATEGORY Single Page

■ 675
PUBLICATION National Post
ART DIRECTOR Leanne M. Shapton
DESIGNER Leanne M. Shapton
ILLUSTRATOR Wesley A. Bedrosian
PUBLISHER Southam Inc.
ISSUE March 11, 1999
CATEGORY Single Page

■ 676
PUBLICATION National Post
ART DIRECTOR Leanne M. Shapton
ILLUSTRATOR Thomas Libetti
PUBLISHER Southam Inc.
ISSUE December 9, 1999
CATEGORY Single Page

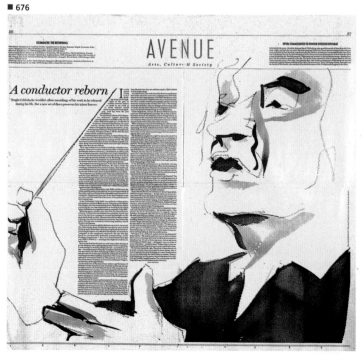

677

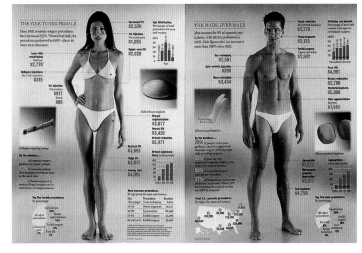

679

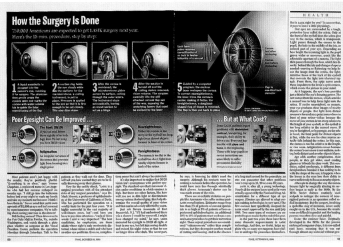

678

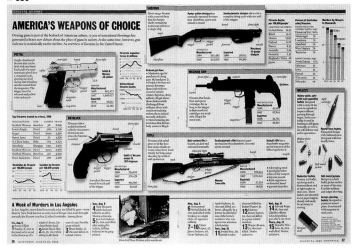

680

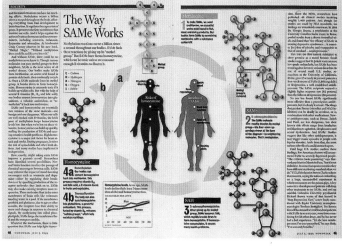

681

■ 677

PUBLICATION Time
DESIGN DIRECTOR Arthur Hochstein
ART DIRECTOR Joe Zeff
DESIGNER Ed Gabel
ILLUSTRATOR Ed Gabel
PUBLISHER Time Inc.
ISSUE November 29, 1999
CATEGORY Information Graphics

■ 678

PUBLICATION Time
DESIGN DIRECTOR Arthur Hochstein
ART DIRECTOR Joe Zeff
DESIGNER Joe Zeff
ILLUSTRATOR Ed Gabel
PUBLISHER Time Inc.
ISSUE October 11, 1999
CATEGORY Information Graphics

■ 679

PUBLICATION Newsweek
DESIGN DIRECTOR Lynn Staley
ART DIRECTOR Bonnie Scranton
DESIGNER Bonnie Scranton
PHOTOGRAPHER Tom Haynes
PUBLISHER The Washington Post Co.
ISSUE August 9, 1999
CATEGORY Information Graphics

■ 680

PUBLICATION Newsweek
DESIGN DIRECTOR Lynn Staley
ART DIRECTOR Bonnie Scranton
DESIGNER Bonnie Scranton
PHOTOGRAPHERS Bill Watzler, Burk Uzzle
PUBLISHER The Washington Post Co.
ISSUE August 23, 1999
CATEGORY Information Graphics

■ 681

PUBLICATION Newsweek
DESIGN DIRECTOR Lynn Staley
ART DIRECTOR Karl Gude
DESIGNER Bonnie Scranton
PUBLISHER The Washington Post Co.
ISSUE July 5, 1999
CATEGORY Information Graphics

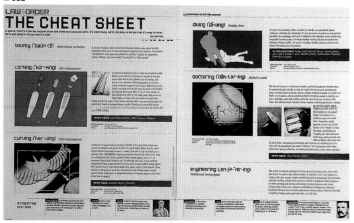

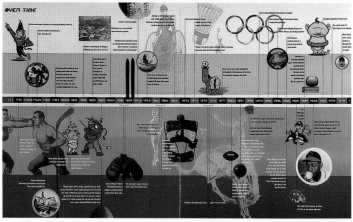

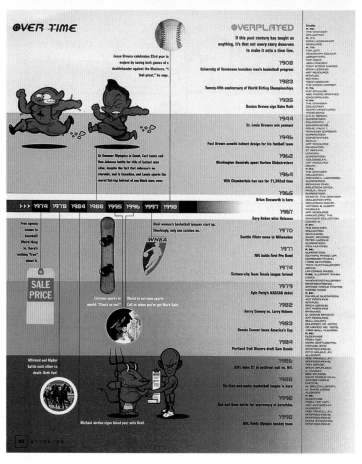

■ 682
PUBLICATION ESPN
DESIGN DIRECTOR Peter Yates
DESIGNERS Peter Yates, Gabe Kuo
PHOTOGRAPHER Nitin Vadukul
PUBLISHER Disney Publishing Worldwide
ISSUE November 1, 1999
CATEGORY Information Graphics

■ 683
PUBLICATION ESPN
DESIGN DIRECTOR F. Darrin Perry
ART DIRECTOR Peter Yates
DESIGNER F. Darrin Perry
ILLUSTRATOR Raul Ferran
PUBLISHER Disney Publishing Worldwide
ISSUE July 26, 1999
CATEGORY Information Graphics

Recognizing the little masterpieces that work so hard to communicate big ideas in a small amount of space.

Senior Assoc. Art Director, *Smart Money*

spots

CHRISTINE CURRY
Illustration Editor, *The New Yorker*
CHAIRPERSON

MELINDA BECK
Illustrator

TERESA FERNANDES
Design Consultant

MARK SHAW
Art Director, *Blaze*

HANNAH MCCAUGHEY
Senior Assoc. Art Director, *Esquire*

AMY ROSENFELD
Art Director, *Smart Money*

■ 684
BEST IN SHOW
ILLUSTRATOR Jason Holley
TITLE Principal Snyder
ART DIRECTOR Geraldine Hessler
PUBLICATION Entertainment Weekly
PUBLISHER Time Inc.
ISSUE October 1999

685

686

688

687

689

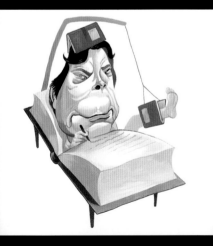

■ 685
ILLUSTRATOR Thomas Fuchs
TITLE The Best and Worst of 1999
ART DIRECTOR Geraldine Hessler
PUBLICATION Entertainment Weekly
PUBLISHER Time Inc.
ISSUE December 24, 1999

■ 686
ILLUSTRATOR Anita Kunz
TITLE John Meets Paul
ART DIRECTOR Geraldine Hessler
PUBLICATION Entertainment Weekly
PUBLISHER Time Inc.
ISSUE April 1999

■ 687
ILLUSTRATOR Anita Kunz
TITLE Cher
ART DIRECTOR Geraldine Hessler
PUBLICATION Entertainment Weekly
PUBLISHER Time Inc.
ISSUE Winter 1999

■ 688
ILLUSTRATOR Anita Kunz
TITLE No Chance In Hell...
ART DIRECTOR Traci Churchill
PUBLICATION Fortune Small Business
PUBLISHER Time Inc.
ISSUE April 2000

■ 689
ILLUSTRATOR Scott Laumann
TITLE Plotting a Winning Business Strategy
ART DIRECTORS Victoria Beerman, Erika Gomez
PUBLICATION Sales & Marketing Management
PUBLISHER Bill Communications
ISSUE February 2000

■ 690
ILLUSTRATOR Marc Lacaze
TITLE Letters
ART DIRECTOR Pamela Berry
PUBLICATION Travel & Leisure
PUBLISHER American Express Publishing Co.
ISSUE August 1999

■ 691
ILLUSTRATOR Zohar Lazar
TITLE You've Got Photos
ART DIRECTOR Pamela Berry
PUBLICATION Travel & Leisure
PUBLISHER American Express Publishing Co.
ISSUE April 2000

■ 692
ILLUSTRATOR Zohar Lazar
TITLE Family Routes
ART DIRECTOR Pamela Berry
PUBLICATION Travel & Leisure
PUBLISHER American Express Publishing Co.
ISSUE June 1999

■ 693
ILLUSTRATOR Zohar Lazar
TITLE I'll Take That For You, Sir
ART DIRECTOR Pamela Berry
PUBLICATION Travel & Leisure
PUBLISHER American Express Publishing Co.
ISSUE March 2000

■ 694
ILLUSTRATORS Paul Corio, Ross MacDonald,
Kelly Alder, Drew Friedman, Peter Kuper,
Jack Gallagher, Mike Gorman, Charlene Potts,
Ingo Fast, Steve Brodner, Michael Klein,
Bob Eckstein, Scott Menchin, Mark Matcho,
Jordin Isip, Melinda Beck, Marcellus Hall,
Stan Shaw, Glenn Head, Bill Russell,
Eric Palma, Mark Zingarelli, Gary Panter,
Jason Schneider, Michael Dougan,
Geoffrey Grahn, Stephen Savage
TITLE P.O.V.'s 20th Century, A to Z
ART DIRECTORS Florian Bachleda, Pino Impastato
PUBLICATION P.O.V.
PUBLISHER B.Y.O.B./Freedom Ventures, Inc.
ISSUE December 1999

■ 695
ILLUSTRATOR Polly Becker
TITLE Home Borrowing
PUBLICATION Money
ART DIRECTOR Maryann Salvato
PUBLISHER Time Inc.
ISSUE March 2000

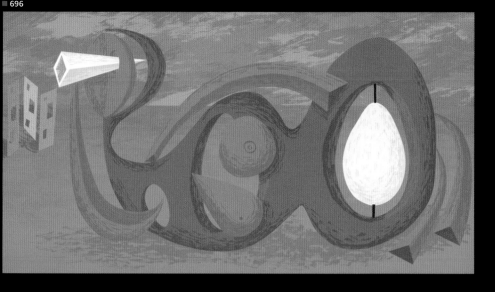

spots

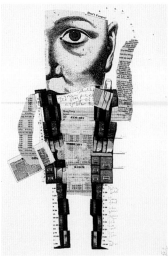

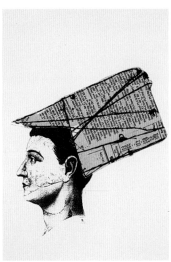

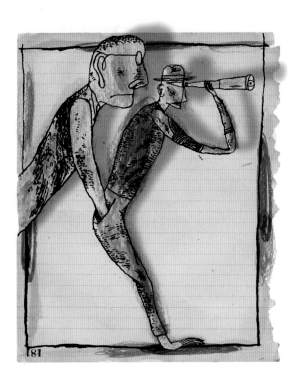

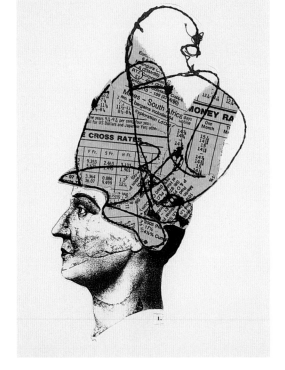

■ 698
ILLUSTRATOR Daniel Adel
TITLE Celebrity Death Lunch
ART DIRECTOR Joseph Heroun
PUBLICATION Boston Magazine
PUBLISHER Boston Magazine
ISSUE September 1999

■ 699
ILLUSTRATOR Henrik Drescher
TITLE Giving Grats a Closer Look
ART DIRECTOR Laura Zavetz
PUBLICATION Bloomberg Wealth Manager
PUBLISHER Bloomberg L.P.
ISSUE April 19, 2000

■ 700
ILLUSTRATOR Sibylle Schwarz
TITLE In Fine Form
ART DIRECTORS Frank Tagariello, Carol Layton
PUBLICATION Bloomberg Personal Finance
PUBLISHER Bloomberg L. P.
ISSUE April 1999

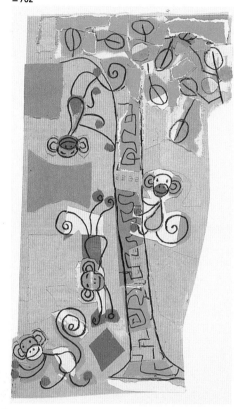

spots

■701
ILLUSTRATOR Matthew Martin
TITLE Who's On The M&A Bill Of Fare?
ART DIRECTOR Frank Tagariello
PUBLICATION Bloomberg Personal Finance
PUBLISHER Bloomberg L. P.
ISSUE July/August 1999

■702
ILLUSTRATOR Catherine Lazure
TITLE Monkeying with Accepted Wisdom
ART DIRECTORS Frank Tagariello, Carol Layton
PUBLICATION Bloomberg Personal Finance
PUBLISHER Bloomberg L. P.
ISSUE March 2000

■703
ILLUSTRATOR Esther Watson
TITLE It's In The Fine Print
ART DIRECTOR Frank Tagariello
PUBLICATION Bloomberg Personal Finance
PUBLISHER Bloomberg L. P.
ISSUE January/February 2000

■704
ILLUSTRATOR Nick Dewar
TITLE Food Lovers Tell All!
ART DIRECTOR Lou DiLorenzo
PUBLICATION Food & Wine
PUBLISHER American Express Publishing Co.
ISSUE October 1999

■705
ILLUSTRATOR Sarah Wilkins
TITLE 20 Wines For 2000
ART DIRECTOR Lou DiLorenzo
PUBLICATION Food & Wine
PUBLISHER American Express Publishing Co.
ISSUE December 1999

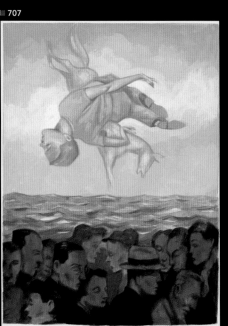

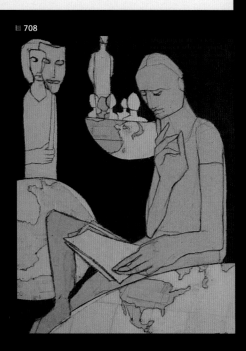

706
ILLUSTRATOR Tim Bower
TITLE A Course Of One's Own
ART DIRECTORS John Korpics, Erin Whelan
PUBLICATION Esquire
PUBLISHER The Hearst Corporation-Magazines Division
ISSUE April 1999

707
ILLUSTRATOR Tim Bower
TITLE A Fool's Proxy
ART DIRECTOR Angela Reichers
PUBLICATION Harpers
ISSUE October 1999

708
ILLUSTRATOR Tifenn Python
TITLE A Message For World Theatre Day
ART DIRECTOR Kitty Suen
PUBLICATION American Theatre
ISSUE April 2000

709
ILLUSTRATOR Joel Holland
TITLE One Step Over the Line
ART DIRECTORS Amy Rosenfeld, Stacy Wakefield
PUBLICATION SmartMoney
PUBLISHER Dow Jones & Hearst Corp.
ISSUE February 2000

710
ILLUSTRATOR Joel Holland
TITLE Age Discrimination
ART DIRECTORS Robert Mansfield, Anton Klusener
PUBLICATION Forbes
PUBLISHER Forbes Inc.
ISSUE April 27, 2000

■711

■714

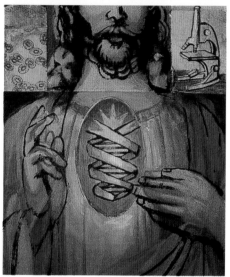

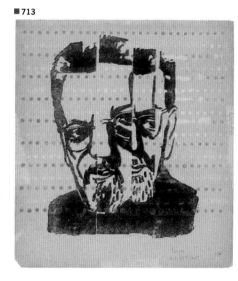

■713

■715

■712
ILLUSTRATOR Hadley Hooper
TITLE The Atlantic Monthly
ART DIRECTOR Elizabeth Urrico
PUBLICATION Atlantic Monthly
ISSUE September 1999

■713
ILLUSTRATOR Hadley Hooper
TITLE Portrait of Bernd Zimmermann
ART DIRECTOR Owen Phillips
PUBLICATION The New Yorker
PUBLISHER Condé Nast Publications, Inc.
ISSUE April 1999

■716

■715
ILLUSTRATOR Jordin Isip
TITLE Vital Signs
ART DIRECTOR Janine Thomas
PUBLICATION Emerge
PUBLISHER Black Entertainment
ISSUE June 1999

■711
ILLUSTRATOR Hadley Hooper
TITLE The Ultimate Hypothesis
ART DIRECTOR Tony Lane
PUBLICATION Forbes ASAP
PUBLISHER Forbes Inc.
ISSUE October 1999

■714
ILLUSTRATOR Jordin Isip
TITLE Taking Aim at that Nightmare Bug
ART DIRECTOR Richard Demler
PUBLICATION BusinessWeek
PUBLISHER The MacGraw-Hill Companies, Inc.
ISSUE November 1999

■716
ILLUSTRATOR Jordin Isip
TITLE No Secrets
ART DIRECTORS Robert Kanes, Barbara Adamson
PUBLICATION PC World
PUBLISHER International Data Group
ISSUE July 1999

spots

717
ILLUSTRATOR Riccardo Vecchio
TITLE Shostakovich
ART DIRECTOR Christine Curry
PUBLICATION The New Yorker
PUBLISHER Condé Nast Publications, Inc.
ISSUE April 1999

■718
ILLUSTRATOR Riccardo Vecchio
TITLE Not One Less
ART DIRECTOR Owen Phillips
PUBLICATION The New Yorker
PUBLISHER Condé Nast Publications, Inc.
ISSUE February 2000

719
ILLUSTRATOR Steve Brodner
TITLE The West Wing
ART DIRECTOR Christine Curry
PUBLICATION The New Yorker
PUBLISHER Condé Nast Publications, Inc.
ISSUE April 2000

720
ILLUSTRATOR Gerard Dubois
TITLE Infrared
ART DIRECTOR Owen Phillips
PUBLICATION The New Yorker
PUBLISHER Condé Nast Publications, Inc.
ISSUE February 2000

721
ILLUSTRATOR Edward Gorey
TITLE The Little Black Dress...
ART DIRECTOR Christine Curry
PUBLICATION The New Yorker
PUBLISHER Condé Nast Publications, Inc.
ISSUE April 17, 2000

■722
ILLUSTRATOR Edel Rodriguez
TITLE Bobby Hutcherson
ART DIRECTOR Owen Phillips
PUBLICATION The New Yorker
PUBLISHER Condé Nast Publications, Inc.
ISSUE January 2000

723

 725

 727

724

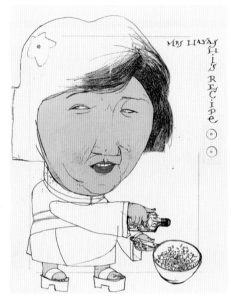 728

726

■ 723
ILLUSTRATOR Richard Merkin
TITLE James Thurber
ART DIRECTOR Owen Phillips
PUBLICATION The New Yorker
PUBLISHER Condé Nast Publications, Inc.
ISSUE January 2000

■ 724
ILLUSTRATOR David Hughes
TITLE Poisoner
ART DIRECTOR Christine Curry
PUBLICATION The New Yorker
PUBLISHER Condé Nast Publications, Inc.
ISSUE April 1999

■ 725
ILLUSTRATOR Al Hirschfeld
TITLE Wendy Wasserstein
ART DIRECTOR Christine Curry
PUBLICATION The New Yorker
PUBLISHER Condé Nast Publications, Inc.
ISSUE April 1999

■ 726
ILLUSTRATOR Cornel Rubino
TITLE The Music Room
ART DIRECTOR Owen Phillips
PUBLICATION The New Yorker
PUBLISHER Condé Nast Publications, Inc.

■ 727
ILLUSTRATOR Lara Tomlin
TITLE Breakdown
ART DIRECTOR Owen Phillips
PUBLICATION The New Yorker
PUBLISHER Condé Nast Publications, Inc.
ISSUE January 2000

■ 728
ILLUSTRATOR Sergio Ruzzier
TITLE Epidemic!
ART DIRECTOR Owen Phillips
PUBLICATION The New Yorker
PUBLISHER Condé Nast Publications, Inc.
ISSUE June 7, 1999

■ 729

■ 731

■ 733

■ 730

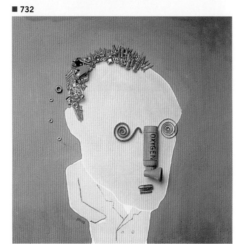

■ 732

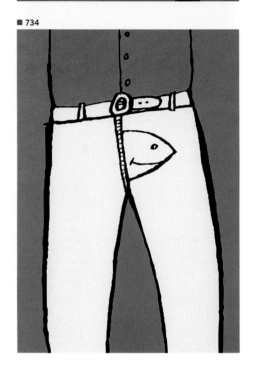

■ 734

729
ILLUSTRATOR Benoit Van Innis
TITLE Stuart
ART DIRECTOR Christine Curry
PUBLICATION The New Yorker
PUBLISHER Condé Nast Publications, Inc.
ISSUE April 2000

■ **730**
ILLUSTRATOR Andrea Ventura
TITLE Elias Canetti
ART DIRECTOR Christine Curry
PUBLICATION The New Yorker
PUBLISHER Condé Nast Publications, Inc.
ISSUE April 1999

■ **731**
ILLUSTRATOR Hanoch Piven
TITLE Jon Stewart
ART DIRECTOR John Giordani
PUBLICATION Details
PUBLISHER Condé Nast Publications, Inc.
ISSUE January 1999

■ **732**
ILLUSTRATOR Hanoch Piven
TITLE Dennis Hopper
ART DIRECTOR John Giordani
PUBLICATION Details
PUBLISHER Condé Nast Publications, Inc.
ISSUE March 1999

■ **733**
ILLUSTRATOR Hanoch Piven
TITLE Steve Martin
ART DIRECTOR John Giordani
PUBLICATION Details
PUBLISHER Condé Nast Publications, Inc.
ISSUE June 1999

■ **734**
ILLUSTRATOR Scott Menchin
TITLE Pisces
ART DIRECTOR Ronda Thompson
PUBLICATION Details
PUBLISHER Condé Nast Publications, Inc.
ISSUE March 1999

spots

■ 735
ILLUSTRATOR Christoph Niemann
TITLE One Louvre
ART DIRECTORS Brandon Kavulla, Dwayne Shaw
PUBLICATION Vibe
PUBLISHER Miller Publishing Group
ISSUE April 1999

■ 736
ILLUSTRATOR Stephen Kroninger
TITLE Let Me Ride
ART DIRECTORS Meegan Barnes, Robert Newman
PUBLICATION Vibe
PUBLISHER Miller Publishing Group
ISSUE February 2000

■ 737
ILLUSTRATOR Saiman Chow
TITLE Homeboy Shopping
ART DIRECTOR Ronda Thompson
PUBLICATION Vibe
PUBLISHER Miller Publishing Group
ISSUE March 2000

■ 738
ILLUSTRATOR Glenn Hilario
TITLE Pisces
ART DIRECTOR Ronda Thompson
PUBLICATION Vibe
PUBLISHER Miller Publishing Group
ISSUE February 2000

■ 739

■ 740

■ 741

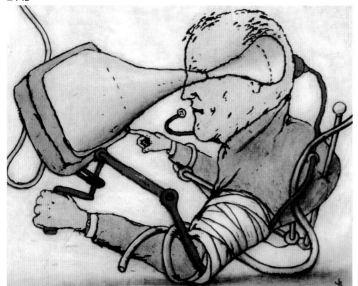

■ 742

■ 743

■ 744

■ 739
ILLUSTRATOR Charles Burns
TITLE Mystery Men
ART DIRECTOR Geraldine Hessler
PUBLICATION Entertainment Weekly
PUBLISHER Time Inc.
ISSUE April 30, 1999

■ 740
ILLUSTRATOR Roberto Parada
TITLE The Dead Zone
ART DIRECTOR Geraldine Hessler
PUBLICATION Entertainment Weekly
PUBLISHER Time Inc.
ISSUE June/July 1999

■ 741
ILLUSTRATOR Peter Kuper
TITLE All the Rage
ART DIRECTOR Minh Uong
PUBLICATION The Village Voice
PUBLISHER VV Publishing Corp.

■ 742
ILLUSTRATOR Jonathan Rosen
TITLE A New Pain In The Neck
ART DIRECTOR Dave Allen
PUBLICATION PC Computing
ISSUE April 2000

■ 743
ILLUSTRATOR Joe Ciardiello
TITLE All That Jazz
ART DIRECTOR Stephen Fay
PUBLICATION The Wall Street Journal Weekend
PUBLISHER Dow Jones & Co., Inc.
ISSUE April 23, 1999

■ 744
ILLUSTRATOR Dusan Petricic
TITLE Family Ties, Severed Roots
ART DIRECTORS Stephen Fay, Andrew Horton
PUBLICATION The Wall Street Journal Weekend
PUBLISHER Dow Jones & Co., Inc.
ISSUE August 27, 1999

student competition

Established in 1995, this competition honors the life and work of B.W. Honeycutt. It recognizes exceptional design by students with awards and three cash prizes; the B.W Honeycutt Award of $2500 and second and third prizes of $1000. This juried competition acknowledges the student designer and the teachers of graphic design who develop their unique talents.

Chairperson
GAIL ANDERSON
Senior Art Director, *Rolling Stone*

PAUL ROELOFS
Art Director, eve.com,

Judges
RINA MIGLIACCIO
Art Director, *Us Weekly*

DEB BISHOP
Art Director,
Martha Stewart Baby and *Martha by Mail*

* Please note that the following student work was completed to assignment specifications for the Society of PUBLICATION Designers. It is intended for PUBLICATION only in the SPD PUBLICATION Design Annual.

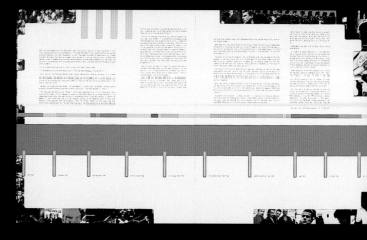

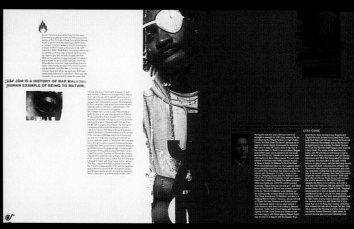

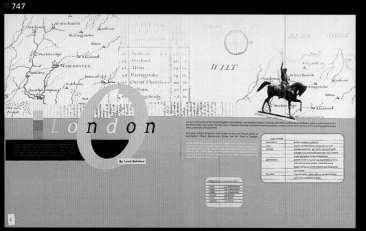

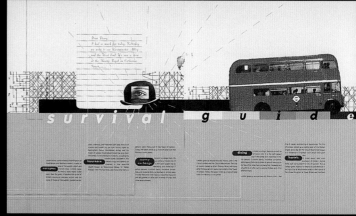

AWARD WINNERS ■ Student competition

745
B.W. HONEYCUTT AWARD WINNER
DESIGNER Kerry Edward
TITLE U2
SCHOOL Fashion Institute of Technology, New York City
INSTRUCTOR Susan Cotler Block

746
SECOND PRIZE AWARD WINNER
DESIGNER Jen Yung Liao
TITLE Def Jam
SCHOOL Maryland Institute College of Art, Baltimore
INSTRUCTOR Ellen Lupton

747
THIRD PRIZE AWARD WINNER
DESIGNER Lillian Ng
TITLE London
SCHOOL Fashion Institute of Technology, New York City
INSTRUCTOR Susan Cotler Block

748
DESIGNER Donna D'Alfonso
TITLE Fiona Apple
SCHOOL Philadelphia University
INSTRUCTOR Malka Michelson

749
DESIGNER Stephen Penning
TITLE Radiohead
SCHOOL Philadelphia University
INSTRUCTOR Malka Michelson

750
DESIGNER SoYoung Oh
TITLE Tokyo
SCHOOL Maryland Institute College of Art, Baltimore
INSTRUCTOR Ellen Lupton

751
DESIGNER Jeremy R. Hoffman

"Fast As You Can..."

"Music stems from my emotions, I can feel in my veins."

**example a.
(radiohead)**

JUMP OUT OF
BED AS SOON
AS YOU HEAR
THE ALARM
CLOCK. BRUSH
YOUR TEETH.
YOU MAY ALSO
FIND IT USEFUL
SPENDING FIVE
MINUTES EACH
MORNING
SAYING TO
YOURSELF :
"EVERY DAY IN
EVERYWAY I
AM GETTING
BETTER AND
BETTER"
PERHAPS IT IS
A GOOD IDEA
TO START A
NEW DAY WITH
THE RIGHT
FRAME OF

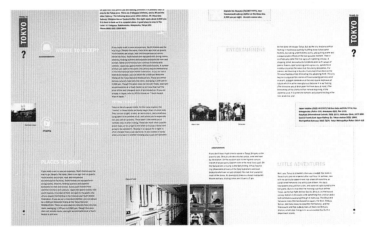

we hope that you choke...that you choke

TOKYO

NIAGARA FALLS

student competition ■ MERIT

index

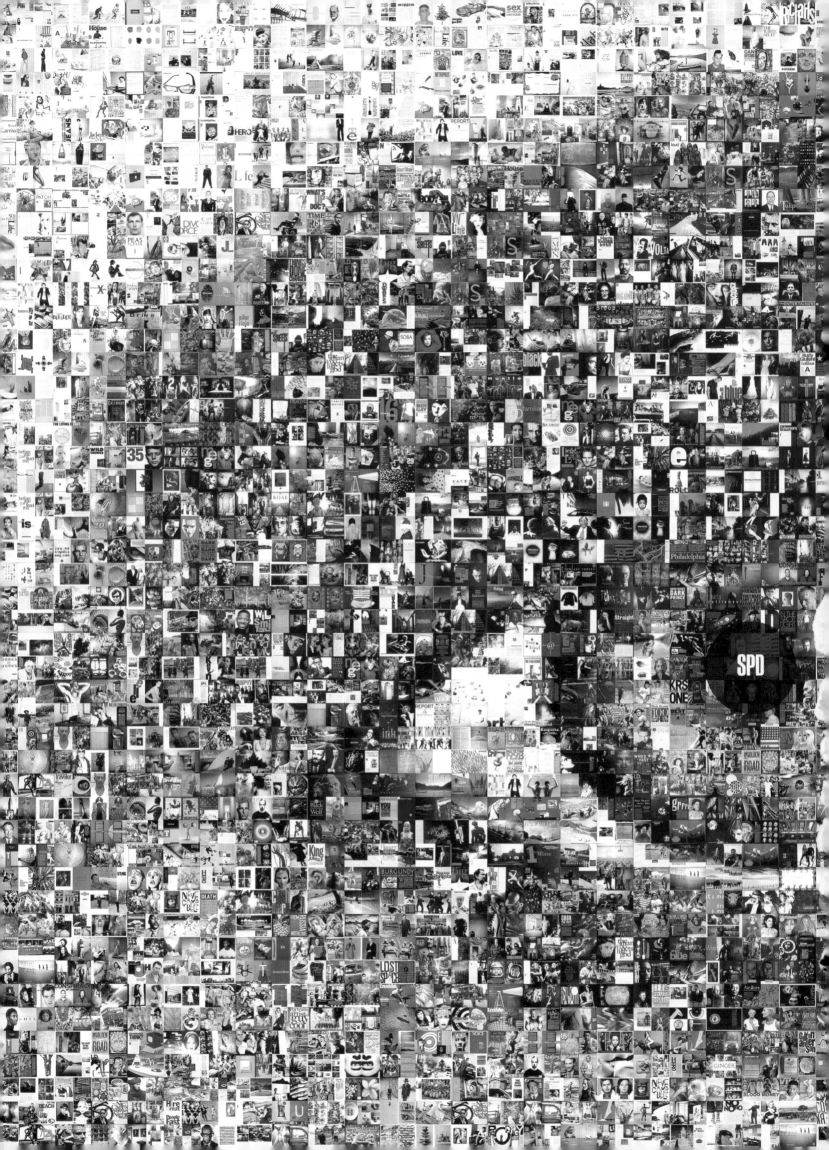